THE BALLAD IMAGE

ESSAYS PRESENTED TO
BERTRAND HARRIS BRONSON

EDITED BY JAMES PORTER
WITH A FOREWORD BY WAYLAND D. HAND

THE BALLAD IMAGE

ESSAYS PRESENTED TO
BERTRAND HARRIS BRONSON

EDITED BY JAMES PORTER
WITH A FOREWORD BY WAYLAND D. HAND

Center for the Study of Comparative Folklore & Mythology
University of California, Los Angeles
Los Angeles, 1983

Center for the Study of Comparative Folklore & Mythology
University of California, Los Angeles

Library of Congress Cataloging in Publication Data

Main entry under title:

The Ballad Image.

    Includes index.
    1. Bronson, Bertrand Harris, 1902- 2. Ballad
Folksong — Addresses, essays, lectures. 1. Porter, James
II. Series.

ISBN 0-912513-00-4

Library of Congress Catalog Card Number: 83-71827

Acknowledgements

The Editor wishes to thank the following persons for their help: Wayland Hand, for continual encouragement; Mildred Bronson, for many kindnesses and practical suggestions; Patrick Ford, Director of the Center for the Study of Comparative Folklore & Mythology, for clearing the way to publication; Frances Farrell, for assistance in providing photographic prints; Richard Keeling, for expert music copying; Judith McCulloh, Bill Nicolaisen, Joan Ruman Perkal, and Ralph Rader for advice and information.

Acknowledgement should also be made to the following for permission to reproduce materials: The Bodleian Library, Oxford, England; The Henry Francis du Pont Winterthur Museum; The Houghton Library, Harvard University; The Huntington Library, San Marino; The Library Company of Philadelphia; Massachusetts Historical Society; The Mitchell Library, Glasgow, Scotland; The Metropolitan Museum of Art; The Museum of Fine Arts, Boston; The Pennsylvania Academy of the Fine Arts, Philadelphia.

Contents

Foreword

From the time of Francis James Child in the last half of the nineteenth century, ballad scholarship in America has not been surpassed, and rarely rivalled, anywhere in the world. To the long and distinguished list of workers who have held aloft the scholarship of Child — Francis Barton Gummere, George Lyman Kittredge, Phillips Barry, Reed Smith, Gordon Hall Gerould, Helen Hartness Flanders, H. M. Belden, Helen Creighton, Samuel P. Bayard, and a few others — should be added the last and in many ways the most direct and illustrious descendant of Child himself, Bertrand Harris Bronson. Of all those mentioned, save Kittredge, Bronson is the only one to have worked with the total corpus of the English and Scottish popular ballads.

The comparison does not end here. In his work with the ballad texts Child became a master of the ballad poetry in the over three hundred individual ballads and almost thirteen hundred textual redactions. These longer variants, moreover, were permeated with what Child was accustomed to call ballad matters and commonplaces. Similarly, Bronson was to become sovereign in his command of the various tune families and individual musical motifs that found their way from ballad to ballad over many centuries of time. To cope with such a formidable bulk of material, whether texts or tunes, both men were forced to become master editors. As Bronson has shown in a series of important papers beginning in the early 1940s, tunes exert a greater control over texts than texts do over tunes, and present-day ballad scholarship has become a more demanding task than it was in Child's day when the principal concern was with ballad poetry.

Since the publication of Bronson's monumental *Traditional Tunes of the Child Ballads*, published in four small folio volumes by Princeton University Press (1959–72), it is now *de rigeur* to study the texts of ballads, wherever possible, in the musical matrix to which they are traditionally bound. In connection with the interdependence of texts and tunes, it is interesting to note that, when

the multi-volume *Deutsche Volkslieder* was being planned in the
late 1920s, the editors made provision for musicologists to sit with
literary editors in compiling the life histories of individual ballads.

It is one of the ironies of scholarship in a field that has featured
song, and even the dance, from early English times, that it should
have taken three quarters of a century to move from Child's notions
of ballad poetry to the idiom of folk music itself, and to the artistic
legacy of folk music and folk ballad, sung and performed. One
further irony of this American concern with the English and Scottish
popular ballads—that dates from 1857 in Child's earliest edition of
the ballads—is the fact that the musical counterparts to the ballad
poetry of the British Isles (compiled in the massive final ten-part
work of Child, 1882–98) have been recovered in large part a whole
continent removed. So complete, then, has been the wedding of
poetic and musical traditions of the English-speaking world that
one has come to speak of this basic unity of Anglo-American balladry.

Sharing the limelight with the two Americans Child and Bronson
in this international undertaking, and serving as a generational link
between the two, was the Englishman Cecil Sharp, who collected
living Anglo-American ballads on both sides of the Atlantic. Sharp's
researches in the Southern Appalachians during the first World War
and in the 1930s took place at a time when the real extent of traditional English song and balladry in America was first becoming
known. These old-country songs and ballads had quietly maintained
themselves in the Southern Highlands, and elsewhere, for more
than two-and-a-half centuries. The recovery of the old songs and
ballads, and the country dances too, provide the most eloquent
American examples to date of the archaism of the fringe and its
corollaries of cultural lag and sequestration. An actual example
worth noting is Sharp's observation that he had found the English
country dances to be performed with greater beauty and fidelity
in the Carolina mountains than he had ever seen them danced on
the English heath itself.

Since the ballads themselves spanned continents within the
Anglo-American continuum, and centuries in their spread and
development, it might be profitable to dwell a bit on the legacy
of Child's scholarly work in the hands of his two principal successors.
In contrast to Child, both Sharp and Bronson were musically
trained, but Bronson, a scholar in eighteenth-century English literature and folklore, possessed the literary and philological training for
ballad scholarship which the genial English schoolmaster lacked.
Even before he came to America for his remarkable field researches,
Sharp worked with a small but select cadre of English folk song and
ballad collectors to supply tunes and extend the musical apparatus
for the Child ballads. Sharp added notably to these researches as
a result of his collecting trips in the Southern Appalachians, made

in 1916–18 in company with Maud Karpeles. Coming at the end of the group of American scholars mentioned above, most of whom contributed to the musical study of the ballads, and drawing upon them and others as well as upon Sharp, Bronson was able to supply the complete musical compendium to Child in his four handsome volumes of *The Traditional Tunes.*

After examining the musical notation and indexing systems of Sigurd Bernhard Hustvedt and others for the demanding work at hand, Bronson turned to the modern machine storage and retrieval systems that were just coming into use. Starting with musical analysis which he punched into IBM cards, beginning in the late 1940s, and watching developments in the emerging field of computer science over the next three decades, Bronson was able not only to assemble requisite information for the *Traditional Tunes* but eventually to put the entire Child corpus on computer tapes, variants and all.

During these fruitful years when Bronson was busily reworking the numerous "tune families" of the Child ballads, intimates of the sage of Berkeley looked on in wonderment as this last exemplar of unhurried eighteenth-century scholarship was himself caught up in the hustle and bustle of twentieth-century computer technology, as the last bastions of the Humanities were breached. In his epochal essay, "Mechanical Help in the Study of Folk Song" (*Journal of American Folklore,* 62 [April 1949]), Bronson sought to free himself of charges of philistinism by stating that "the machine is not asked to do what a machine should not attempt: it cannot solve aesthetic problems on the basis of figures, but where facts and figures are necessary, it can give factual answers with startling economy of time and effort, and free the student for questions of a higher order."

There were other paradoxes, too, wherein Bronson was to emerge from his eighteenth-century world and come to grips with the new folklore and ballad scholarship that was taking shape around him in America. The Folksong Revival that set in during the 1950s was not the anathema to him that it was to many another of his colleagues. He spoke with unstinting praise, for example, of Kenneth S. Goldstein's work, and particularly of the five-album anthology of Child ballads on the Riverside label. Most typical of Bronson as the gentleman and scholar that he is, however, was his reception of wandering "folksongers," as he called them, who made pilgrimages to Berkeley to meet him. Like as not they ended up being taken to lunch at UC Berkeley's congenial faculty club or, better still, being bidden to tea at his home, an elegant afternoon ritual at 927 Oxford Street.

The tribute paid to Bronson in these pages by colleagues on both sides of the Atlantic comes at the end of the proverbial fourscore years, and an academic career spanning some sixty years. It began in 1918 when he first went off to the University of Michigan (B.A. 1921), then to Harvard (M.A. 1922), and then on to Oxford as a Rhodes scholar (1922–25), followed by a year of teaching at Michigan (1925–26). He received the doctorate at Yale in 1927, and joined the faculty at Berkeley the same year. There he has remained throughout a long and brilliant career that has seen many academic and professional honors come his way. Bronson "retired" in 1970.

This is the Bertrand H. Bronson whom I have known for more than forty years. Like all who have had this privilege, I have found Bert's warmth and human quality equal to his prodigious scholarship, and with them I stand in awe of his unexampled perseverance and dedication.

Wayland D. Hand

Introduction

The essays in this volume form a modest tribute to the foremost living ballad scholar in Europe and America. As occasional toilers in the same vineyard, the contributors and the Editor can only express admiration for the sustained effort and combination of lucidity and thoroughness that characterize the four volumes of *The Traditional Tunes of the Child Ballads,* surely the finest achievement of ballad scholarship this century. We can likewise grasp the catholic range of interests, within the field of traditional song, in his collected essays that span nearly thirty years, *The Ballad As Song* (1969). We wonder, in the end, how Bronson ever found time to make the significant contributions he did to *litterae humaniores,* from his studies of Chaucer in the 1930s and his two-volume biography of the crusty English antiquarian, Joseph Ritson (1938), to the essays on the music and poetry of the Enlightenment (and especially those on Johnson and his circle) in the 1940s and 1950s.

This book, then, is an act of homage to Bronson's accomplishment as a ballad scholar, and the papers are exclusively on topics in the traditional song of Britain, Ireland, and North America. To attempt a comprehensive reflection of Bronson's interests in other fields would have been to court an unwelcome heterogeneity of theme, and moreover, substance has been a primary editorial consideration. The number of contributors had therefore to be limited, and the Editor hopes that those who were unable to add their salute will forgive this underlying principle. To those who detect a high proportion of papers on Scottish material, the Editor can only confess that this surely reflects the traditional attraction to Scottish song that scholars from Ramsay and Ritson in the eighteenth century have continued to feel.

The twelve essays fall largely into groups that deal with issues in ballad scholarship: the study of individual ballads, stability and variation in texts and tunes, the creative role of singers, and problems in the oral re-creation of folksong. The first group includes a variety of perspectives: W. F. H. Nicolaisen selects "Sir Patrick

Spens" (Child 58) for a study of the tension between imitation and variation in a ballad text when it undergoes translation; Emily B. Lyle discusses ancient concepts of music and the seasons that lie behind the text of "King Orpheus" (Child 19); and Tristram Potter Coffin considers the four famous riddling ballads (Child 1, 2, 3, 46) in terms of their possible origin in love-joust situations.

The two papers that follow address the problem of stability and variability in traditional song. The often perplexing question of song identity, text identity, or tune identity—more familiar in studies of the ballad proper—is tackled by Judith McCulloh in an analysis of the more intractable lyric song tradition in the United States. The Editor then examines a complex of songs and tunes, mainly Scottish, originating in the late seventeenth century and proposes a three-stage diachronic model to clarify development of the complex. As a centerpiece essay on a neglected theme in folk-song scholarship, Archie Green's discussion of iconographic evidence makes clear its promise as source research for students of American folk music.

Traditional singers come next into focus. Two papers deal with singers from diverse Northeast traditions: first, Herschel Gower evaluates the influence of Jeannie Robertson, the Traveller singer from Aberdeenshire, on the Folksong Revival of the 1950s and 1960s; and Edward D. Ives, adding to his previous studies of Larry Gorman, Lawrence Doyle, and Joe Scott, delineates another singer-composer from the Maritime Provinces, Joe Smith.

The final segment of this volume is taken up with the theory of oral re-creation, first offered in a developed way by A. B. Lord for the composition and performance of epic song, and later adapted by several scholars as a hypothesis for the production of traditional ballad texts. David Buchan, in a look at one of the rarer specimens in Child, treats the idea of re-creation on both compositional and functional levels in "Hugh Spencer's Feats in France" (Child 158). Citing evidence from French and Irish traditions as well as from British or American, Hugh Shields draws attention to a characteristic element of ballad style, the rhetorical use of "impossibles." A position he adopted twenty years ago in opposing the idea of oral re-creation as the primary creative fact in balladry is continued by Albert B. Friedman; memorization, he believes, is a more plausible explanation for stability in ballad variants. Finally, D. K. Wilgus exemplifies Lord's concept of "tension of essences" in relation to a series of "murdered sweetheart" ballads in American tradition.

These papers convey not only the preoccupations of the individual authors but suggest, too, the range of scholarly topics illuminated by Bertrand Bronson in his life's work. As with Maud Karpeles's appraisal of Cecil Sharp, we perceive plainly the integration of Bronson's faith and works through his belief in the staying power and common virtues of traditional song. It is to him that we owe our contemporary conception of the ballad as song; and it is because of him that our image of the ballad, with its dual aspect of words and music, has become a lasting reality.

James Porter

Tabula Gratulatoria

Gerald Abraham
Sussex, England

Roger D. Abrahams
Claremont College
Claremont, California

R. Gerald Alvey
University of Kentucky
Lexington, Kentucky

Flemming G. Andersen
Odense University
Odense, Denmark

Samuel G. Armistead
University of Pennsylvania
Philadelphia, Pennsylvania

Shirley L. Arora
University of California
Los Angeles, California

Anneli Asplund
Finnish Literary Society
Helsinki, Finland

Sheridan Baker
Ann Arbor, Michigan

F. W. Bateson
Buckinghamshire, England

Samuel Baud-Bovy
Geneva, Switzerland

Ernest W. Baughman
Albuquerque, New Mexico

Richard Bauman
University of Texas
Austin, Texas

Hermann Bausinger
Ludwig Uhland Institut
Germany

Samuel P. Bayard
Pennsylvania State College
Pennsylvania

Bruce A. Beatie
Cleveland State University
Cleveland, Ohio

Horace P. Beck
Ripton, Vermont

Dan Ben-Amos
University of Pennsylvania
Philadelphia, Pennsylvania

Robert D. Bethke
University of Delaware
Delaware

Richard Bevis
Vancouver, Canada

Ludvik Bielawski
Akademie Nauk
Warsaw, Poland

Edward Bloom
Brown University
Providence, Rhode Island

Olav Bø
University of Oslo
Olso, Norway

The Bodleian Library
Oxford, England

Artur Bohnet
University of Alberta
Alberta, Canada

George W. Boswell
Mississippi State University
Mississippi

The British Library
London, England

Mary Ellen Brown
Indiana University
Bloomington, Indiana

Morris Brownell
University of Nevada
Reno, Nevada

Jan H. Brunvand
University of Utah
Salt Lake City, Utah

Rolf W. Brednich
Georg-August Universität
Göttingen, Germany

David Buchan
Memorial University
St. John's, Newfoundland
Canada

Linda Burman-Hall
University of California
Santa Cruz, California

Howard Burton
Riverside, California

David Bynum
Harvard University
Cambridge, Massachusetts

Cambridge University Library
Cambridge, England

J. Douglas Canfield
Tucson, Arizona

Nicholas Carolan
Dublin, Ireland

Paulo de Carvalho Neto
University of California
Los Angeles, California

Mrs. W. M. Chace
Palo Alto, California

Clare College
Cambridge, England

James Clifford
New York, New York

Tristram P. Coffin
University of Pennsylvania
Philadelphia, Pennsylvania

Anne Cohen
Pacific Palisades
California

Norm Cohen
Los Angeles, California

David Colbert
University of Washington
Seattle, Washington

Francis M. Collinson
Innerleithen, Scotland

Patricia L. Conroy
University of Washington
Seattle, Washington

Helen Creighton
Dartmouth, Nova Scotia
Canada

Peter Crossley-Holland
University of California
Los Angeles, California

Daniel Crowley
University of California
Davis, California

Keith K. Cunningham
University of Arizona
Flagstaff, Arizona

Erik Dál
University of Copenhagen
Copenhagen, Denmark

Linda Dégh
Indiana University
Bloomington, Indiana

Walter Deutsch
Vienna, Austria

Deutsches Volksliedarchiv
Freiburg, Germany

Jürgen Dittmar
Deutsches Volksliedarchiv
Freiburg, Germany

Charles Franklin Doe Library
University of California
Berkeley, California

Vincent Duckles
University of California
Berkeley, California

Duke University Library
Durham, North Carolina

Alan Dundes
University of California
Berkeley, California

Wolfram Eberhard
University of California
Berkeley, California

Arthur C. Edwards
Los Angeles, California

Carol Edwards
University of California
Los Angeles, California

Albert Elkus
University of California
Berkeley, California

Oskár Elschek
Slovak Academy of Sciences
Bratislava, Czechoslovakia

David Engle
Valley Center, California

David Evans
Memphis State University
Memphis, Tennessee

Burt Feintuch
Western Kentucky University
Bowling Green, Kentucky

William Ferris
New Haven, Connecticut

The Folklore Society
London, England

Patrick W. Ford
University of California
Los Angeles, California

David W. Foster
Arizona State University
Tempe, Arizona

Edith Fowke
Downsview, Ontario
Canada

David B. Fowler
University of Washington
Seattle, Washington

Albert B. Friedman
Claremont College
Claremont, California

Robert A. Georges
University of California
Los Angeles, California

Edith Gerson-Kiwi
Jerusalem, Israel

Henry Glassie
University of Pennsylvania
Philadelphia, Pennsylvania

Kenneth S. Goldstein
University of Pennsylvania
Philadelphia, Pennsylvania

Herschel Gower
Vanderbilt University
Nashville, Tennessee

Ronald Grambo
Oslo, Norway

Archie Green
San Francisco, California

John Greenway
University of Colorado
Boulder, Colorado

Neil R. Grobman
University of Oregon
Eugene, Oregon

Gordon S. Haight
Woodbridge, Connecticut

Herbert H. Halpert
St. John's, Newfoundland
Canada

Wayland D. Hand
University of California
Los Angeles, California

Bess Lomax Hawes
National Endowment for the Arts
Washington, D.C.

Charles Haywood
New York, New York

Hamish Henderson
University of Edinburgh
Edinburgh, Scotland

Karl-Ivar Hildeman
University of Stockholm
Stockholm, Sweden

The Huntington Library
San Marino, California

Joseph C. Hickerson
Library of Congress
Washington, D.C.

Christine R. Hilary
Northampton, Massachusetts

M.J.C. Hodgart
Brighton, England

Bengt Holbek
Copenhagen, Denmark

Otto Holzapfel
Odense University
Odense, Denmark

Lauri Honko
Nordic Institute of Folklore
Turku, Finland

Volodymyr Hoshovskij
Erevan, Soviet Union

Agnes Hostettler
Charlotte, North Carolina

S.F.D. Hughes
Purdue University
Lafayette, Indiana

Edward D. Ives
University of Maine
Orono, Maine

Alan Jabbour
American Folklife Center
Washington, D.C.

Bruce Jackson
State University of New York
Buffalo, New York

William A. Jackson
Houghton Library
Harvard University
Cambridge, Massachusetts

Carolyn E. Jakeman
Houghton Library
Harvard University
Cambridge, Massachusetts

Michael O. Jones
University of California
Los Angeles, California

Bengt Jonsson
Stockholm, Sweden

Robert M. Jordan
University of British Columbia
Vancouver, British Columbia
Canada

Charles W. Joyner
St. Andrews College
Laurinburg, North Carolina

Ed Kahn
Los Angeles, California

Israel J. Katz
York College, New York

Harold Kelling
Boulder, Colorado

Peter Kennedy
London, England

Joseph Kerman
University of California
Berkeley, California

King's College Library
University of Aberdeen
Aberdeen, Scotland

Ernst Klusen
Institut für Musikforschung
Neuss, Germany

Maria Kosová
Slovak Academy of Sciences
Bratislava, Czechoslovakia

Thorkild Knudsen
Holstebro, Denmark

Ildikó Kríza
Hungarian Academy of Sciences
Budapest, Hungary

Raimund Kvideland
University of Bergen
Norway

Zmaga Kumer
Slovenian Academy of Sciences
Ljubljana, Yugoslavia

Donatien Laurent
Brest, France

G. Malcolm Laws, Jr.
University of Pennsylvania
Philadelphia, Pennsylvania

Edward B. Lawton
University of California
Berkeley, California

Library of the Society of
Antiquaries
Newcastle-upon-Tyne
England

Michael Licht
University of Texas
Austin, Texas

Herman Liebert
Yale University Library
New Haven, Connecticut

George List
Indiana University
Bloomington, Indiana

Alan Lomax
New York, New York

Eleanor R. Long
Los Angeles, California

Albert B. Lord
Harvard University
Cambridge, Massachusetts

Emily B. Lyle
University of Edinburgh
Edinburgh, Scotland

Ewan MacColl
Beckenham
Kent, England

John MacQueen
University of Edinburgh
Edinburgh, Scotland

Maynard Mack
New Haven, Connecticut

William H. McCarthy, Jr.
Houghton Library
Harvard University
Cambridge, Massachusetts

Judith McCulloh
University of Illinois Press
Champaign, Illinois

Basil Megaw
University of Edinburgh
Edinburgh, Scotland

Keyes D. Metcalf
Harvard College Library
Harvard University
Cambridge, Massachusetts

Ernst Erich Metzner
Universität Frankfurt
Frankfurt, Germany

The Mitchell Library
Glasgow, Scotland

Robin Morton
Belfast, Ireland

Patrick B. Mullen
Ohio State University
Columbus, Ohio

Tom Munnelly
Miltown Malbay
Co. Clare, Ireland

Ailie Munro
University of Edinburgh
Edinburgh, Scotland

Joseph Nagy
University of California
Los Angeles, California

The National Library of Scotland
Edinburgh, Scotland

Bruno Nettl
University of Illinois
Urbana, Illinois

Venetia Newall
The Folklore Society
London, England

W.F.H. Nicolaisen
State University of New York
Binghamton, New York

John D. Niles
University of California
Berkeley, California

Mortan Nolsøe
Tórshavn, Faroe Islands

Holger O. Nygard
Duke University
Durham, North Carolina

Felix J. Oinas
Indiana University
Bloomington, Indiana

Vésteinn Ólason
University of Iceland
Rejkjavik, Iceland

Harry Oster
University of Iowa
Iowa City, Iowa

Sean Ó Suilleabháin
Dublin, Ireland

Americo Paredes
University of Texas
Austin, Texas

Sandy Paton
Sharon, Connecticut

Roger deV. Renwick
University of Texas
Austin, Texas

Kenneth Peacock
Museum of Man
Ottawa, Canada

Suzanne Peterson
University of Washington
Seattle, Washington

John Pope
New Haven, Connecticut

James Porter
University of California
Los Angeles, California

Frank Purslow
Cecil Sharp House
London, England

Richard Purdy
New Haven, Connecticut

Ralph Rader
University of California
Berkeley, California

Benjamin Rajeczky
Hungarian Academy of Sciences
Budapest, Hungary

Inkeri Rank
University of California
Los Angeles, California

Gordon N. Ray
John Simon Guggenheim
Foundation
New York, New York

Willard Rhodes
Columbia University
New York, New York

W. Edson Richmond
Indiana University
Bloomington, Indiana

Ralph Rinzler
Smithsonian Institution
Washington, D.C.

John D. Robb
University of New Mexico
Albuquerque, New Mexico

Stanley R. Robe
University of California
Los Angeles, California

Warren E. Roberts
Indiana University
Bloomington, Indiana

Neil V. Rosenberg
Memorial University of
Newfoundland
St. John's
Newfoundland, Canada

Angus Ross
Sussex, England

Klaus Roth
Universität Münster
Germany

Nils Schiørring
University of Copenhagen
Copenhagen, Denmark

Peggy Seeger
Beckenham
Kent, England

Pete Seeger
New York, New York

L.W. Sharp
Edinburgh University Library
Edinburgh, Scotland

Leslie Shepard
London, England

Helena M. Shire
Cambridge, England

Joseph Silverman
University of California
Santa Cruz, California

W. Douglas Simpson
Aberdeen University Library
Aberdeen, Scotland

Carleton Sprague Smith
New York Public Library
New York, New York

Erik Sønderholm
University of Copenhagen
Copenhagen, Denmark

Mrs. Barry Spachs
Wellesley, Massachusetts

Ellen B. Stekert
University of Minnesota
Minneapolis, Minnesota

Stephen Stern
University of California
Los Angeles, California

Doris and Erich Stockmann
Akademie der Wissenschaften
Berlin, Germany

Wolfgang Suppan
Institut für Musikethnologie
Graz, Austria

John Szwed
University of Pennsylvania
Philadelphia, Pennsylvania

Randall Thompson
Cambridge, Massachusetts

James Thorpe
Huntington Library
San Marino, California

Jeff Todd Titon
Tufts University
Medford, Massachusetts

Barre Toelken
University of Oregon
Eugene, Oregon

Stefaan Top
Catholic University
Leuven, Belgium

John Traugott
University of California
Berkeley, California

F. McD. C. Turner
Magdalene College Library
Oxford, England

Judith W. Turner
University of Santa Clara
Santa Clara, California

Lajos Vargyas
Institute of Musicology
Budapest, Hungary

Mrs. Ursula Vaughan Williams
English Folk Dance and Song
Society
London, England

Karel Vetterl
Slovak Academy of Sciences
Bratislava, Czechoslovakia

Donald J. Ward
University of California
Los Angeles, California

Ruth H. Walker
University of Chicago
Chicago, Illinois

Rainer Wehse
Georg-August Universität
Göttingen, Germany

Jerome Wenker
San Francisco, California

Part 1:
The Study of Individual Ballads

Theodor Fontane's "Sir Patrick Spens"

W. F. H. Nicolaisen

It may seem inappropriate, in a volume of essays dedicated to the greatest ballad scholar this century has known, to include a study which completely ignores tunes. Like no other, Bronson has taught us—or reminded us of—the close interdependence of text and melody, meter and rhythm, syntactic unit and musical phrase, verbal texture and singability in the ballad: ballads are there to be sung. Where Child investigated a literary sub-genre, Bronson has examined and substantiated for us a rounded musico-literary form —the song that tells a story. The Child Ballads are now the Bronson Ballads.

The topic of this appreciative essay does, nevertheless, demand almost exclusive concentration on the text of a certain ballad, just as it requires a relative neglect of those important facets of oral transmission which have become so central to modern scholarly preoccupations in the field of traditional balladry. Instead of concentrating on the ballad as re-created performance, it will be concerned with the problem of linguistic transferability of narrative substance as well as the translatability of story-shaping form. But despite its use of singular, suspiciously definitive, written texts it will have as its subject the tension which may arise between imitation and variation as a result of the conscious, deliberate "rendering" of ballad texts into a language other than that through which they were originally transmitted.

As illustration, the main focus will be on the German version of a Scottish traditional ballad—Theodor Fontane's "Sir Patrick Spens."[1] There are several persuasive reasons for this choice: Fontane (1819–1898), although perhaps better known as a novelist and as a writer of forceful prose, is one of the great exponents of the German literary ballad in the nineteenth century. His "Archibald Douglas" and his "Die Brück' am Tay" ("The Tay Bridge"),[2] one inspired by a Scottish historical event, the other by a contemporary Scottish disaster, must be among the most frequently anthologized pieces of German poetry. Having become acquainted in 1848 with both Bishop Percy's *Reliques of Ancient English Poetry* and Sir Walter Scott's *Minstrelsy of the Scottish Border,* Fontane acknowledged the continued strong influence of these two works on his literary taste and outlook[3] and, in the decade which followed, tried his hand at the translation and re-creation of several of the ballads contained in them. Some of these, "Sir Patrick Spens" among them, had been translated a number of times into German before, from the 1770s onward,[4] and it is therefore possible for us to compare Fontane's version with an earlier rendering by that giant of German folklorists, Johann Gottfried Herder (1744–1803).[5] In addition, there are three different versions by Fontane of the ballad in question, showing slight but significant differences in the wording of some stanzas and consequently offering an opportunity for further comparison within the general framework of the author's own intentions. For these and other reasons the situation is therefore not at all unlike that encountered in the folk-cultural situation, and a terminological classification into type, oicotype, and variant by no means as exotic as it may at first appear. We also have the further advantage, not only of Fontane's own comments on the literary genre of the *Kunstballade,* but also of his views on its folk-cultural model; we benefit, too, from the availability of a certain amount of important biographical material and other relevant sources. Naturally, "Sir Patrick Spens" is not the only ballad which might have been exploited suitably for our purposes but it is certainly one of the best. In the table which follows, the first column provides the Percy version (Child 58 Aa) of 1765 which both Herder and Fontane used, the second Herder's translation (1778), and the third Fontane's rendering, as it first appeared in the annual *Argo* in 1854[6] and then in the collected edition of his ballads in 1861.[7]

While Herder only had the Percy "original" available to him since the *Minstrelsy of the Scottish Border* was not published until 1802, Fontane had the choice of using either Percy's or Scott's version as his model, a choice which was not really difficult for him and which he justified in no uncertain manner:

> Dr. Percy and others have taken great trouble to discover the historical fact which might be the basis of this in truth old and frequently translated ballad. Their endeavors have remained in vain. Walter Scott did have other designs in mind concerning this poem. For him it was not motivated enough and he thought it quite necessary to invent additional motives before including it in his 'Minstrelsy of the Scottish Border'. In my view, he has gone completely astray in this respect, and in place of such a thoroughly poetical, perhaps even

because of its mysteries and its semi-obscurity attractive poem, he has patched together a moderately motivated story which lacks nothing but — the living breath. I find it incredible that there have been translators of decided talent who preferred Scott's improvement for the worse to the touchingly beautiful original[8]

— no punches pulled here by a Scott admirer! It has sometimes been claimed that Fontane nevertheless "followed" Scott,[9] but there appears to be no evidence for this assertion in Fontane's version apart from the slight breach of principle implicit in the addition of a stanza (7a) to Percy's text. These additional four lines are, however, not based on Scott or on any other source but must be ascribed to Fontane himself.

Phrases used in this passage such as "thoroughly poetical," "attractive in its mysteriousness," "touchingly beautiful" are perhaps not the most plausible explanations for his choice, but elsewhere Fontane is more persuasive by describing "Sir Patrick Spens" as "the most ancient historical ballad in Scottish folk poetry, having been created about 1300."[10] His overriding interest in the ballad as "the poetic expression of outstanding historical events,"[11] or as poetic history, and his delight in such stylistic qualities as "brevity, conciseness of expression, the magic of semi-darkness, simplicity and melodiousness, depth of feeling, natural grace . . . "[12] of necessity resulted in his preference for the Percy version. Whether Fontane was right in his assumption of the ballad's considerable antiquity is of little concern, and the presentation of arguments supporting or contradicting his opinion lies outside the scope of this study. It is quite sufficient to state that he undoubtedly regarded the version printed in Percy's *Reliques* as close to the "original" which, as his comments on the Robin Hood cycle of ballads demonstrate, may be easily discerned once the "variants" have been discarded.[13]

Fundamentally, then, Bishop Percy's version is more or less a definitive text to Fontane such as he himself would produce as a creative poet. That this stance does not automatically infer invariability is inherent in his attitude towards his own poetry, which he treats as a skilled craftsman who is never totally satisfied and therefore always looking for improvements. Fontane calls himself a "potterer"[14] several times, each new edition of his poems (including his ballads) sees him at work revising and reshaping, and his "Sir Patrick Spens" shows the signs of sensitive artistic responsibility as much as any of his other works, through the number of published textual variations which the ballad displays on different occasions. It is, of course, somewhat ironic in a way that the Percy "original" is itself probably a composite version since it is said to have been "given from two M.S. copies, transmitted from Scotland,"[15] but that fact, too, is not really relevant in this context, for our main

	Sir Patrick Spence (Percy 1765)	Der Schiffer (Herder 1778)	Sir Patrick Spens (Fontane 1852/54)
1	The king sits in Dumferling toune, / Drinking the blude-reid wine: / O quhar will I get guid sailòr, / To sail this schip of mine?	Der König sitzt in Dumferlingschloss, / Er trinkt blutrothen Wein. / "O wo treff ich ein'n Segler an, / Dies Schiff zu segeln mein?"	Der König sitzt in Dumferlin-Schloss, / Er trinkt blutroten Wein: / "Wer ist mein bester Segler? / Er muss in See hinein!"
2	Up and spak an eldern knicht, / Sat at the kings richt kne: / Sir Patrick Spence is the best sailòr, / That sails upon the se.	Auf und sprach ein alter Ritter, / (Sass rechts an Königs Knie), / "Sir Patrik Spence ist der beste Segler / Im ganzen Land allhie."	Sprach da ein schottischer Ritter / (Er stand an des Königs Seit'): / "Der beste, das ist Sir Patrick / Im Lande weit und breit."
3	The king has written a braid letter, / And signd it wi' his hand; / And sent to to Sir Patrick Spence, / Was walking on the sand.	Der König schrieb ein'n breiten brief / Versiegelt ihm mit seiner Hand, / Und sandt' ihn zu Sir Patrick Spence, / Der wohnt' an Meeres Strand.	Der König schrieb einen offenen Brief, / Einen Brief mit eigner Hand — / Sir Patrick schritt am Meere / Hin über den knirschenden Sand.
4	The first line that Sir Patrick red, / A loud lauch lauched he: / The next line that Sir Patrick red, / The teir blinded his ee.	Die Erste Zeil Sir Patrik las, / Laut Lachen schlug er auf; / Die zweite Zeil Sir Patrik las, / Eine Thrän' ihm folgte drauf.	Er sah auf die erste Zeile / Und lachte, als er sie sah, / Er las die zweite Zeile, / Nicht weiter las er da.
5	O quha is this has don this deid, / This ill deid don to me; / To send me out this time o' the zeir, / To sail upon the se?	O wer, wer hat mir das gethan? / Hat wehgethan mir sehr! / Mich auszusenden in dieser Zeit! / Zu segeln auf dem Meer.	Sein Auge stund in Tränen: / "Wem tat ich also weh, / Zu schicken in dieser Sturmzeit / Mich über die weisse See?
6	Mak hast, mak haste, my mirry men all, / / Our guid schip sails the morne.	Macht fort, macht fort, mein' wackre Leute, / Unser gut Schiff segelt morgen.	Zu Schiff nun, liebe Mannen, / Wir segeln vor Tagesschein!"

	Scots	German	German
	O say na sae, my master deir, For I feir a deadlie storme.	"O sprecht nicht so, mein lieber Herr, Da sind wir sehr in Sorgen."	Da sprach ein alter Matrose: "Sir Patrick, das kann nicht sein.
7	Late late yestreen I Saw the new moone Wi' the auld moone in hir arme; And I feir, I feir, my deir mastèr, That we will com to harme.	Gestern Abend sah ich den neuen Mond, Ein Hof war um ihn her. Ich fürcht', ich fürcht', mein lieber Herr, Ein Sturm uns wartet schwer."	Ich hört' in meiner Koje Die Windsbraut, wie sie gelacht, Und der neue Mond hielt den alten Im Arme die letzte Nacht." *
7a			Es kam der nächste Morgen, Sie gingen all an Bord, Sir Patrick und die Seinen Und mancher schottische Lord.
8	O our Scots nobles wer richt laith To weet their cork-heild schoone; Bot lang owre a' the play wer playd, Thair hats they swam aboone.	O edle Schotten, sie wussten lang, Zu wahr'n ihr Korkholzschu; Doch lang überall das Spiel gespielt, Schwammen ihre Hüte dazu.	Im Winde flaggten die Wimpel, Hoch tanzten Schiff und Flut? Drei Tage, da schwamm auf dem Meere Nur noch ein bebänderter Hut. *
9	O lang, lang, may thair ladies sit Wi' thair fans into their hand, Or eir they se Sir Patrick Spence Cum sailing to the land.	O lang, lang mögen ihre Frauen sitzen, Den Fächer in ihrer Hand; Eh je sie sehn Sir Patrik Spence Ansegeln an das Land.	Nun sitzen viel schöne Frauen Mit ihren Fächern am Strand Und warten auf Sir Patrick, Auf dass er steig' an Land.
10	O lang, lang, may the ladies stand Wi' thair gold kems in their hair, Waiting for their ain deir lords, For they'll se thame na mair.	O lang, lang mögen ihre Frauen stehn Den Goldkamm in dem Haar, Und warten ihrer lieben Herr'n, Sie sehn sie nimmer gar.	Alle tragen sie Kämme mit Goldschmuck Und blicken hinaus aufs Meer, Doch sie erharren keinen Und sehen keinen mehr.
11	Have owre, have owre to Aberdour, It's fiftie fadom deip: And thair lies guid Sir Patrick Spence, Wi' the Scots lords at his feit.	Dort über, hinüber nach Aberdour! Tief funfzig Fad'n im Meer, Da liegt der gute Sir Patrick Spence, Sein' Edlen um ihn her.	Fünfzig Faden tief und tiefer, Da pflegen sie all der Ruh: Sir Patrick und die Seinen Und die schottischen Lords dazu.

concern must obviously be with Fontane's attitudes, perceptions and skills.

Fortunately, the purely technical task of listing similarities and differences, omissions and additions, slavish imitations and more literal rewordings has already been attended to. Two dissertations in the early parts of this century performed this service for us. Of these, the earlier, Carl Wegmann's *Theodor Fontane als Übersetzer englischer und schottischer Balladen* (1910) deals mainly with the differences and, without much attention to detail, regards Fontane's German rendering as a "formally perfect, poetic work of art."[16] The later, Hans Rhyn's *Die Balladendichtung Theodor Fontanes mit besonderer Berücksichtigung seiner Bearbeitungen altenglischer und altschottischer Balladen aus den Sammlungen von Percy und Scott* (1914), while making a detailed comparison stanza by stanza, also comes to rather superficial conclusions: "the rhythm is handled very well," "the third line of Fontane's is more appropriate," "Fontane seems to have given up the lively repetition [of stanza 6] on purpose," "in [Fontane's] version [of stanza 8] everything is thoroughly distinct and clear," etc.[17] Rhyn, too, though not quite so fulsome in his unqualified praise as Wegmann, appears to prefer Fontane's version, and of his more general conclusions at least three would seem to apply to "Sir Patrick Spens": "Fontane smoothes abrupt transitions; adds new images; usually retains the beauties of the original and multiplies these in many ways."[18]

Naturally, it cannot be our business to indulge in similarly facile comparisons and statements. The question is not whether Fontane's rendering is better or worse than Percy's (or even Herder's) but whether it is successful as a literary ballad with strong folk connections. That is why Herder's earlier version is so instructive, for even the briefest scrutiny shows it to be an attempt at a close, faithful translation of a Scottish ballad into German, not avoiding the resulting syntactic wrenchings, syllabic elisions, and grammatic awkwardnesses. Nothing is added, nothing is taken away, nothing is interpreted. The result is, as intended, a Scottish ballad in German, no more no less, and the original force and flavor are convincingly maintained. This is where its attraction and its worth lie; the translator is simply — no easy task! — a mediator who thrives on invisibility and whose success can be measured largely by the degree of his non-interference. If any German speaker without an adequate knowledge of Scottish English wishes to have a sense of the stylistic characteristics of Percy's version of "Sir Patrick Spens," he must, as in many similar instances, turn to Herder whose German words and rhythms might well be sung to the traditional Scottish tunes. If, on the other hand, the same German speaker wishes to have a satisfying poetic experience in German, while not losing the most central and significant qualities of the Scottish model he must turn to Fontane, the translator as both mediator and re-creator, the poet successfully transcending the imitative act.

Fontane himself was very conscious of this dual role. From April till September 1852 he made his second journey to England, with the avowed purpose of "conducting on the spot more detailed research into old English ballad literature,"[19] the first poetic fruits of which are obviously his translations of "Sir Patrick Spens" and "Edward," both of which he read to the Berlin literary society *Der Tunnel* on November 21 of the same year.[20] While in England — mainly in London, part of the time as a neighbor of Dickens — he also wrote a number of literary essays for several German publications; the study entitled *Die Manufaktur in der Kunst (Manufactured Art)* is a clear indication of his reflective preoccupation with the process of craftsmanlike (artful?) imitation in which he is himself involved. Presenting the human race as "an imitative species whose greatest inclination is imitation," he argues for the existence of a real "art of imitation within art itself,"[21] as a legitimate counterpart to crude deception and falsification, citing as his crown witnesses two "famous names in English literature who were great poets but even greater 'manufacturers': Chatterton and Macpherson."[22] Reading, in places, like an act of self-persuasion, this essay provides a philosophical matrix for his poetic endeavors in the field of ballad re-creation and adaption without which, presumably, his efforts in this direction would have remained halfhearted and less profound, certainly without that encouraging artistic conviction.

As part of a general investigation of the characteristics and categories of "The Old English and Scottish Ballads,"[23] he gains additional strength in his theoretical concepts from a seminal discussion of the role the individual author plays in the creation of folk poetry. Responding to the contemporary view that the period of genuine Scottish folk poetry lay between 1315 and 1745 i.e., between Bannockburn and Culloden (1746), he comments:

> These dates . . . are right as long as one thinks it necessary to retain the old definition of folk poetry, that definition which demands no definitely identifiable author and makes the absence or presence of a *name* the decisive and differentiating criterion. But it might perhaps be high time to give up this old definition once and for all and to make the question as to what constitutes folk poetry dependent only on the tone, the manner, and possibly on the yardstick of the popularity or non-popularity of a song. [Certain German songs] are, although we know the names of their authors, just as much German folksongs as the old German song of the girl and the hazeltree or the old ballad of the Knight of Falkenstein. Nobody had

recognized this truth more clearly than our great authority in matters folksong—Herder; but his example, which he only sketched out rather than fully developed, has *not* been followed. Other views have won the day and are still dominant.

Endless confusion has been caused by the fact that, partly under Walter Scott's leadership, people have become used to speaking of genuine, real folksongs and mere imitations of these. Such a difference does not exist. Real folksongs, too, are imitated folksongs; for everybody who has sung a song, no matter whether today or three centuries ago, has always had in his ear some sound of a known or unknown predecessor, and especially the most genuine and most undisputed folksongs tend to carry this dependency on traditional sounds to an incredible extreme. The contrast between folk poetry and art poetry is ancient but in the same way in which folk poetry and art poetry have *always* existed side by side in all civilized societies, they *still* exist side by side today, and the time has surely come to abandon the old, confusing notion that in any given century—for one society earlier, for another later — folk poetry ceases and art poetry begins.

Art poetry begins and also ends when such events as the great Germanic migrations intervene; but folk poetry continues forever. It has different seasons, it is good or bad, it flourishes and decays, it rules and it serves, but it is always alive, is always there, and it is almost foolish to speak of its demise. It is most foolish, however, to stress the question of named authorship and to let our judgement as to what is a folksong and what is not depend on the question whether we know the author or not. This circumstance is of extreme indifference. The songs of Robert Burns and Allan Ramsay are folksongs as much as the old airs of Queen Mary's times; it does not matter whether a song is a hundred hours old or a hundred years, and in accordance with this justifiable view, Scottish folk poetry flourishes right at this very moment, against all assurances that it died in 1745, having somehow lain among the dead on Culloden field. Burns's songs of 1785 sound the same as the Jacobite songs of 1745; we know who wrote the former but we do *not* know who wrote the latter. That is the whole difference. Folksongs the ones, and folksongs the other; a line has been drawn arbitrarily and a distinction has been made which does not exist in fact.[24]

Despite some understandable nineteenth-century preconceptions this passage, as well as the whole essay of which it is part, may well be looked upon as a lively and well-reasoned contribution to a debate about an issue which still tends to exercise quite a few minds in ballad scholarship. Fontane was clearly no folklorist; he may not ever have understood fully the true nature of folksong, as Gillian Rodger has pointed out;[25] but as a creative artist mediating between the two cultures and their languages he has insights which have eluded many a folklorist. As a writer of ballads, nourished on the one hand by a parental predilection for Scott and on the other by an early educational encounter with the whole of Schiller's balladry,[26] he is closer to the re-creative folk singer than any literary critic is ever likely to be, and is well aware that the long cherished notion of spontaneous creation is a delusion impossible to share by the involved poet/performer. Anonymity in particular is no exclusive passport to folk-cultural authenticity; and the role of the known individual in the creation, adaptation and transmission of folklore is so much more prominent and important than those who should know better are often prepared to acknowledge.

Naturally Fontane's argument is not primarily, perhaps not at all, concerned with oral transmission but with the medium in which he himself is a practitioner: the written text. His "original" is, and his own product will be, a written text but this does not mean a totally different point of view; nor is it completely inappropriate in the case of the English and Scottish traditional ballad which for so long has had a written as well as an oral tradition, the intertwinings of these being sometimes difficult to separate in a world and an era of literate "folk." For him, a ballad tells a story, and whenever possible relates history. "Historical episodes, characters and situations engrossed him far more than the general human themes of the folk-ballad."[27] Having himself used the ballad as the literary form most suited to come to terms with a contemporary disaster ("Die Brück' am Tay"), he sees "the old ballad themes" as having at one time themselves been "current events,"[28] and it is quite natural for him, on his travels through England and Scotland, to visit places whose historical significance has become authenticated through the ballads in which they occur. For "Sir Patrick Spens" he has this scenario in mind:

> It is assumed that the event on which this ballad is based took place under King Alexander III, the last Celtic king of Scotland. His daughter was married to the King of Norway, and he despatched Sir Patrick Spens to Norway in November i.e., in the season of the gales, in order to get news or fetch his daughter. The gale came and all the ships foundered at Aberdour on the Scottish coast. Some say (based on hints which the ballad itself provides) that it was a plot to get rid of Sir Patrick Spens.[29]

This summary is helpful, almost essential, in understanding and assessing Fontane's approach to his task and the means he deploys to accomplish it. In a fashion, it fills gaps in prose which the narrative poetry has left open; and it almost functions like that additional stanza 7a, which in its turn is informed by the author's own commentary and which, together with the completely revised stanza 8, removes the acid judgment expressed in the Percy version on the reluctance of the precious landlubbing, unsuitably-dressed Scottish courtiers when faced with a voyage at the most dangerous time of the year. For Fontane, the lords are simply Scottish, reinforcing the Scottishness of the setting emphasized earlier through the introduction of a "Scottish," not just an "eldern," knight in stanza 2, and like good vassals of the king they board the ship without outward signs of emotion or any symbols of despair. Fontane's own commentary, too, throws light on his interpretive substitution "in dieser Sturmzeit" ("in this season of gales") for Percy's phrase "this time o' the zeir," a substitution further highlighted by the new epithet "white" in the following line. There is obviously a limit to the amount of gaps in narrative which Fontane is willing to tolerate, although he himself creates an additional abrupt transition by eliminating line 3 of stanza 3 in which the actual sending of the king's letter is alluded to, and by replacing it visibly with a dash. This removal does, however, give him an opportunity to devote two lines to Sir Patrick's "walking on the sand," and he does so by the addition not only of the clarifying adverbial phrase "am Meere" ("by the sea") but also of a further attributive adjective: the sand becomes "knirschend" ("crunching"), an epithet which appeals to our aural and tactile senses in the same way in which "weisse See" ("white sea") speaks to our imagination through the sense of vision. Contrary to folk-narrative practice, which tends to leave such matters to the listener's imagination, the poet's sea has to be "white," the sand "crunching," the season "stormy," the sailor "old," and the ladies have to be "beautiful." This deliberate infusion of epithets is even more noticeable in the ballad version quoted to illustrate his essay of 1861. There stanzas 9 and 10 read:

> Nun sitzen viel schöne Frauen
> Mit blitzenden Fächern am Strand,
> Und stützen die weisse Stirne
> Auf ihre weisse Hand.
>
> Sie tragen goldene Kämme
> Und starren hinaus aufs Meer,
> Doch sie erharren keinen
> Und sehen keinen mehr.[30]

In this variant the fans have become "blitzend" ("flashing"), the ladies brows and hands "weiss" ("white"), and their combs, as in the original, "golden." The repetition of "weiss," the internal rhymes "sitzen — blitzen (den) — stützen" and "starren — erharren," and the syntactic parallelism of the last two lines (with its repetition of "keinen"!) bear witness to an intensity of construction and density of linguistic texture found neither in Percy/Herder, with its own texturing devices, nor in Fontane's own "definitive" version. Nevertheless, not even here does Fontane attempt to recapture the severe, lament-like, incrementally-repetitive sequence of the two "O lang, O lang" quatrains.

For some reason, it is in fact stanza 9 which appears to have received a greater share of Fontane's "pottering" attention than any other portion of the ballad, but this impression may be more apparent than real insofar as it is one of only three stanzas included in three different contexts by the author. In a vignette of a journey to Loch Leven Castle—obviously part of his journey through Scotland with Bernhard von Lepel in 1859 but not included in his travelogue *Beyond the Tweed*—he makes reference to the geographical framework of "Sir Patrick Spens" by quoting stanzas 1, 9, and 10, the first and the last in a form identical with the essay version. The first two lines of stanza 9, however, read:

> Nun sitzen viel schöne Frauen
> Bei Aberdour am Strand,[31]

anticipating the place name of Percy's eleventh stanza by making it the location of the waiting widows-to-be rather than of their husbands' watery grave. He thus avoids being drawn into the controversy regarding the precise place where the disaster occurred. Because there are two Scottish places named *Aberdour,* both have been claimed in connection with this ballad. Child without equivocation spoke for the Aberdeenshire *Aberdour*[32] but Fontane had no doubt that it was the *Aberdour* situated not many miles east of *Dunfermline,* overlooking the Firth of Forth from the north. Crossing the firth from Leith to North Queensferry he saw "on his right the village of *Aberdour.* This name recalls one of the most beautiful and oldest of Scottish ballads, the ballad of Sir Patrick Spens,"[33] just as Dunfermline is for him the place where the "old ballad king drank the 'blude-reid wine'."[34] These are only two telling examples of what Gillian Rodger has called Fontane's reliance "on the evocative power of place-names."[35] These provide him with a sense of location and geographical space similar to the sense of chronological space supplied by the names of historical characters and important battles. "From Bannockburn to Culloden" is Fontane, "from 1314 to 1745 (1746)" is the history book. The wine-sipping king who sends Sir Patrick Spens and many Scottish nobles to their deaths carouses at Dunfermline, the bereaved women wait in vain at Aberdour. On at least three occasions,[36] Fontane asks friends for names to flesh out poems on which he is working, for, as he writes to Friedlaender in 1888: "One needs the stimulus names give and the knowledge that a certain amount of factual information lies beside them—and out of this consciousness of ownership one can then create."[37] The contents of names, their onomastic meaning, so to speak, becomes available as an author's resource; and he can be as generous or as miserly as he wishes with it, especially when his readers/listeners have no interfering contents of their own to bring to these names—Dunfermline, Aberdour, Sir

Patrick Spens. In view of Fontane's delight in, and creative use of, names it is slightly surprising that the name *Aberdour* does not appear in his "definitive" version. Is this an indication of complete withdrawal from a toponymic controversy? Did uncertainty in an issue like this act as an irritant so annoying that it prevented him from using the name at all iconically?

There is no such problem regarding the titular hero of the ballad. One cannot even imagine Fontane contemplating an anonymous title like Herder's "Der Schiffer" ("The Skipper"). This ballad is not about a nameless hero—none of his ballads are—and for good measure Percy's "my master deir" (Herder: "mein lieber Herr," Fontane's essay version: "Lieb Herre") also becomes "Sir Patrick" in the "definitive" stanza 6 which, in conjunction with the stanza which follows, turns out to be among the most drastically altered of the whole ballad. The set of changes introduced, mostly in the cause of clarity, is complex and interdependent and has as much to do with structural concepts as with narrative continuity and an overwhelming sense of inescapable, impending doom. Its initial reason may well lie in the previous stanza where Fontane decided to substitute "Sturmzeit" ("season of gales") for "this time o' the zeir" (Herder is halfway: "in dieser Zeit"). This substitution would have made the later "I feir a deadlie storme" redundant or at least repetitive, and Fontane is thus forced into repatterning the affected eight lines and into introducing a new image. He begins this task by inserting a statement about the identity of the speaker of the warning derived from the portents of popular weather lore (6:3). This is, of course, uncharacteristic of the ballad, as well as unnecessary in the structuring of ballad dialogue through formal means i.e., change of speaker at the caesura or at the end of a stanza. The inserted line also simply confirms what we know, or have at least suspected, already: it is a sailor who speaks, a common man, one of the folk. That it is an "old sailor" we might also have guessed, but Fontane's explicit introduction of the notions of age and long service is designed to reinforce the dilemma in which Sir Patrick finds himself. Not only does his own experience as a sailor—after all, he is the best in the land—tell him that this is the wrong time of the year to go to sea and that the risks he is about to take are far too great, but the trustworthy voice of folk wisdom interpreting the weather signs in its own way comes, not unexpectedly but more ominously, to the same conclusion. As if one warning were not enough! Loyalty to one's king is doubly challenged, since disaster is now no longer just possible but certain.

In Percy's version, the very real fear of the seafaring folk, as expressed by their representative, is put into words three times: "I feir a deadlie storme" (6: 4) and "I feir, I feir, my deir master, that we will com to harme" (7: 3-4). The most central and most striking image of the whole ballad, that awesome, frightening heavenly spectacle of "the new moone wi' the auld moone in hir arme" (7: 1-2) has had its effect—the ships' crews are so afraid that, in an unprecedented step, the most senior of them is sent to the admiral, "the best sailor that sails upon the se," to give humble but insistent voice to their trembling. Fontane retains the central spectre in a most effective translation—"der neue Mond hielt den alten im Arme die letzte Nacht"—but, having preempted the possibility of mentioning its dreadful consequences in his previous "Sturmzeit," decides to re-emphasize the uncontrollable power of the irrational by paralleling the portentous apparition seen by so many in the sky of the night before with a personal experience in the privacy of the sailor's own sleeplessness—"I heard in my berth the *Windsbraut* laughing"—(7: 1-2). One may agree or disagree whether this second superstition is effective or not; I, for one, see in it an unfortunate addition although it takes the whole process of "folk fear" one step further from the sagacious interpretation of weather lore into the inexplicable terrain of personified superstition. Not only does it seem to weaken the impact of the central symbol presented by Percy's "original," it also introduces a superstition apparently confined, in this particular form, to the German-speaking world since it represents a late folk-etymological re-interpretation of an obsolescent medieval German word meaning simply something like "whirlwind."[38] From a Scottish point of view this is an unforgivable folk-cultural clash; in a German ballad it may perhaps not be as incompatible, though hardly supportable even, in terms of structure.

Despite these modifications, however, the basic architectonics of the ballad remain intact. Fontane, although re-creating a ballad within the compass of his own stylistic and narrative craftsmanship, does not have Scott's editing ambitions directed at making the ballad tell the full story. He does not regard the Percy version as a fragment or in any way defective but rather as the "good, old original" which legitimately displays the acknowledged ballad characteristics of terseness, abrupt transitions, suggestiveness, etc. Even his undeniable attempts at clarifying augmentation do not seriously violate the principal qualities of ballad style. Indeed, as we have already seen, Fontane effectively creates a new gap in narrative continuity in one place (stanza 3) by replacing Percy's third line "And sent it to Sir Patrick Spence" with a dash.

That Fontane's "Sir Patrick Spens" might well have been a very different ballad without the availability and influence of Herder's translation is almost self-evident. His youthful enthusiasm may at one stage have prompted him to compete with the "old master," but later in life he was less sure about the results of this competition. As he admitted in a letter to Erich Schmidt of October 7, 1896:

> I translated it [Percy's version of "Edward"] when I was quite young and at that time intended to show old Herder how it should be properly done. Four years ago, however, when the most recent edition of my poems appeared, I came to the conclusion, although somewhat late, that my ding-dong translation [Tamtamübersetzung] had nothing to offer when compared with the magnificent simplicity of the old superintendent general (or whatever he was), and at that time I atoned for my sin by eliminating the ballad [from that edition].[39]

He had written in a similar vein to Detlev von Liliencron on May 11, 1889, with regard to his translation of the "Chevy Chase" ballad:

> I still remember that, almost fifty years ago, I made up my mind to translate the Chevy-Chase better than Herder and even deluded myself into thinking that I had succeeded. Now I am all for Herder and shudder at my wonderful identical rhymes.[40]

Although read to the *Tunnel* on the same day as "Edward" and obviously written at the same time with the same intentions in mind, "Sir Patrick Spens" escapes Fontane's self-critical verdict and subsequent excision. Perhaps its indebtedness to Herder is too great to allow it to be seen as a serious and true competitor. In fact, after the first two lines we cannot even be sure whether we are about to read Herder, or Fontane who has also retained such Herderisms as the etymologically-cognate "Segler" for "sailor" (1: 3), the substitution of an affirmation of country-wide fame for the mere assertion of seafaring skills (2: 4), the additional adverbial phrase "am Meere" (3: 3; Herder: "an Meeres," 3: 4), but otherwise introduces many words and phrases of his own and, as we have already seen, redistributes certain lines, as for example in the transfer of the last line of stanza 4 to the beginning of stanza 5. Sometimes he makes use of other sources; his phrase "einen offenen Brief" (3: 1) for Herder's "ein'n breiten Brief" (Percy's "a braid letter") stems from a footnote in Percy's edition[41] which glosses "braid" as "open." Perhaps the most crucial change comes in the stress pattern, for only in the first lines of stanzas 1 and 3 does Fontane preserve the four stresses which are a regular feature of Percy's and Herder's 4, 3; 4, 3 pattern; all other lines, in whatever position, have three stresses so that the basic stanza scans 3, 3; 3, 3. Because of the highly inflected nature of German many more bisyllabic words of a "stress-unstress" model are required. Fontane uses these regularly as the final words in the non-rhyming first and third lines (apart from the first lines of stanzas 1 and 3, of course, for obvious metric reasons) but avoids bisyllabic rhymes, whereas Herder is forced to use them once (6: 2 and 4). It seems highly unlikely therefore that the Fontane ballad might be sung to any of the traditional tunes.[42]

When all is said and done, Fontane's "Sir Patrick Spens" turns out to be, in its own right, a well-crafted ballad which can take its place unselfconsciously in any edition of the author's poetry. It is not "a mere translation" but a successful and acceptable variant within the written corpus of versions of Child 58.[43] That it is in German rather than in English becomes almost immaterial insofar as the verbal disagreement among the Scottish-English variants themselves is considerable although not as extensive as in certain other traditional ballads. There is never any doubt that all versions are variants of the same ballad type, and this includes Fontane's rendering. Its dependence on its original with regard to narrative structure, word choice, and basic stylistic features is finely balanced by an independent handling of the metric arrangement, the inclusion of additional imagery, and the introduction of certain modifications aimed at clarifying the ballad story for the German reader unfamiliar with Scottish affairs. Its narrative substance remains well intact and its effectiveness as a poem in its own right is never in dispute. At the same time, it is not undermined by the tension arising from the wish to imitate and the need to innovate, but thrives on it, while effectively bridging the gap between folk ballad and literary poem.[44] Because of its mediating position and dual function it is, like Fontane's other literary re-creations of Scottish and English traditional ballads, certainly worth the folklorist's attention.

NOTES

[1]See, for example, Theodor Fontane, *Sämtliche Werke*, ed. Walter Keitel, vol. 6 (Munich: Carl Hauser, 1964), pp. 137–39.

[2]Ibid., pp. 9–12, 285–87.

[3]Theodor Fontane, *Von Zwanzig bis Dreissig. Sämtliche Werke*, vol. 15 (Munich: Nymphenburger Verlagsbuchhandlung, 1967), p. 163.

[4]For a list of these translations see Francis James Child, *The English and Scottish Popular Ballads*, vol. 2 (Boston: Houghton, Mifflin and Co., 1886), p. 20.

[5]*Herders Sämtliche Werke*, ed. Bernard Suphan, vol. 25 (Berlin: Weidmannsche Buchhandlung, 1885), pp. 175–76. It was originally published in *Volkslieder*, part 1 (Leipzig: Weygandsche Buchhandlung, 1778), pp. 89–91. A similar comparison was made by Ernst Kohler in his Berlin dissertation of 1939, *Die Balladendichtung im Berliner "Tunnel über der Spree"* (Berlin: Ebering, 1940), pp. 270–81. Apart from some obvious statements of fact, however, and certain unavoidable conclusions derived from them, there is little in Kohler's treatment which impinges on the present argument and approach. It is, for instance, not a concern of ours whether Fontane's rendering is a more or less "faithful" translation than Herder's.

[6]*Argo*, Belletristiches Jahrbuch für das Jahr 1854. Edited by T. Fontane and F. Kugler (Dessau: Katz, 1854).

[7]Theodor Fontane, *Balladen* (Berlin: Wilhelm Hertz, 1861).

[8]Comments in *Argo*, 1854, pp. 229–36 (see Keitel, Fontane *Sämtliche Werke* 6, p. 898). All translations are mine. It has, of course, been shown since that Scott did not "invent" his additional material but obtained it from other versions of the ballad. For a synopsis see Charles G. Zug III, "The Ballad Editor as Antiquary: Scott and the *Minstrelsy*," *Journal of the Folklore Institute*, 13 (1976), 68, and "The Ballad and History: The Case for Scott," *Folklore*, 89 (1978), 230. Zug calls Scott's final version "overstuffed."

[9]Theodor Fontane, *Balladen und Gedichte. Sämtliche Werke*, vol. 20 (Munich: Nymphenburger Verlagshandlung, 1962), p. 759. See also vol. 31, no. 2 (1974), p. 687. Cf. Sir Walter Scott's *Minstrelsy of the Scottish Border*, vol. 1, ed. T. F. Henderson (Edinburgh: W. Blackwood and Sons, 1902), pp. 224–30.

[10]Theodor Fontane, *Aufsätze zur Literatur. Werke und Schriften*, vol. 28 (Frankfurt/M.: Ullstein, 1979), p. 175.

[11]Ibid., p. 173.

[12]Ibid., p. 165.

[13]Ibid., p. 147.

[14]See, for example, his letter to Paul Lindau, February 13, 1885, in Richard Brinkmann, *Theodor Fontane*, part 1: Dichter über ihre Dichtungen, vol. 12, no. 1 (Munich: Heimeran, n.d.), p. 132.

[15]Thomas Percy, *Reliques of Ancient Poetry* (London: John Templeman et al., 1839), p. 20.

[16]Carl Wegmann, *Theodor Fontane als Übersetzer englischer und schottischer Balladen* (Münster: Westfälische Vereinsdruckerei, 1910), p. 50.

[17]Hans Rhyn, *Die Balladendichtung Theodor Fontanes mit besonderer Berücksichtigung seiner Bearbeitungen altenglischer und altschottischer Balladen aus den Sammlungen von Percy und Scott*, Sprache und Dichtung 15 (Bern: A. Francke, 1914), pp. 61–66.

[18]Ibid., p. 113.

[19]"Autobiographie Fontanes für Ignaz Hub, 1864," *Sämtliche Werke*, vol. 15 (Munich: Nymphenburger Verlagshandlung, 1967), p. 431.

[20]Wegmann, *Theodor Fontane als Übersetzer*, p. 5. Fontane translated altogether twelve ballads from Percy's *Reliques*, six from Scott's *Minstrelsy*, and three from J. S. Moore's *Pictorial Book of Ballads* (London, 1847).

[21]Theodor Fontane, *Ein Sommer in London. Sämtliche Werke*, vol. 17 (Munich: Nymphenburger Verlagshandlung, 1963), p. 50.

[22]Ibid., p. 52.

[23]"Die alten englischen und schottischen Balladen," *Aufsätze zur Literatur*, pp. 142–82. First published in *Morgenblatt für Gebildete Leser*, 55 (Stuttgart: Cotta, 1861), nos. 6, 7, 9, and 10 (Feb. 5–Mar. 5).

[24]Ibid., pp. 163–65.

[25]Gillian Rodger, "Fontane's Conception of the Folk-Ballad," *The Modern Language Review*, 53 (1958), 44–58.

[26]Theodor Fontane, *Meine Kinderjahre. Sämtliche Werke*, vol. 14 (Munich: Nymphenburger Verlagshandlung, 1961), pp. 88, 137.

[27]Rodger, "Fontane's Conception," p. 50.

[28]Letter to Paul Schlenther, June 30, 1889, in Brinkmann, *Theodor Fontane*, p. 154.

[29]*Aufsätze zur Literatur*, p. 173.

[30]Ibid., p. 175.

[31]"Lochleven-Castle," *Sämtliche Werke*, vol. 18 (Munich: Nymphenburger Verlagshandlung, 1963), p. 420. First published in *Die Presse* (Vienna) 12, no.

333 (December 23, 1859). This has been included in Theodor Fontane, *Across the Tweed* (London: Phoenix House, 1965), p. 207, but a curious rearrangement of the text, as well as a return to the Percy "originals," do not give any impression of the flavor of Fontane's translations and obscure the variations. An informative assessment of Fontane's travels through Scotland is to be found in Gotthard Erler, "Fontane in Schottland," *Fontane Blätter*, 3, no. 1 (1973), 124-33.

[32]Child, *The English and Scottish Popular Ballads*, vol. 2, p. 20.

[33]"Lochleven-Castle," p. 420.

[34]Ibid.

[35]Rodger, "Fontane's Conception," p. 56.

[36]Letters to Richard Béringuier, October 5, 1885 (Brinkmann, *Theodor Fontane*, p. 139), Detlev von Liliencron, January 19, 1889 (Brinkmann, ibid., p. 148), and Georg Friedlaender, February 3, 1888 (Brinkmann, ibid., p. 145).

[37]February 6, 1888 (Brinkmann, ibid., p. 145).

[38]See Hanns Bächtold-Stäubli, *Handwörterbuch des deutschen Aberglaubens*, vol. 9 (Berlin: Walter de Gruyter, 1938-41), cols. 636-40.

[39]Brinkman, *Theodor Fontane*, p. 181.

[40]Ibid., p. 149.

[41]Percy, *Reliques*, p. 20.

[42]Bertrand Harris Bronson, *The Traditional Tunes of the Child Ballads*, vol. 2 (Princeton, N.J.: Princeton University Press, 1962), pp. 29-36.

[43]Child, *The English and Scottish Popular Ballads*, vol. 2, pp. 20-32.

[44]See also Wolfgang Kayser, *Geschichte der deutschen Ballade* (Berlin: Dunker und Dünnhaupt, 1936), p. 276.

"King Orpheus" and the Harmony
of the Seasons

Emily B. Lyle

In the Scottish ballad of "King Orpheus" (Child 19),[1] after Orpheus has finished playing his pipes to the fairy people, he is asked what he would like to have as reward for his playing and he asks for his queen, Isabel, the Scottish Eurydice, and takes her safely back home. I want here to focus on the musical performance which leads to this happy outcome for it is, as we shall see, in a way comparable to the much more obviously splendid harmony of the spheres which Orpheus is described as hearing in another Scottish work, the fifteenth-century *Orpheus and Eurydice* of Robert Henryson:

> In his passage amang the planetis all,
> He herd a hevynly melody and sound,
> Passing all instrumentis musicall,
> Causid be rollyng of the speris round.[2]

Henryson is writing in the Neoplatonic tradition and his learned treatment of the theme of the harmony of the spheres falls readily into place in the line of development of classical thought in Western literature. The treatment of music in the ballad does not do so and I shall argue that it belongs to a very early conceptual framework which preceded the idea of the harmony of the spheres and was largely replaced by it in the mainstream of Western tradition. I am, I believe, making the point about the ballad music for the first time but I am not breaking new ground in claiming that the harmony of the spheres is a development from an earlier concept. M.L. West notes with approval that Walter Burkert "has suggested, on the basis of several ancient references and parallels among other peoples, that the later theory of a harmony of the planetary spheres developed from a simpler conception of a

correspondence between the four seasons and four notes or inter-
vals."[3] It is this "simpler conception" that is in question here but
in my view the correspondence cannot be understood in terms of
the relatively late four seasons. The Indo-European year had three
seasons only—summer, winter, and spring—and it is to this group
of three seasons that the three types of music in "King Orpheus"
may be seen to correspond.

The different kinds of music that Orpheus plays are defined
by their influence. The first kind causes "noy" (grief) and the
second "joy" while the third has a comforting effect—it could
have made a sick heart "heal" (well). The ballad lines are:

> First he played the notes of noy,
> Then he played the notes of joy,
>
> And then he played the gaber reel,
> That might a made a sick heart heal.[4]

The romance of *King Orphius,* which is the source of the ballad,
has unfortunately survived only in fragmentary form and does
not include the section where Orpheus plays in the hearing of the
fairy people and so it is impossible to say whether the three types
of music occurred there. Later in the narrative, however, Orpheus
has occasion to play the third type of music with its power of
healing grief when his host, the burgess, is overcome with sorrow:

> He begouithe to weip with this
> That was the worthiest, I wis.
> Than Orphius tuik his hairp with this
> For to comfort the burgess
> And sa he did into that stound,
> The hairp it gaif sick anc sound.[5]

In this text from a sixteenth-century manuscript Orpheus plays
the harp and not the pipes as in the ballad and it is in connection
with the harp that the concept of the three types of music is
familiar in the Celtic tradition to which the motif in the ballad
apparently belongs. In Irish, the three strains are called *goltraige,
gentraige,* and *súantraige* (music that provokes tears, music that
provokes laughter, and music that induces sleep). There is a
superficial difference between the sleep-inducing music here and
the healing music in "King Orpheus" but at a deeper level the
difference is resolved for the type of music which took its name
from the power to send to sleep was also a healing music which
brought relief from suffering by means of sleep, as in the description of the effect of the music emitted by the three gold apples
on the fairy branch in *The Adventure of Cormac Mac Airt:* "at
that melody the men of the world would sleep, and neither sorrow

nor affliction would oppress the people who hearkened to that melody."[6]

According to an Irish triad these three types of music are the "three things that constitute a harper"[7] and a skilled performer was expected to excel in all three. In *The Second Battle of Moytura* when Lug claims to be a harper he is called on to demonstrate his skill and does so by playing in the three different ways:

> "Let a harp be played for us," say the hosts. So the warrior played a sleep-strain for the hosts and for the king the first night. He cast them into sleep from that hour to the same time on the following day. He played a wail-strain, so that they were crying and lamenting. He played a smile-strain, so that they were in merriment and joy.[8]

In several Irish stories the performance of the three types of music culminates with the musician playing the sleep music which leaves him in control of the situation. At a later point in *The Second Battle of Moytura* the Dagda, accompanied by Lug and Ogma, enters the hall of their enemies, the Fomorians, and summons his harp which is hanging on the wall:

> Then the harp went forth from the wall, and kills nine men, and came to the Dagda. And he played for them the three things whereby harpers are distinguished, to wit, sleep-strain and smile-strain and wail-strain. He played wail-strain to them, so that their tearful women wept. He played smile-strain to them, so their women and children laughed. He played sleep-strain to them, and the hosts fell asleep. Through that (sleep) the three of them escaped unhurt from the Fomorians though these desired to slay them.

In an Arabic parallel, where the musician also slips away after the sleep music has taken effect, the emphasis is on the musician's mastery and we are given a little more information about his playing. It appears from the alteration of the strings that the different kinds of music are played in different modes.

> The prince then ordered some of the most eminent performers of instrumental music to be brought in, but not one of them could touch his instrument without exciting Abū Nasr's disapprobation. "Have you any skill in this art?" said Saif ad-Dawlat. — "I have," replied the other, and drawing a case from beneath his waistband, he opened it and produced a lute. Having tuned it, he began to play and cast all the company into a fit of laughter. He then undid the strings and, having tuned it in another manner, he played again and drew tears from their eyes. Mounting it a third time, in a different key, he played and set them all asleep, even the door-keepers, on which he took the opportunity of retiring and left them in that state.[9]

In Arabic tradition the various melodic and rhythmic modes were related to individual strings of different pitches as shown, for example, in this description of the effect of the string called *zīr* (C):

What appears through the movements of the *zīr* string in the action of the soul, are the joyful, glorious, victorious actions, and hardness of heart and courage, and so forth. And it is related to the nature of the *mākhurī* rhythm and what resembles it, and there results from the faculty of this string and this rhythm that they strengthen the yellow bile, moving it, and silencing the phlegm, quenching it.[10]

In Ireland, too, each kind of music is found related to a single string. *The Lay of Caoilte's Urn* gives a full account of a harp with three strings each of which is associated with the effect of one of the three types of music:

> The household harp was one of three strings,
> Methinks it was a pleasant jewel:
> A string of iron, a string of noble bronze,
> And a string of entire silver.
>
> The names of the not heavy strings
> Were *Suantorrglés; Geantorrglés* the great;
> *Goltarrglés* was the other string,
> Which sends all men to crying.
>
> If the pure *Goiltearglés* be played
> For the heavy hosts of the earth,
> The hosts of the world without delay
> Would all be sent to constant crying.
>
> If the merry *Gentorrglés* be played
> For the hosts of the earth, without heavy execution,
> They would all be laughing from it,
> From the hour of the one day to the same of the next.
>
> If the free *Suantorrglés* were played
> To the hosts of the wide universe,
> The men of the world, — great the wonder, —
> Would fall into a long sleep.[11]

The three kinds of music, then, as played by Orpheus in the ballad belong to a tradition where they are associated with three strings, presumably giving out notes of different pitches as in the more fully documented Arabic material. It is now possible to turn to the connection claimed by Burkert between the notes and the seasons. The three strings are not directly linked with the seasons in the Irish tales, although the Dagda's summons to his harp in *The Second Battle of Moytura* does include the words, "Come summer, Come winter!", but they are connected quite explicitly in an account of the invention of the lyre written in Greek. According to Diodorus Siculus, Hermes "made a lyre and gave it three strings imitating the seasons of the year; for he adopted three tones, a high, a low, and a medium; the high from the summer, the low from the winter, and the medium from the spring."[12] Similarly Boethius, who includes autumn among the seasons, speaks of Mercury as the inventor of a lyre with four strings each of which has its equivalent season.[13]

As long as the connection is confined to that between a note and a type of music, it can be thought to depend on a musical association of some kind, but once each note is linked with a season it becomes completely clear that a system of correspondences is being referred to and such a system, by its nature, is not going to be confined to a single set but will involve a whole network of correspondences, some of which may be quite arbitrary. We are entering a different realm of thought from that of logical statement, a realm that Burkert sees as satisfying some of the same requirements as the later scientific thinking:

> Order and pattern . . . which the human spirit craves, are to be found not only in the form of conceptual rigor and neatly logical structure, but, at an earlier level, in richness of mutual allusiveness and interconnection, where things fit together "symbolically."[14]

Strangely enough, it is Plato's *Republic,* the very work which formulated the conception of the harmony of the spheres, which also gives us a particularly clear insight into the simpler conception of the harmony of the three notes, but before considering the *Republic* it will be as well to have a closer look at the three notes themselves. Part of their symbolic force seems likely to have lain simply in the ordering of high, low and intermediate pitch, but the notion of harmony comes over particularly strongly when the three notes are concordant and it seems possible that the use of three concordant notes was not confined to Greece, although the examples come from there. The Greek scale referred to is that where the note of lowest pitch (*hypate*) and the note of highest pitch (*nete*) are an octave apart while the intermediate note (*mese*) is a fourth above *hypate* and a fifth below *nete.*[15] Of the three, *mese* is in the position of control as one can see, for instance, in a reference by Plutarch to a cosmic scheme in which "the sun himself as *mese* holds the octave together."[16]

Turning now to Plato, we find that he expresses in the *Republic* a system of correspondences by threes on the social, psychological and physical planes. Society is divided into three groups: 1 rulers, 2 soldiers, and 3 farmers "and the rest." Man's soul has three divisions: 1 the rational, 2 the spirited, and 3 the appetitive; and his body has three parts: 1 head, 2 upper body, and 3 lower body. The threes correspond and have a hierarchical order which at one point Plato expresses by reference to metals of descending values.[17] These correspondences can be tabulated as:

1	rulers	rational	head	gold
2	soldiers	spirited	upper body	silver
3	farmers	appetitive	lower body	iron and bronze

Plato also makes the musical comparison. In the just state, all parts are ruled by justice which assures that each part does what is fitting to it; similarly, the just man will have all parts of his soul acting in harmony. A man will be just "when he has bound together the three principles within him, which may be compared to the higher, lower, and middle notes of the scale. . . ."[18] However, Plato does not say which note corresponds to which place in his hierarchical ordering and the matter gave rise to speculation among commentators. One solution of the problem was the simple and natural one of equating the two extreme notes with the extremes of the body—head and lower body—leaving *mese* to be equated with the upper body,[19] but Plutarch seems closer to Plato's thinking when he concludes that the controlling power of *mese* belongs to the rational part, the head. He argues that, although by "local position" the head is at one extreme, the top, we should pay attention to function rather than to position:

> In fact it is incidental that in the body of man the rational part has been situated as first in local position; but the foremost and most sovereign function belongs to it as *mese* in relation to the appetitive as *hypate* and to the spirited as *nete* inasmuch as it slackens and tightens and generally makes them harmonious and concordant by removing the excess from either. . . .[20]

This gives the head as equivalent to the note of intermediate pitch while the upper and lower body are equivalent to the notes of extreme pitch. The correspondences, while functionally satisfying, are certainly awkward to envisage and Plato's treatment of the tripartite soul in the *Phaedrus* should probably be brought in here for it suggests a different triple division of the human frame which gives the head in the central position. In this work the rational part, the head, is viewed as a charioteer driving two horses, the white one on the right representing the spirited (which is related elsewhere to the upper body) and the black one on the left representing the appetitive (which is related elsewhere to the lower body).[21] Plato is glancing at a body-part correspondence which I think may prove very helpful in establishing the early system of cosmic harmony, but the present point is that it is possible

to equate the right and left sides of the body with the extreme
notes and the head as center with *mese*. There is now no conflict
between our understanding of function and the immediate image
of the intermediate element in the middle position.

In addition to the reference to the harmony of the three notes,
the *Republic* offers some comments on the musical modes and
their influence in the course of the discussion of education.[22]
Plato approves of only two modes, Phrygian and Dorian, which
he associates with courage and moderation. As he is concerned
with educating the upper levels of the hierarchical society it seems
highly probable that the Phrygian mode, linked with courage,
is considered appropriate to his class of soldiers while the Dorian
mode, linked with moderation, is appropriate to his class of rulers.
The Lydian and Ionian modes which are used for dirges and
laments or are linked with drunkenness, softness and idleness,
are rejected as educationally unsuitable and are apparently appropriate to the rest of the people. The "dirges and laments" in the
Republic are clearly equivalent to the "notes of noy" in "King
Orpheus" and I take it that the "notes of joy" are at the opposite
extreme, while the power to allay grief found in the music of
healing links this type of music to the moderation of the Dorian
mode. It is now possible to suggest how the three kinds of music
in "King Orpheus" connect with the sequence of correspondences
that has emerged from this discussion of Diodorus Siculus and
Plato:

winter	spring	summer
hypate	*mese*	*nete*
left side of body	head	right side of body
lower body	head	upper body
appetitive	rational	spirited
farmers	rulers	soldiers
iron and bronze	gold	silver
Lydian and Ionian modes	Dorian mode	Phrygian mode

music of grief	music of healing	music of joy

The correspondences in Plato have been thought to be the
result of Oriental influence[23] and it is certainly possible to point
to parallels in Indian sources. The three parts of the soul in Plato
may be compared with the three *guṇas* or constituents of Nature
in Sāṃkhya philosophy—*sattva, rajas* and *tamas*.[24] The three parts
of the body distinguished in the *Śatapatha-Brāhmaṇa* are "what
is below the navel, what is above the navel and below the head,
and the head itself,"[25] and in the *pravargya* ritual the three parts
of the body are connected with the three classes of society—*brah-*

min, kṣatriya and *vaiśya* (priest, warrior and farmer).[26] Similarly, in the horse sacrifice the three parts of the horse's body are marked out with three different metals, including gold and silver.[27] The three classes of society are linked with the three seasons.[28] The *Rigveda* "was and is sung to three notes."[29]

However, we find some of the same correspondences when we turn to the West. In *Celts and Aryans* Myles Dillon, agreeing with Dumézil's finding about the tripartite division of society, connects the Irish *fili, flaith* and *aithech* with the Indian *brahmin, kṣatriya* and *vaiśya*.[30] The triple division of the body is clearly indicated in Irish legend by the red lines round the neck and waist of Lugaid of the Red Stripes,[31] and we have seen above that there were three harp strings, each of which was of a different metal. It may be that the Greeks were able to draw something from the common Indo-European heritage as well as borrowing specifically Eastern developments of ideas of cosmos. At any rate, the Greek interest in music has supplied a point of contact for the sequence of the three kinds of music in "King Orpheus" and allows us to set it in a probable context where it can be seen as one of the foundation elements in a general fitting together or *harmonia* that can be expressed in terms of music or, with equal aptness, in terms of the seasons of the year.

NOTES

[1]The ballad has no known traditional title. Child named it "King Orfeo" after the Middle English romance which has been called both *King Orfeo* and *Sir Orfeo*, but it seems more appropriate now to name it after the recently-discovered Scottish romance, *King Orphius*, to which it is more closely related. Since there is no reason to retain the romance's sixteenth-century spelling for the ballad, I have named it "King Orpheus."

[2]*The Poems of Robert Henryson*, ed. Denton Fox (Oxford: Clarendon Press, 1981), p. 139. For background, see John MacQueen, "Neoplatonism and Orphism in Fifteenth-Century Scotland. The Evidence of Henryson's *New Orpheus*," *Scottish Studies*, 20 (1976), 69-89, and Kathi Meyer-Baer, *Music of the Spheres and the Dance of Death: Studies in Musical Iconology* (Princeton, N.J.: Princeton University Press, 1970).

[3]M. L. West, *Early Greek Philosophy and the Orient* (Oxford: Clarendon Press, 1971), p. 217. West refers to Walter Burkert, *Weisheit und Wissenschaft: Studien zu Pythagoras, Philolaos und Platon* (Nuremberg: Erlanger, 1962), pp. 333-35. In the English translation now available, *Lore and Science in Ancient Pythagoreanism*, trans. Edwin L. Minar, Jr. (Cambridge, Mass.: Harvard University Press, 1972), the equivalent pages are 355-57.

[4]These lines are from the earliest known version of the ballad, which was recorded by Bruce Sutherland at Gloup, Orkney, in 1865, published in *The Shetland News* in 1894, and reprinted by Patrick Shuldham-Shaw in "The Ballad

King Orfeo," Scottish Studies, 20 (1976), 124–26. Other traditional versions may be found in Francis James Child, *The English and Scottish Popular Ballads*, 5 vols. (Boston: Houghton, Mifflin and Co., 1882–98), vol. 1, p. 217, and Bertrand H. Bronson, *The Traditional Tunes of the Child Ballads*, 4 vols. (Princeton, N.J.: Princeton University Press, 1959–72), vol. 1, p. 275. The precise meaning of "gaber" is uncertain since the word does not occur elsewhere.

[5]Marion Stewart, *"King Orphius,"* Scottish Studies, 17 (1973), 6, lines 81–86. In this quotation, abbreviations have been expanded, punctuation and capitalization added, and the letters "y" and "v" replaced by "th" and "w."

[6]Vernam Hull, *"Echtra Cormaic Maic Airt,* The Adventure of Cormac Mac Airt," *Publications of the Modern Language Association*, 64 (1949), 877.

[7]*The Triads of Ireland*, ed. Kuno Meyer (Dublin: Hodges, Figgis, and Co., 1906), p. 16, no. 122.

[8]The quotations are of paragraphs 73 and 164 as translated by Whitley Stokes in *Revue Celtique*, 12 (1891), 81, 109, except that I have substituted "joy" for "joyance" and "Dagda" for "Dagdae." The word *cruit*, translated by Stokes as "harp," could apply to either the harp or the lyre. Joan Rimmer notes in *The Irish Harp* (Cork: The Mercier Press, 1969), pp. 9–13, 22, that the earliest iconographical evidence for the fully-framed triangular harp is of the ninth century A.D., and that the stringed instrument in use among the Celts at an earlier period was probably a U-shaped lyre.

[9]*Ibn Khallikan's Biographical Dictionary*, translated from the Arabic by Baron W. Mac Guckin de Slane, 4 vols. (Paris: Académie des Inscriptions et Belles-Lettres, 1843–71), vol. 3, p. 309.

[10]H. G. Farmer, "The Influence of Music. From Arabic Sources," *Proceedings of the Musical Association*, 52 (1925–26), 99–100, quoting Al-Kindi. Farmer shows that melodic modes were also associated with the different strings in *An Old Moorish Lute Tutor* (Glasgow: Civic Press, 1933), pp. 8–15, 38–39.

[11]The quotation is from Eugene O'Curry, *On the Manners and Customs of the Ancient Irish*, 3 vols. (London, Edinburgh, Dublin, New York: Williams & Newgate, 1873), vol. 3, pp. 223–24. For a complete version of *The Lay of Caoilte's Urn* with translation and notes, see *Duanaire Finn: The Book of the Lays of Fionn*, vol. 1, ed. Eoin MacNeill (London: Irish Texts Society, 1908), pp. 38–45, 140–49, and vol. 3, ed. Gerard Murphy (Dublin: Irish Texts Society, 1953), pp. 36–40, 274. For the playing of the three types of music on a *timpán* with three strings, see *Cath Maige Mucrama: The Battle of Mag Mucrama*, ed. Máirín O Daly (Dublin: Irish Texts Society, 1975), pp. 40–41.

[12]Diodorus of Sicily, *The Library of History*, I.16.1–2, trans. C.H. Oldfather (London and New York: Loeb, 1933), vol. 1, p. 53. In *Diodorus Siculus Book 1: A Commentary* (Leiden: Brill, 1972), pp. 17 and 78–79, Anne Burton notes that chapter 16, "which discusses Hermes or the Egyptian Thoth, suggests an equal mixture of ideas" from Greece and Egypt and that the god's association with music "must come from the Greek tradition." Cf. the harmony of the three seasons played by Apollo in Orphic Hymn 34, where winter is related to the low note (*hypate*), summer to the high note (*nete*), and spring to "the Dorian"; see *Orphei Hymni*, ed. Guilelmus Quandt (Berlin: Weidmann, 1962), p. 27, and *The Orphic Hymns*, trans. Apostolos N. Athanassakis (Missoula, Montana: Scholars Press, 1977), pp. 48–49, 124.

[13]"De Musica," 1.2 and 1.20. J.-P. Migne, *Patrologiae Cursus Completus. Series Latina* 63 (Paris: J.-P. Migne, 1882), cols. 1174–75, 1183.

[14]Burkert, *Lore and Science*, p. 399.

[15]I.e., C, F, C' in the key of C. The four-stringed lyre of Boethius has the same gamut, his additional note being *paramese* i.e., G in the key of C.

[16]Plutarch's *Moralia*, ed. F.C. Babbitt and others (Cambridge, Mass. and London: Harvard University Press, 1927–69), vol. 13, part 1, p. 331, "On the

Generation of the Soul in the Timaeus," 1029A and note *e*; cf. *Moralia*, vol. 9, p. 277, "Table-Talk" IX. 14, 745.

[17]*The Republic*, trans. H. D. P. Lee (Harmondsworth: Penguin, 1955), 414–15, pp. 159–61. For the divisions of the body, see 588–9, pp. 365–67, and Francis M. Cornford, *Plato's Cosmology: The "Timaeus" of Plato translated with a running commentary* (London: K. Paul, Trubner & Co., 1937), 69A–71A, pp. 279–86.

[18]*The Republic of Plato*, trans. B. Jowett, 3d ed. (Oxford: Clarendon Press, 1888), 443, p. 137.

[19]See Plutarch, "Platonic Questions," Question IX and notes. *Moralia*, vol. 13, part 1, pp. 91–103.

[20]"Platonic Questions," IX, 1009A. *Moralia*, vol. 13, part 1, pp. 100–1. I have adapted the translation to give the Greek names of the notes and the term "the spirited."

[21]*Phaedrus*, trans. Walter Hamilton (Harmondsworth: Penguin, 1973), 246, 253, pp. 50–51, 61–62.

[22]*Republic*, 398–99. On the influence of the Phrygian and Dorian modes cf. Aristotle, *Politics*, 1340b: "Another mode is specially calculated to produce a moderate and collected temper; this is held to be the peculiar power of the Dorian mode, while the Phrygian mode is held to give inspiration and fire." *The Politics of Aristotle*, trans. Ernest Barker (Oxford: Clarendon Press, 1946), p. 344. These modes are not, of course, the same as the later church modes known by these names; see M. Kolinski, "Modes, Musical," in the *Encyclopaedia Britannica*, 15th ed. (Chicago: Benton, 1974), *Macropaedia*, vol. 12, pp. 295–98.

[23]*Plato: Republic Book X*, ed. John Ferguson (London: Methuen, 1957), pp. 69–70, 93; S. Radhakrishnan, *Eastern Religions and Western Thought*, 2d ed. (London: Oxford University Press, 1940), pp. 147–49; Edward J. Urwick, *The Message of Plato: A Re-Interpretation of the "Republic"* (London: Methuen & Co., Ltd., 1920), pp. 15–41.

[24]J. Gonda, *Triads in the Veda* (Amsterdam, Oxford, New York: North-Holland Publishing Company, 1976), p. 208.

[25]Gonda, *Triads*, p. 96. *Śatapatha-Brāhmaṇa*, trans. Julius Eggeling, Sacred Books of the East, vol. 44 (Oxford: Clarendon Press, 1900), 12.9.1.7.

[26]J. A. B. van Buitenen, *The Pravargya: An Ancient Indian Iconic Ritual* (Poona: Deccan College Postgraduate and Research Institute, 1968), pp. 124–25.

[27]P.-E. Dumont, *L'Aśvamedha: Description de Sacrifice Solennel du Cheval dans le Culte Védique* (Paris: P. Guenther, 1927), pp. 277, 339.

[28]*Śatapatha-Brāhmaṇa*, Sacred Books of the East, vol. 12 (Oxford: Clarendon Press, 1882), 2.1.3.5.

[29]*Grove's Dictionary of Music and Musicians*, 5th edition, ed. Eric Blom (London: Macmillan and Co., 1954), vol. 4, pp. 456–60, "Indian Music"; cf. *The New Oxford History of Music*, vol. 1: *Ancient and Oriental Music*, ed. Egon Wellesz (London: Oxford University Press, 1957), pp. 199–201, and O. Gosvami, *The Story of Indian Music: Its Growth and Synthesis* (Bombay: Asia Publishing House, [1957]), pp. 4–7.

[30]Myles Dillon, *Celts and Aryans: Survivals of Indo-European Speech and Society* (Simla: Indian Institute of Advanced Study, 1975), pp. 96–97.

[31]*Cóir Anmann (Fitness of Names)*, in *Irische Texte*, ed. Whitley Stokes and E. Windisch, 3d series (Leipzig: S. Birzel, 1891–97), pp. 332–33.

Four Black Sheep Among the 305

Tristram Potter Coffin

To the best of my speculation, the ballad form developed from the custom of reciting and singing narrative obituary verse. The ins and outs of this theory have already had as much attention as present evidence will allow in articles by me and my former student, Robert Bethke, and in a definitive book by my son, Mark T. Coffin.[1] At present my thoughts on the matter have hardened along these lines: narrative verses were commonly recited and sung at funerals in Western Europe during the Middle Ages; some of these narratives were significant enough or memorable enough to be sung long after the occasion for which they were composed had been forgotten; from them, gradually, a secular song form which we now call the ballad was developed. As this evolution took place, the new ballads were influenced poetically, musically, and structurally by other forms in circulation at the time, drawing from, mingling with, in turn influencing carols, Latin hymns, saints' legends, *romances, lais,* and folktales. But most of all, one has to acknowledge the centrifugal pull of the ballad: it has always drawn more flotsam and jetsam toward it than it has let escape.

Today, the various types of Western European ballads are generically defined as narrative folksongs. In Britain, the older or "traditional" ballads tend to focus on the climax of this narrative, and many of them like "Lord Randal" or "The Maid Freed from the Gallows" are puzzling in their lack of detail and proper motivation. But all the traditional British ballads have or show they once had fully developed plots, and in most cases the scholar who assembles variants can reconstruct enough of the action to ease frustration. There are, however, four riddle ballads in Child which pose something of an enigma in themselves for they neither have, nor seem ever to have had, any sort of complete plot structure. They are songs built on a simple incident, in this case a meeting of two people, and are no closer to being narrative songs than many of the American love lyrics such as "Green Grows the Laurel" or "Birmingham Jail."

The ballads in question are Child 1–3 and 46: "Riddles Wisely Expounded," "The Elfin Knight," "The Fause Knight Upon the Road," and "Captain Wedderburn's Courtship." The last, "Captain Wedderburn's Courtship," is typical. The "story" involves nothing but the meeting of a man and a girl to decide whether or not they are to sleep together. The variants imply no further action: the man may conquer; the girl, who normally poses the questions, may confound him; she may even force him to marry her as a condition — but there is nothing to the matter other than a meeting and some riddles which lead to a frankly sexual decision. "Captain Wedderburn's Courtship" is quite sparse in action when compared to a riddle ballad like Child 47, "Proud Lady Margaret," which is structured and narratively set the way other Child ballads are.

Although the texts in Child have been tampered with,[2] the story of "Proud Lady Margaret" is clear enough: an amorous girl, like the girl in "Captain Wedderburn's Courtship," is in the habit of testing her suitors by means of riddles. In this case, however, the riddles seem to be devised to eliminate unworthy "heirs" to her father's lands. The result of failure is death. A knight, who reminds the girl of her dead brother, approaches and expresses his love. She poses the riddles and is surprised at his adeptness in answering them.

> "You may be my match, kind sir,
> You may be my match and more . . ."

she says, in Child's B version and is willing to give herself over. However, the knight turns out to be the dead brother after all, and even though she still expresses a willingness to "go with him" he rejects her, moralizing to her:

> 'Leave off your pride, jelly Janet,' he says,
>   'Use it not any more;
> Or when you come where I have been
>   You will repent it sore . . .'[3]

The plot is a classic traditional ballad plot. Unlike "Captain Wedderburn's Courtship" where the riddling is the purpose of the song, the riddling here is merely a device integrated into a story of a father who has lost his heir and who, in league with his daughter, has decided that only the man who answers her riddles can have her and his estates. Those who fail are to die. The brother, perhaps unable to rest because the girl's "pride" disturbs him, returns from the dead and resolves the situation by humbling his haughty sister. "Proud Lady Margaret" has the exact structure that a Child ballad with riddles might be expected to have. MacEdward Leach once suggested that "one might think that the riddles here are intrusive,"[4] and the Child E text neither includes them nor needs them. One could never say that about "Captain Wedderburn's Courtship." Child 46 without riddles would be nothing.

There are six riddle ballads in the Child canon. One, "King John and the Bishop" (Child 45), can be dismissed from this discussion. It is a simple song version of a widely distributed folktale and really is more joke than test anyhow. Moreover, it does not involve sex or sexual symbolism. Child 1-3 and "Captain Wedderburn's Court-ship" are the interesting ones; they are the "black sheep" among the flock of 305.

My guess is that Child 1-3 and 46 derive from "love-joust" songs and not from the places that balladry normally derived its stories. This is not to say that, as they stand, they should not be called traditional ballads or that they should have been omitted from the Child canon. Rather, I am suggesting that they derive from a form of song that once had a quite different purpose from telling a story and that they reflect backgrounds not to date associated with balladry.

To my knowledge there has been no discussion of the relationships of the "love-joust" or "love-riddling" song and balladry. In fact, there has been precious little discussion of "love-riddling" in Britain at all. In Anglo-American scholarship, the articles of Edwin Loeb are as good a place to start as any; on pp. 71-77 of *The Proper Book of Sexual Folklore,* I spent some time on Loeb's theories concerning the "love proverb" (as he calls it), its relationship to bundling and the growth of romantic love, and more recent cus-toms which reflect such things.[5] To put it simply, Loeb believes that when people reach the cattle-owning (i.e., property-owning) stage they begin to postpone marriage, creating a period when young men and girls are sexually anxious and yet frustrated. Socie-ties have to acknowledge this frustration and in many cases do so by allowing premarital sexual play (normally without intercourse). Out of this semi-permissiveness and its frustrations comes romantic love. In areas ranging from China to Southwest Africa, India to Switzer-land, Loeb sees antiphonal love-singing (almost always taking pro-verbial quatrain form) as offering young people in property-oriented societies a means of pairing up during festivals or at other selected times for what bundling or sporting is allowed. The quatrains Loeb cites, like this one from Sumatra,

"From where, sister, comes the leech?"
  "From the rice field, down to the river."
"From where, sister, comes love?"
  "From the eyes, down to the heart."[6]

are more riddles than proverbs, and in actuality it is riddling and part-riddle, part-proverb song that is used to open the way.

Loeb is not, of course, the only scholar to see the relationship of riddles to courtship patterns. I cite other examples in *The Proper Book of Sexual Folklore,* even quoting the sweeping statement of the Chadwicks in *The Growth of Literature*[7] that "the ability to answer riddles is a test frequently applied to a suitor who asks for the hand of a lady in marriage." Furthermore, one may note that Loeb believes the love-sonnet to have derived from the "love-proverb," and that although such ideas may be rather tenuous, Shakespeare does introduce Romeo to Juliet through a sonnet used exactly as a love-proverb might be used. Romeo's famous speech as he meets Juliet for the first time begins: "If I profane with my unworthiest hand. . . ." It is the first of four sonnet lines. She replies with four more, and so they challenge each other through their introduction until he kisses her and she, to everyone's understanding, has given herself to him "by the book."

Shakespeare knew, and Shakespeare's audience knew, of such ways. At May Day, Whitsunday, Midsummer, Christmas and the like men and women paired up with a license they did not have at other times. The custom stretched far back, a vestige of days and ways long forgotten. And it was through these customs, frowned on as they were by the more urbane and the more clerical, that many a boy and girl entered into a relationship that would eventually result in marriage. Selection of partners was done in various ways: physical games in which boys pulled or tried to pull girls across to them; games of rhyme and reason, blindman's buffs, dances, lotteries were used — all of them, through accepted means of cheating, allowed the boys to select the one they wished and the girls to go with or turn away their suitors. Riddling was one of the devices, and it is most likely that a song like "Captain Wedderburn's Courtship" simply records a joust selection process once common enough in the British Isles.

Child's texts of "Captain Wedderburn's Courtship" are not particularly old, though the riddles, dating at least to the fifteenth century, are. The best one can say for the ballad is that it preserves an old situation and old riddles in a literary text. "Riddles Wisely Expounded" is another story. This ballad also dates at least as far back as fifteenth century, when the text printed by Child[8] was recorded in a book acquired by Walter Pollard of Plymouth in the twenty-third year of Henry VI (1444–5). It is, incidentally, the only Child ballad extant in American tradition that can demonstrably be shown to derive from the Middle Ages. The story of the contest between the maiden and the fiend is well known, the latter seeking to become the girl's leman and evidently having the power to compel her if she cannot confound him. She escapes by answering his riddles and naming him. This earliest text, homiletic in nature, may well be a churchly variant in which the Blessed Virgin defeats her major adversary, Satan Himself. At least MacEdward Leach found a riddle ballad in Labrador which the informant said was locally known as "The Devil and the Blessed Virgin Mary" and which was about just such a narrow escape for Mary. Admitting that "no version of Child 1 names Mary" (the word *virgo* in the title *Inter Diabolus et Virgo,* meaning maiden or virgin in that sense), Leach goes on to speculate that

> . . . there was (is?) a story (probably, rather than a ballad) in which the Virgin nonplussed the Devil and thus unmasked him by her clever answers to his riddles. From such a story a ballad was made; that ballad was, I believe, the prototype of Child 1, A*. . . .[9]

Actually, his Labrador text is a mixture of Child 1 and "Captain Wedderburn's Courtship," the title under which Leach finally decided to list it. He believes that the extraordinary popularity of the Wedderburn ballad in the eighteenth and nineteenth centuries confused the "The Devil and the Blessed Virgin Mary" text, corrupting it to such an extent that it became more like Child 46 than its original Child 1 form.

Whatever the situation in Labrador, "Riddles Wisely Expounded" has generally become romantic as it has survived into more recent times. Later texts either involve a situation where a man says he will marry a certain girl if she can reply correctly to his riddles, or a situation in which a girl who has "set her cap" for a certain man compels him to marry her by the same device. If the ballad did evolve from a homiletic tale about Satan and Mary as Leach thinks, the modern variants tend to be love-jousts not unlike the one in "Captain Wedderburn's Courtship" or the ones behind the sexual riddling discussed by Loeb.

Child 2, "The Elfin Knight," is about a young lady who hears an elf-knight blow his horn on a hill telling whoever will listen that "the wind has blown his plaid away." Recognizing that the "plaid away" statement means the elf-knight is no virginal lover, she wishes him to be hers. He appears and is willing, if she will perform an impossible task — usually the making of a shirt or sark without seam, needlework, or such. She replies with tasks of her own, and tells him that he can have his shirt (this also appears to symbolize her compliance) when he accomplishes them. Evidently, she is going "to keep her maidenhead." This ballad is widely recalled and in its "Scarborough Fair" variant is one of the rare Child ballads that might be recognized as a "pop song" in America today. Recent texts have dropped the elf-knight and replaced him with an everyday knight or more usually an everyday man so that the song has become no more than a pre-sexual joust of riddling, the girl confounding her would-be lover.

In his unpublished notes for "The Ballad" section of Wells's *Manual*,[10] Leach speculates (somewhat in contradiction of his remarks above) that the lover in "Riddles Wisely Expounded" was, like the lover in "the Elfin Knight," "probably originally a fairy lover, who is rationalized into the devil, and who in turn is rationalized into a knight or gay cavalier." Meanwhile, Kenneth Peacock discovered an "Elfin Knight" text in Newfoundland which has no love-play at all, but which is a contest between the Devil and an old woman.[11] Roger Renwick, who considers this text in his notes in the most recent edition of *The British Traditional Ballad in North America*,[12] comes to no firm conclusion about it except that it has borrowed heavily, perhaps from Child 1 or 3 or 46, certainly from Child 278 ("The Farmer's Curst Wife") and Mother Goose rhymes.

There is also Child 3, "The Fause Knight Upon the Road." This too is a riddle ballad, although sometimes it is not recognized as such. It is always homiletic, all texts describing a contest in which a devil or "fause knight" (elf-knight?) is thwarted by a witty child. The song is known in North America, though scarcely common, and seems to owe its recent popularity to its inclusion in songsters such as *The American Songster* and *Charley Fox's Minstrel's Companion*.[13] It is also strikingly like the homiletic variants of Child 1 and even Child 2. In fact, Child 1 and Child 3 have mingled sufficiently in Canada to cause a number of scholars to prick up their ears. Roger Renwick notes again the interrelationships between Child 1, 2, 3 and 46-47 not only in their use of similar riddle patterns, but in their use of figurative references to sex.[14] He is, of course, supported by Barre Toelken's article on these points.[15] One certainly does not have to stretch one's thoughts to conclude that "The Fause Knight Upon the Road" may also once have been a riddling contest ballad.

The confusion in Leach's writings on Child 1 and in Renwick's attempts to explain the Canadian Child 2 and Child 3 traditions characterize all scholarship about "Riddles Wisely Expounded," "The Elfin Knight," and "The Fause Knight Upon the Road." The three always end up being "interrelated": mixtures in some sequence of old fairy lover or Devil tales which have ultimately been rationalized into everyday jousts between everyday couples. Yet all are known to contain highly suggestive and frequently ancient sexual riddling. The other possibility—that the everyday love-joust is the oldest theme in these songs and accounts for the presence of the sexual riddles, that as they came in contact with balladry and balladeers these challenge songs developed along more complex

story lines of elfin seductions and churchly struggles — does not seem
to have occurred to anyone. After all, we know there was riddling
for pre-sexual purposes in Britain. We also know the riddles incor-
porated into Child 1-2 and 46 are old, far older than any ballad
use of them. Toelken has demonstrated quite clearly that the riddles
of these ballads, and in particular those of "The Elfin Knight," are
filled with sexual implications and ambiguities.[16] His study even
makes it possible to see the girl in "The Elfin Knight" posing seemingly impossible tasks that if understood and performed would in
fact make the man her lover. There are also the refrains. Those
common to Child 1 mentioning "juniper, gentian, and rosemary"
or "bonnie broom," and those in Child 2 concerning "rosemary and
thyme" and "ivy and holly," make blunt references to sex-related
plants which frequent the literature of love and seduction throughout British tradition. Continually, these riddle ballads come back
to the opening scene in Child 2 H:

> 'Come, pretty Nelly, and sit thee down by me.
>   Every rose grows merry wi thyme
> And I will ask you questions three,
>   And then thou wilt be a true lover of mine.'

One could argue that Child 1-3 and 46 are not in actuality ballads
at all, but a separate form, hovering between narrative and lyric
and centering on a simple sexual decision. I do think a pretty good
case could be made for that opinion. But I also remember that
David C. Fowler has made it quite clear that the British ballad
(much less the European ballad) is not merely one form of narrative
song, but a continually changing genre.[17] I have already stressed
that it has incredible centrifugal pull and has drawn all kinds of
song matter into its canon. The chances are, thus, that Child 1-3
and 46 represent the influence of the love-joust on balladry rather
than survivals of actual love-joust songs themselves. It is hard to
make headway against the fact that all of the texts of "Captain
Wedderburn's Courtship" and all the romantic texts of "Riddles
Wisely Expounded" and all the everyday texts of "The Elfin Knight"
are modern; that the homiletic and fairy texts of all three songs are
the most traditional; and that there is no actual love-joust text of
"The Fause Knight Upon the Road." One has to believe that the
modern texts represent what one might call "a return to the love-
joust."

I repeat what seems to have happened. Love-joust situations,
their songs, and their riddles came in contact with balladry and
its balladeers. Some of them entered the canon, where they survived
either as pure man-woman songs quite in the style of "Captain
Wedderburn's Courtship" or where their riddles were re-set into

more fanciful contests between threatening fairies and mortal girls or between the Devil (devil) and the Virgin (virgin). At the same time, the love-joust in its various forms of dance, game, and wit was working its influence on seduction and courtship literature at folk and more urbane levels. The sonnet, almost a riddling game, that Romeo and Juliet compose is not greatly different from the challenges of aphorism that bring Beatrice and Benedict together in *Much Ado About Nothing* or that start the seduction of the heroine by the rake in a Restoration comedy. Nor is it unlike a Fred Astaire-Ginger Rogers dance or an operatic duet. So it is normal that songs like Child 46 or Child 2 were most often rendered as clear-cut seduction or love-match songs in the seventeenth, eighteenth, and nineteenth centuries. Their coy riddling, even if a somewhat archaic process, was still understood symbolically if not literally by the public at large.

What we have, then, is a complexion. Exactly what happened in any specific variant of say "Riddles Wisely Expounded" or "The Elfin Knight" is hard to say. Leach may be correct that there was an early folktale in which Mary thwarted Satan, and it is possible this folktale became a ballad (Child 1, A*) just as "Kaiser und Abt" became Child 45. And there certainly are plenty of stories of elfin lovers who threaten young ladies. One of these could have become a ballad too. There is also no telling what Canadian tradition shows. The Newfoundland text of "The Elfin Knight" which involves an old woman and the Devil may be an ancient survival "at the periphery" or a modern recasting, as may the Labrador "Captain Wedderburn's Courtship"–"Riddles Wisely Expounded" mix. But one thing is, I think, clear. Overall, Child 1–3 and 46 (the "black sheep") reflect an influence on balladry that has not to date been given much attention. There is no escaping the fact that these four ballads rhyme into an enigma. It is appropriate that the solution to the enigma appears to lie in riddling itself.

NOTES

[1]See Mark Tristram Coffin, *American Narrative Obituary Verse and Native Balladry* (Norwood, Pa.: Norwood Editions, 1975). On page 3, footnote 4, complete references to Bethke's and my own writings on narrative obituary verse are given.

[2]See Francis James Child, *The English and Scottish Popular Ballads,* 5 vols. (New York: Dover Publications, 1965), vol. 1, pp. 425–26. All references to Child texts are to this reprint of the original edition of 1882–1898.

[3]Ibid., p. 428, stanzas 19 and 26.

[4]MacEdward Leach, *The Ballad Book* (New York: A. S. Barnes, 1955), p. 162.

[5]See Edwin Loeb, "Courtship and the Love Song," *Anthropos,* 45 (1950), pp. 821–51, and "The Function of Proverbs in the Intellectual Development of Primitive Peoples," *Scientific Monthly,* February 1952, pp. 100–4; good bibliographies

are included. *The Proper Book of Sexual Folklore* was published by Seabury Press, New York, 1978.

⁶See Loeb, *Scientific Monthly,* p. 103.

⁷H. M. and N. K. Chadwick, *The Growth of Literature* (Cambridge: Cambridge University Press, 1940).

⁸Child, vol. 5, p. 283.

⁹MacEdward Leach, *Folk Ballads and Songs of the Lower Labrador Coast* (Ottawa: National Museum of Canada, 1965), p. 28.

¹⁰See John Edwin Wells, *A Manual of the Writings in Middle English, 1050–1400* (New Haven: Yale University Press; H. Milford: Oxford University Press, 1916–). Leach died before his contribution was accepted. The typescript is in my possession.

¹¹*Songs of the Newfoundland Outposts* (Ottawa: National Museum of Canada, 3 vols., 1965), vol. 1, p. 6.

¹²Tristram Potter Coffin, *The British Traditional Ballad in North America* (Austin: University of Texas Press, 1977): Third Edition with a Supplement by Roger DeV. Renwick, pp. 209–10.

¹³*The American Songster* (Philadelphia: W. A. Leary, 1945); *Charley Fox's Minstrel's Companion* (Philadelphia: Turner & Fisher, 1858).

¹⁴See Coffin-Renwick, *The British Traditional Ballad,* pp. 209–11, where the whole matter is treated and documented.

¹⁵J. Barre Toelken, " 'Riddles Wisely Expounded'," *Western Folklore,* 25 (1966), 1–16.

¹⁶Ibid.

¹⁷David C. Fowler, *A Literary History of the Popular Ballad* (Durham: Duke University Press, 1968).

Part 2:
Stability and Variability in Traditional Song

The Problem of Identity
in Lyric Folksong

Judith McCulloh

What gives a song identity? The answer to this question becomes more complex as the units of text that may be rearranged— that is, shifted to different positions within the song—grow smaller. Songs with sequential structure, with or without a plot, such as "Barbara Allen," "Billy Venero," "The Lumberman's Alphabet," and "The Twelve Days of Christmas," are the easiest to identify. They proceed from beginning to end, logical and predictable in outline if not in detail. The entire text, in effect, becomes the basic rearrangeable unit. Such pieces offer us an obvious and convenient basis for study. Ballads, particularly, have been outlined, christened, and numbered. Along with other neatly structured traditional genres, such as the folktale, riddle, and proverb, they have enjoyed spirited and extensive examination.

At the opposite end of the spectrum are those pieces, some of our lyric songs, blues, and worksongs, for instance, in which single lines of text and even half-lines form the minimal units. The "Reuben"/ "900 Miles" complex offers a convenient illustration.[1] One of the earliest notations we have is this 1905 couplet from South Carolina:

> Reuben he got drunk, he pawned his watch and trunk,
> He was ten thousand miles from his home.[2]

In other versions, after a first line of the type just cited, the second line is unpredictable, though it may refer to gold (money or jewelry) or home. Often a line similar to the second one above follows one of the type "If this train runs right I'll be home (see my woman) tomorrow (Saturday) night," but that is not certain either. Moreover, the resultant couplets may show up anywhere in the song.

Much of our English-language repertoire falls short of this extreme, but not by too much. The "and other" sections in folksong collections with "ballad and other" arrangement abound in move-able stanzas of typically two, three, or four lines. These are some-times called floating stanzas, particularly if they become attached to ballads. Actually, certain stanzas float more freely than others and may be found in a wider variety of contexts.

These basic textual units may also form clusters that we sense intuitively. That is, we come to recognize that we have met certain stanzas of one song also in another song, though not necessarily in the same order, and eventually we are no longer surprised to find them together. Thus some lyric material has been named (I am using "lyric" broadly here, to mean "nonsequential"): "John Henry," "I Shall Not Be Moved," "The Wagoner's Lad," "O Waly Waly," "Nine Pound Hammer," "Reuben"/"900 Miles," "In the Pines"/"The Longest Train." Pinning down what is essential to these clusters and what their outer boundaries are, though, is another matter. Lacking a thorough overview, each person has to rely on his own notion of precisely what the song comprises, and that depends on prior exposure, good memory, and a sense of proper fit. Thus Henry M. Belden described these last two stanzas of "Look Up, Look Down That Lonesome Road" in the Frank C. Brown collection as "bits of the floating lyric of the folk, likely to appear in almost any love song":

> The blackest crow that ever was seen
> Was flying from pine to pine, my love,
> Was flying from pine to pine.
>
> The longest train that ever had run
> Was going down old Georgia line, my love,
> Was going down old Georgia line.[3]

A variant perspective came from J. E. Mainer, the North Carolina fiddler who organized one of the most important early, transitional country music string bands: "Judith that Verse you rote are not suposed to be in the longest train. the verse you seaid were in the song the dove that flys from pine to pine. that verse is in several different songs. Just because you can put some verses in anothr some people does this. and they ruin the hole song."[4]

A provocative intermediate type of song is the blues ballad, which acts like other lyric songs (hence "blues") but is considered a form of narrative by most of those who have examined and written about it (hence "ballad"). Here, the underlying story is so well known to both singer and audience, or the narrative pattern so well estab-lished, that it need not be directly reconstructed. An oblique refer-ence, an editorial comment, of even one verse, will suffice; temporal sequence will be loose, or non-existent. A blues ballad might be prompted by a well-known local event, such as a crime or accident

("Railroad Bill," "Casey Jones"), or by an event of national impact, such as the assassination of a president ("Whitehouse Blues"); or it might be built on a narrative pattern familiar because of its use in countless other ballads ("The Coon Can Game").[5] It is the awareness of the story behind the song, first by the folk, then by the folklorist, that is cited to justify regarding blues ballads as narratives. Again, though, we should expect these different participants to have variant perceptions of the "same" tradition.

How do we make sense of such songs? Most folklorists have resorted to general and overlapping categories of subject, style, function, and origin for their nonballad material, even while recognizing the illogical nature of such an approach. When Belden first received the typescript for that part of the Brown collection he was to edit, for instance, he lamented, "Anything like a scientific classification of folksong seems, from the composite nature of many of the individual items, impossible." A year later, after having worked out suggestions for ordering the items, he concluded that "this whole *song* section is pretty much, to me, a labyrinth without the necessary clue."[6] Eventually he assigned the following headings for volume 3: "Courting Songs," "Play-Party and Dance Songs," "Lullabies and Nursery Rhymes," "Jingles about Animals," "Work Songs," "Folk Lyric," "Satirical Songs," "Songs of Prisoners and Tramps," "Martial, Political, and Patriotic Songs," "Blackface Minstrel and Negro Secular Songs," "Religious Songs."[7]

Subject categories like these offer some unity and convenience, and can be turned to advantage, say, in providing a ground for historical, cultural, socio-economic, or psychological commentary.[8] But if we become interested in a particular item in one of the subject groupings, we cannot assume that there are not related songs in other sections. The safest procedure is to note any editorial cross-references, then systematically work through the entire volume (not to mention, in the case of the Brown collection, volumes 2, 4, and 5 also) from cover to cover. For all practical purposes, we have abandoned the headings and are back to the beginning.

Lacking even the hint of a narrative touchstone, as some blues ballads may provide, one logical solution is to deal with lyric songs on their own structural terms: stanza by stanza, couplet by couplet, line by line. The smallest rearrangeable unit of text, in other words, is the largest unit with which rigorous study can begin. We can find comments throughout Anglo-American folksong literature similar to Newman I. White's (here concerning black repertoire)—"Practically the only fixed element is the stanza or phrase, and that is only relatively fixed"[9]—whether as observation or complaint. Surely the prospects of hunting and gathering, cross-referencing, and simply keeping track of apparently endless numbers of juxtaposed stanzas constitute much of the reason folk lyric "seems to have scared off and discouraged scholars."[10]

Some limits obviously have to be set, and the material should suggest its own best method of identification and analysis. Within a single performance of a lyric song, unless the singer uses one unit as a chorus or otherwise repeats it, or gives it as a title, all parts of the song must be accepted as equally important. The song *is* that particular performance; its identity is ready-made, and analysis, stanza by stanza, becomes a relatively straightforward task.[11]

If we have several overlapping pieces rather than just one text, the problem of what to use as a take-off point, as a control, becomes more complicated. A scale of relative importance should begin to take shape, though, along the lines of the intuitively sensed clusters of textual units I mentioned earlier. Some stanzas or lines appear more often, others less often. Once we have a notion of what seems to be the core of the lyric, the most constant, essential, and identifying components, we have something to go on. If we suspect, for example, that it is stanzas of the type A, B, and C that hold a group of songs together, then we can proceed systematically to gather all the variants we can find with stanzas A, B, and C and note what patterns emerge. Now, this kind of hunch may or may not prove sufficient. It might turn out that stanza C does not occur that often after all, or only in one sub-cluster. Or it might be necessary to go back and pick up songs containing stanza D, which at first did not seem crucial but which took on more significance as more and more texts came to light. In any event, this is a reasonable way to begin.[12]

So far I have said nothing about music, although these lyrics obviously were and are sung. In a sense my discussion parallels the customary way in which lyric folksong clusters have been studied: texts first, tunes incidentally (perhaps). One reason for this uneven approach has been the relative unavailability of tune transcriptions. Another is the general reluctance to make use of nonarchival sound recordings. Still another relates to the problem of textual control: if the texts to be studied are not limited in any way, neither will the associated tunes be limited; and since tunes can lead notoriously independent lives, the task of tracing them as well as an infinity of textual components becomes doubly discouraging. Even starting with a given — the texts of the Child ballads — Bertrand Bronson's studies of the associated tunes represent an occupation encompassing more than half our traditional lifespan.[13]

We know that thorough consideration of the music accompanying narrative songs can sometimes shed light on their history and on textual relationships with other songs. Bronson notes, for instance, that a few variants of "Young Hunting" (Child 68) that begin with the sound of a distant horn are set to a tune associated with "Lady

Isabel" (Child 4), a ballad that in its earlier texts made much of the sound of a horn. He speculates that either the horn motif was borrowed from "Lady Isabel," bringing the tune along, or the common use of that tune facilitated bringing the horn motif into "Young Hunting."[14] Elsewhere he suggests that if Child had paid more attention to the music of his ballads, especially to their refrains, he would have rearranged his variants in many cases.[15] Some of the blues ballads that have been studied show similar ties. Marina Bokelman, for example, uses melodic evidence to point out textual borrowing from one reworking of "The Coon Can Game" to another.[16] Noting that the tune of the Carter Family's "Cannon Ball" is close to that of Charlie Poole's "White House Blues," Neil Rosenberg suggests that the Carters may have borrowed their "from Buffalo to Washington" refrain from the Poole version.[17]

That music can take on special structural importance in songs without plot or sequence is not a new observation. Thus D. K. Wilgus defined folk-lyric as "a folksong lacking a coherent, developed narrative, often consisting of images held together by a tune or mood."[18] Or Henry C. Davis, writing about black folksong in South Carolina: "Stanzas of one song may serve in another with only the tune and the chorus to bind them together.[19] E. C. Perrow interpreted this phenomenon more negatively: ". . . some songs have become hopelessly confused with others. This fact is due chiefly, I think, to the comparative scarcity of melodies, one melody being made to serve for several songs." He did not sense any relative priority of text and tune: "I am sure that it has been only with the greatest difficulty that I have been able to separate some of the songs in this collection from others sung to the same tune, and I am not sure now that I have not put some stanzas in the wrong songs."[20]

Just as a textual unit or image may serve different functions in different songs — here advancing the narrative, there setting the mood — we should expect the role of music to differ from one song to the next. Logic suggests a kind of complementary distribution: the less stable and predictable the textual structure, the more essential and identifying the music. Tradition, however, is not so neatly logical. How often and to what degree this kind of distribution actually holds true can be determined only by case studies of a number of text-tune complexes; the few observations we do have are not unanimous. In this they parallel Bronson's findings, that some text-tune associations are tighter than others: a given Child ballad may appear with just one or with a number of distinct tunes; it may have its own characteristic tune(s) or share its tune(s) with other songs.[21] At one extreme, according to J. W. Allen, the tunes associated with the three songs that Cecil Sharp combined to form "O Waly Waly" gave little help in typifying the groups, although there was some similarity of tunes in one of these groups.[22] At the other extreme, I have concluded after long listening that except for obvious imitations of Cousin Emmy's "Ruby," the Woody Guthrie-Cisco Houston "900 Miles," and Hedy West's "500 Miles," the tune is the only predictable element in the whole "Reuben"/"900 Miles" complex.

Another parallel may be drawn to textual analysis: the size of the basic musical unit will differ from one song to the next. Whether it corresponds to a textual stanza, couplet, line, or half-line will become clearer as examples of the song accumulate. The smaller the unit, the more complex any description of the tune(s) must be. Indeed, from a musical perspective, the prospect of tracing and studying such musical motifs or commonplaces—should we call them floating bits of tune?—is even more overwhelming than working with textual units, if only because we lack the tools to locate them, or even any obvious way to recognize them. Again, we are dependent upon prior exposure, good memory, and, even with access to mechanical aids, inspired reflection.[23]

There is one aspect to this kind of traditional song (lyric, non-sequential) that is rarely reflected in our printed collections, namely, the give and take between voice and instrument when the song is accompanied. In 1893, Lila Edmands gave this glimpse of mountaineers on Roan Mountain, North Carolina: "These people have a peculiar way of picking the banjo, of which it is impossible to give any idea in writing out the tunes. They also play an interlude between each stanza, which sometimes exceeds the length of the measures sung."[24] Robert W. Gordon described how stanzas "leap out singly and with startling effect from the background of the instrumental music."[25] As early as 1927, hillbilly record catalogues distinguished between "vocal records" and "instrumental records with singing"; not all the items in each category fit the heading, but at least someone in the industry recognized the difference and tried to cope with it.[26] Accounts of the blues generally acknowledge the way instrumental accompaniment complements and comments on the vocal line.[27]

Usually, though, we find printed only the words to such songs, written in a block as if they had been sung one stanza immediately after the other. Unless we have access to sound recordings, or unless the collector tells us otherwise,[28] we would naturally assume this to be the case. If there is music, it will typically be of one stanza, perhaps with variants, to give the tune rather than the overall form of the piece. Surely all the songs in volumes 3 and 5 of the Brown collection, to take a convenient example, were not sung at a clip in their natural settings. "High Topped Shoes," we learn fortuitously from one of Frank C. Brown's informants, "was primarily a fiddle

and banjo instrumental piece with only two or three verses for singing."[29] Robert Gordon's observations of banjo songs and fiddle
songs in that same area also testify otherwise.[30]

No doubt this pattern of (sporadic) alternation between vocal and
instrumental segments facilitated development of the blues ballad
tradition, and maintained its lyric structure, just as older unaccom-
panied, strophic, steadily progressing melodic conventions helped
shape classic ballad tradition.[31] In this light, it is interesting that
D. K. Wilgus, who proposed the term "blues ballad," had earlier
used "banjo ballad" to describe that phenomenon.[32]

The matter of instrumental accompaniment deserves mention
because it affects what we understand the structure and identity
of a lyric song to be. The way we respond to the text on a printed
page might not be the way we would respond if we heard it sung.
We might find clustering of stanzas within a single performance,
which would suggest that all textual units are not attracted equally
to all other textual units. Or we might realize that a seeming in-
congruity of detail or of logical association of stanzas or images
did not come through as so incongruous after all, because an instrumental interlude separated those portions of text. Generally, there
is no way we can reconstruct how a printed lyric song might have
been performed. At best, we can caution on the point.

These banjo and fiddle songs caught the early attention of Robert
Gordon, to the extent that he devoted two of his *New York Times
Magazine* columns to them. Given his alertness to the interplay
between the various aspects of folk and popular tradition, he was
particularly interested in one "very puzzling group" of banjo songs:
"Old Reuben," "Georgia Buck," and "To the Pines":

> The stanzas are of three lines each (sometimes doubled in "Old
> Reuben") with two short lines and one long. This last long line is
> wailed almost as in the "blues." In fact I strongly suspect that this
> particular group of banjo songs may prove to be important fore-
> runners of the blues. The group seems to be more recent than the
> songs first quoted ["Honey, Where You Been So Long" and "Little
> Bonnie Blue-Eyes"], and to have more connection with individual
> authorship than with pure folk composition. But whatever their
> origin, the folk are certainly making them over, and they are now
> "folk-songs in the making."[33]

Indeed, the "To the Pines" that Gordon had recorded from Bertie
May Moses at Morganton, North Carolina, on December 4, 1925,
proved to be a folksong in the making in ways that he could not
suspect. It represents an early variant of the lyric song best known
as "In the Pines" or "The Longest Train," after the two verses that
typically occur in it, either alone or together. In recent years, two

forms of the song have become momentarily stabilized thanks to influential recordings by Leadbelly and by Bill Monroe.[34] While the texts that have come to light in the past sixty-odd years exhibit a typically wide and bewildering array of configurations, though, they are set to a smaller and more readily classified number of tunes. The relationships among these texts can in fact be clarified, and a probable history of their development can be more convincingly drawn, just because we do have access to the musical side of the tradition.

The following transcription comes from Gordon's 1925 cylinder recording:

TO THE PINES

To the pines, to the pines, where the sun never shines,
Going to shiver where the cold wind blows.

My husband was a railroad man,
Killed a mile and a half from here.

His head was found in a driver's wheel,
His body has not been found.

To the pines, to the pines, where the sun never shines,
Going to shiver where the cold wind blows.

Transportation brought me here,
Takes money to carry me back.

To the pines, to the pines, where the sun never shines,
Going to shiver where the cold wind blows.

A long steel rail that has no end
Has brought me far as here.

[You've] caused me to weep, you've caused me to mourn,
You've caused me to leave my home.[35]

The second and third couplets, and possibly also the last one, appeared later in Leadbelly's repertoire, joined to the text and tune of the "Black Girl" collected by Cecil Sharp and Maud Karpeles from Lizzie Abner, August 18, 1917, in Clay County, Kentucky:

BLACK GIRL

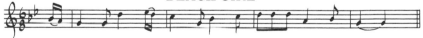

Black girl, black girl, don't lie to me
Where did you stay last night?

I stayed in the pines where the sun never shines,
And shivered when the cold wind blows.[36]

Except for the very unusual minor third (a tell-tale feature inherited by the folk music revivalists), the tune Leadbelly learned for this song represents its most common form. Typically, it is a one-strain melody, that is, two four-measure phrases, each musical phrase corresponding to one textual line, or half a couplet. The tune may be set against an instrumental accompaniment with the harmonic structure I – I – IV – I / I – V – I – I, each chord label standing for one full measure. The stressed pitches at the beginnings of the measures (assuming G as the tonic) typically read out as G – D – C – B (or G) / D – A (or B) – G. The tune is in triple meter. Within each measure the most representative rhythmic pattern is long-short, say, a half-note followed by a quarter note or two eighth notes (or the equivalent in compound meter). This rhythmic pattern is emphasized by the pattern of pitch change; that is, more frequently than not, the pitch of the third beat (the quarter note, or the first eighth note in that beat) is different from that of the first two beats (the half-note). Range is relatively narrow, from the tonic up through the fifth or sixth, occasionally to the octave above, and occasionally, just before the final, to the fifth below.

A secondary form of this tune, encountered less frequently, and mainly of older circulation, reverses the pitches stressed in the first two measures: D – G, rather than G – D. A recording by Georgian Riley Puckett will illustrate:

THE LONGEST TRAIN

The longest train I ever saw
Was on that Chaw-chaw line.

The engine passed at six o'clock
And the cab come round at nine.

The prettiest girl I ever saw
Lived down that railroad track.

Red rosy cheeks and blue eyes fair
And the curls hung down her back.

Little girl, little girl, what have I done
That you must treat me so?

You taken my clothes and throwed 'em outdoors,
And me no place to go.

My darling was killed last Friday night
Just a half a mile from town.

Her head was laying in the car-box floor
And her body has never been found.

The longest train I ever saw
Was on that Chaw-chaw line.

The engine passed at six o'clock
And the cab come round at nine.[37]

Both tune forms belong to a larger family, most handily illustrated by the examples Bronson has brought together for Child 85, "George Collins" (a label I have adopted for convenience). Indeed, part of his account of his variants could have come from my earlier description of the characteristic "In the Pines" tune: "The meter is usually triple (or compound duple). The range is often narrow, and apart from phrasal upbeats on the lower dominant, stays within the tonic and the fifth or sixth."[38]

A few texts of Child 85 have appeared with melodies quite close to that specialized "In the Pines" tune. To Bronson's No. 43, for instance, and the j and k versions he cites but does not print, we may add Lee Monroe Presnell's "George Collins"[39] or, more to the argument here, Dick Justice's "One Cold December Day":

ONE COLD DECEMBER DAY

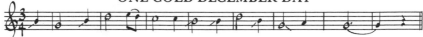

Down by a western water tank
One cold December day,

In a bottom of an empty car
A dying hobo lay.

He had a girl in yonders town,
She dressed of silk so fine.

When she heard that poor old George was dead
She laid her silk aside.

Oh mother, oh mother, let his coffin lid back,
And lay his saddle aside,

So that I can kiss his sweet, pale lips,
Well, I know he'll never kiss mine.

The longest train I ever saw
Was on the Georgie line.

The engine passed at six-fifteen,
The cab rolled by at nine.

Look up, look down this lonesome road,
Hang down your head and cry.

I see a dove in yonders hill,
She's flying from pine to pine.

She's mourning for her own true love,
And why can't I mourn for mine?

The longest train I ever saw
Was on the Georgie line.

The engine passed at six-fifteen,
The cab rolled by at nine.

> Look up, look down this lonesome road,
> Hang down your head and cry.[40]

Bertie May Moses's tune represents the extended family, as does the
following by Bascom Lamar Lunsford:

TO THE PINES

> To the pines, to the pines, where the sun never shines,
> Gonna shiver while the cold winds blow.
>
> Look down, look down that lonesome road,
> Where you and I must go.
>
> The best of friends must part sometime,
> And why not you and I?
>
> Little boy, little boy, where did you stay?
> Where did you stay last night?

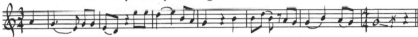

> I stayed in the pines, where the sun never shines,
> I shiver while the cold winds blow.
>
> To the pines, to the pines, where the sun never shines,
> Gonna shiver while the cold winds blow.
>
> The longest train I ever did see
> Was in John Brown's coal mine.
>
> The engine passed at half a past three,
> The cab didn't pass till nine.
>
> To the pines, to the pines, where the sun never shines,
> Gonna shiver while the cold winds blow.
>
> The prettiest girl I ever did see
> Was killed one mile from here.
>
> Her head n was in the driving wheel,
> Her body never was found.
>
> To the pines, to the pines, where the sun never shines,
> Gonna shiver while the cold winds blow.[41]

Other "George Collins" variants resemble these, but with the pitches
that are stressed in the first two measures reversed: D – G, rather
than G – D.

A minority of "In the Pines"/"Longest Train" texts are set to
tunes in duple meter, and of these, the one that occurs frequently
enough to be anticipated is "Reuben"/"900 Miles." Briefly outlined,
this is a one-strain tune in duple meter (a second strain may accommodate a refrain). It stresses the fifth of the scale except at cadence
points, where it descends to the tonic. There may be other momen-
tary diversions to the tonic, or to the upper octave of the tonic.
When there is instrumental accompaniment, it comprises a I chord

throughout, except for a V chord preceding the final cadence.[42]
Daw Henson's "I'm Crazy over You" illustrates the type:

I'M CRAZY OVER YOU

I'm crazy over you and the way that you do,
Oh honey, I'm fool over you.

What have I done, true love, to you
That you've treated me this-a way?

You treated me mean and dirty so long
Till there's nothing goes hard with me.

Look up, look down these lonesome road,
Hang down your head and cry.

Ain't but one woman in this wide world
That does not fear to die.

I'm crazy over you and your little sister too,
Oh honey, I'm fool over you.

The hardest work that I ever done
Was grubbing around that old pine.

The easiest work that I ever done
Was hugging that woman of mine.

I'm crazy over you and the way that you do,
Oh honey, I'm fool over you.

The longest train that I ever rode
Left out of John Brown's coal mine.

The engine passed at six o'clock,
And the cab never passed till nine.[43]

Now, when we look at the texts in this lyric cluster in light of the
tunes—first as they align with either triple or duple meter, and then
as those in triple meter may be further subdivided, into the standard
"In the Pines" tune, or the variant of it noted earlier, or other tunes
associated with "George Collins"—we begin to notice some interesting affiliations. The "in the pines" couplet (and other verses that
tend to appear with it) occurs almost exclusively with triple-meter
tunes, especially the dominant form for which it provides the title;
that bond is exceedingly stable. The "longest train" verse reflects
a different distribution: if it occurs with an "in the pines" couplet,
we can expect to find the "In the Pines" tune; but if it occurs without that couplet, we can expect to find a duple-meter tune. The
verses recounting the accident in which a person is decapitated are

set most often to tunes in duple meter, or to that minority form of the "In the Pines" tune that stresses D - G in the first two measures, or to other "George Collins" tunes; they appear mainly in conjunction with "longest train" verses.

How can we account for these patterns? It seems clear to me that the two textual elements that are now bound into a common lyric cluster once existed as independent songs or clusters: that with the "longest train" verses circulated with a number of tunes in duple meter, particularly the "Reuben"/"900 Miles" tune; that with the "in the pines" verses circulated with the "In the Pines" tune and other "George Collins" tunes. When these two clusters came together, the "In the Pines" tune supplanted the others. Probably the common use of the "in the pines" couplet as a chorus, a role the "longest train" couplet seldom enjoyed, had some influence.

What brought these two songs together in the first place? On the textual side, the obvious link is rhyme—"pine," "shine," "mine," "line," "nine"—with the common theme of darkness, removal, isolation. Odum and Johnson offered the following segment as part of a song "of the mining or railroad camp laborer" from early in this century:

> Goin' take my pick an' shovel—goin' deep down in mine.
> I'm goin' where de sun—don't never shine.[44]

Evidence that this association remains viable is as recent as Merle Travis's "Dark as a Dungeon" or Jean Ritchie's "Blue Diamond Mines."[45]

On the musical side, the similarity of the tunes to which the bulk of these texts are set no doubt blended bits of text in performance and memory. Certainly the process paralleled what Bronson has observed for narrative song: ". . . there may be tunes which, from a relationship half-consciously sensed by the singer, act as the disintegrating and reintegrating agents that gradually win away elements of a ballad, and reestablish these in new contexts, modifying the conduct of the narrative, or otherwise effecting a crossing that produces a new and different species."[46]

For the most part, these are one-strain melodies, that is, two phrases of four measures each, or relatively straightforward expansions of such a unit. In basic outline, they make extensive use of the notes in the I chord. There is considerable playing around with the tonic and the fifth as stressed pitches in measures 1 and 2; they appear in different order, in different octaves, above or below the tonic. A point of difference or clue to identity comes only with measure 3: here the "In the Pines" tunes stress the fourth, rather than the fifth (or another pitch). Given this initial variance in tunes of similar length and outline, it would seem relatively easy for a singer to slip into one or another pattern, depending on how he happened to begin the tune. Not that there was any planned or minutely creeping progression from the "Reuben"/"900 Miles" tune to "In the Pines," say, or the other way around; but the resemblances are sufficient to suggest how one tune might have brought another—and its text—to mind.

What happened when these two lyric clusters began to merge? The "In the Pines" tune, as I mentioned, eventually won out. We can see a transition in those pieces using "George Collins" tunes and the secondary form of the "In the Pines" tune. Musically, they resemble the duple-meter end of the spectrum more than does the dominant form of "In the Pines." Textually, they retain more of the "longest train" and associated verses than do most of the variants set to that standard "In the Pines" tune. Some of the fairly specific and graphic features associated with the "longest train" songs began to be generalized, abbreviated, or dropped. The train, for instance, which earlier was located at Georgia governor Joseph Emerson Brown's coal mines, later simply came "down that Georgia line." The earlier description of the train's engine in terms of where it was gave way to an indication of when it passed by. Verses describing the "prettiest girl" who then lost her head in the driving wheel began to appear with "George Collins" and "In the Pines" tunes, suggesting that they were added mainly after the two original clusters merged; but then that whole sequence was condensed, or eroded altogether. The description of the girl fell away; a train was no longer specified as cause of the accident; the victim became a man rather than a woman. Our most familiar versions, then, by Leadbelly and Bill Monroe, represent later stages in the development of the "In the Pines"/"Longest Train" complex.

As a body, all the songs in this cluster represent at least a century's worth of the coming together and sorting out of many elements, both textual and musical. The patterns we see represent earlier independent components as well as subsequent blends that in their turn became standard models. The popularity of the Leadbelly and Monroe versions reflects the magnetic personalities and powerful musicianship of the performers involved, as well as the impact of mass-media distribution. While taken up by different audiences, each shows some sign of being adapted back into traditional repertoires, more so in the case of Bill Monroe's "In the Pines." How and when conscious creativity or forgetfulness or relationships half-consciously sensed will overcome the force of authority, and how widely, we cannot say. Differing versions, some of obvious vintage, still come to our attention, and the banjo- and fiddle-song traditions that helped create and maintain such clusters as "In the Pines"/ "The Longest Train" still flourish: witness the variants by Maggie

Hammons Parker and Dee Hicks.[47] It may be that in another hundred years the association of Bill Monroe with his version of "In the Pines" and the predominance of his particular tune and textual configuration will have faded, just as the name Joe Brown dropped from the songs and evokes virtually no response today even by Georgians whose grandparents worked at his mines a century ago.

We cannot predict whether the tunes associated with this particular lyric song will continue to provide a more helpful guide than the texts in classifying the variants and clarifying their relationships, in confirming the identity of the song and helping us sense better, for instance, where we have a member of the "In the Pines" family and where we simply have an "in the pines" verse tucked into a quite different song, for reasons we may or may not be able to explain. I suspect, though, that the melodies will in fact speak to us more clearly than the words.

And for other lyric songs, the lesson should by now have been reinforced: where we lack what has been the customary basis for studying traditional song—a text that is narrative or otherwise sequentially structured—there is a complementary element to which we can turn. Bertrand Bronson has reminded us eloquently of the logic and need for considering ballad texts and tunes together; surely for lyric songs the logic and need, and the potential for bringing order out of chaos, are even greater.

NOTES

[1]For a discussion of this song, with an extensive biblio-discography, see Norm Cohen, *Long Steel Rail: The Railroad in American Folkson* (Urbana: University of Illinois Press, 1981), pp. 503-17.

[2]Robert Duncan Bass, "Negro Songs from the Pedee Country," *Journal of American Folklore*, 44 (Oct.–Dec., 1931), 431.

[3]*The Frank C. Brown Collection of North Carolina Folklore*, vol. 3, *Folk Songs from North Carolina*, edited by Henry M. Belden and Arthur Palmer Hudson (Durham, N.C.: Duke University Press, 1952), p. 348.

[4]Mainer to McCulloh, Aug. 22, 1969.

[5]For sample blues ballad studies, see Cohen, *Long Steel Rail*, pp. 122-31 ("Railroad Bill"), 132-57 ("Casey Jones"), 413-25 ("Cannonball Blues"/"Whitehouse Blues"); Neil Rosenberg, "'Whitehouse Blues'—'McKinley'—'Cannonball Blues': A Biblio-discography," *JEMF Newsletter*, 4 (June, 1968), 45-58; Marina Bokelman, "'The Coon Can Game': A Blues Ballad Tradition," Master's thesis, UCLA, 1968; D. K. Wilgus and Lynwood Montell, "Clure and Joe Williams: Legend and Blues Ballad," *JAF*, 81 (Oct.-Dec., 1968), 295-315.

[6]Belden to Newman I. White, May 8, 1945, and May 19, 1946, in Duke University, Perkins Library, Manuscript Dept., Frank C. Brown Papers, Box 71, Folder 6.

[7]For a more detailed overview of the variety of lyric songs, see W. Edson Richmond, "'Just Sing It Yourself': The American Lyric Tradition," in *Our Living*

Traditions, edited by Tristram P. Coffin (New York: Basic Books, 1968), pp. 94–107.

[8]See, e.g., Paul Oliver, *Blues Fell This Morning* (London: Cassell, 1960); idem, *Screening the Blues: Aspects of the Blues Tradition* (London: Cassell, 1968); Charles Keil, *Urban Blues* (Chicago: University of Chicago Press, 1966); Archie Green, *Only a Miner: Studies in Recorded Coal-Mining Songs* (Urbana: University of Illinois Press, 1972).

[9]Newman I. White, *American Negro Folk-Songs* (1928; rpt., Hatboro, Pa.: Folklore Associates, 1965), p. 26.

[10]Tristram P. Coffin, "A Tentative Study of a Typical Folk Lyric: 'Green Grows the Laurel,' " *JAF,* 65 (Oct.–Dec., 1952), 341. Cf. Jan Brunvand, *The Study of American Folklore: An Introduction* (New York: W. W. Norton, 1968), p. 144.

[11]For examples of such analysis, see Zonweise Stein, " 'John Brown's Coal Mine,' " *Kentucky Folklore Record,* 7 (Oct.–Dec., 1961), 147–58; Francis Lee Utley, "The Genesis and Revival of 'Dink's Song,' " in *Studies in Language and Literature in Honour of Margaret Schlauch,* edited by Mieczysław Brahmer et al. (Warsaw: Pánstwowe Wydawnietwo Naukowe, 1966), pp. 457–72.

[12]Coffin, " 'Green Grows the Laurel,' " e.g., focuses on one stanza — the chorus.

[13]Bertrand Harris Bronson, *The Traditional Tunes of the Child Ballads,* 4 vols. (Princeton, N.J.: Princeton University Press, 1959–72). Norman Cazden's extensive research on a Catskills collection reached print only after his death, in *Folk Songs of the Catskills,* edited and annotated, with a study of tune formation and relationships, by Norman Cazden, Herbert Haufrecht, and Norman Studer, and their companion volume *Notes and Sources for Folk Songs of the Catskills* (Albany: State University of New York Press, 1982). Other valuable longterm projects remain unpublished.

[14]Bronson, *Traditional Tunes,* vol. 2 (1962), p. 60. He made this point earlier in "The Interdependence of Ballad Tunes and Texts," *California Folklore Quarterly,* 3 (July, 1944), 199.

[15]Bronson, "Interdependence," p. 190.

[16]Bokelman, " 'Coon Can Game,' " pp. 82–83, 102.

[17]Rosenberg, " 'Whitehouse Blues,' " p. 55. For transcriptions of these two recordings, see Cohen, *Long Steel Rail,* pp. 413–14.

[18]D. K. Wilgus, *Anglo-American Folksong Scholarship since 1898* (New Brunswick, N.J.: Rutgers University Press, 1959), p. 432.

[19]Henry C. Davis, "Negro Folk-Lore in South Carolina," *JAF,* 27 (July–Sept., 1914), 240.

[20]E. C. Perrow, "Songs and Rhymes from the South," *JAF,* 25 (Apr.–June, 1912), 145, and 28 (Apr.–June, 1915), 182.

[21]See, e.g., Bronson, *Traditional Tunes,* vol. 1 (1959), pp. xix, 9, 143, 191, 237, 409, and *passim* in other headnotes.

[22]J. W. Allen, "Some Notes on 'O Waly Waly,' " *Journal of the English Folk Dance and Song Society,* 7 (Dec., 1954), 167.

[23]Cf. Samuel P. Bayard, "Aspects of Melodic Kinship and Variation in British-American Folk-Tunes," in *Papers Read at the International Congress of Musicology* [1939], edited by Arthur Mendel, Gustave Reese, and Gilbert Chase (New York: American Musicological Society, 1944), pp. 125–26; Bronson, *Traditional Tunes,* vol. 1, p. xxv; A[nne] G. G[ilchrist], review of *Spiritual Folk-Songs of Early America* by George Pullen Jackson, *JEFDSS,* 3 (Dec., 1938), 214.

[24]Lila Edmands, "Songs from the Mountains of North Carolina," *JAF,* 6 (Apr.–June, 1893), 131.

[25]Robert W. Gordon, "Folk-Songs of America: Fiddle Tunes," *New York Times Magazine,* Nov. 27, 1927, p. 14.

[26]Catalog supplement to Columbia *Old Familiar Tunes,* Oct. 11, 1927.

[27]See, e.g., David Evans, *Tommy Johnson* (London: Studio Vista, 1971), p. 49; Jeff Todd Titon, *Early Downhome Blues: A Musical and Cultural Analysis* (Urbana: University of Illinois Press, 1977), p. xvi.

[28]Writers whose first love is instrumental tradition do better on this score. See, e.g., Ira W. Ford, *Traditional Music of America* (1940; rpt., New York: Da Capo Press, 1978), p. 27.

[29]"High Topped Shoes," sung by Houston and Wiseman, in *Brown Collection*, vol. 5, *The Music of the Folk Songs*, edited by Jan Philip Schinhan (Durham, N.C.: Duke University Press, 1962), pp. 215-16; information from Myron Houston, relayed in Scotty Wiseman to McCulloh, Aug. 29, 1969.

[30]Robert W. Gordon, "The Folk-Songs of America: Banjo Tunes," *New York Times Magazine*, Jan. 1, 1928, pp. 10, 15 (reprinted with minor revisions in *Folksongs of America* [Washington, D.C.: National Service Bureau publication 73-S, Dec., 1938], pp. 78-84); "Folk-Songs of America: Fiddle Tunes," *New York Times Magazine*, Nov. 27, 1927, pp. 14, 23 (reprinted, with minor changes in the body of the article and extensive reworking of the introduction, in *Folksongs of America*, pp. 71-77).

[31]See, e.g., Bronson's discussion in *Traditional Tunes*, vol. 1, p. xii.

[32]D. K. Wilgus, " 'Arch and Gordon,' " *KFR*, 6 (Apr.-June, 1960), 53.

[33]Gordon, *Folksongs of America*, p. 84. See also n. 30 above.

[34]Leadbelly, "Black Girl," *Rock Island Line*, Folkways FA 2014 (recorded 1941-46); idem, "Black Girl," *Leadbelly Memorial, III*, Stinson SLP 48 (recorded 1941-46); idem, "Where Did You Sleep Last Night," *Leadbelly Sings Ballads of Beautiful Women and Bad Men*, Sutton SU 278 (recorded Feb. 17, 1944, in New York City); Bill Monroe, "In the Pines," Bluebird 8861 (recorded Oct. 2, 1941, in Atlanta), reissued on *The Father of Bluegrass Music*, Camden CAL 719; idem, "In the Pines," Decca 28416 (recorded July 18, 1952, in Nashville), reissued on *Bill Monroe's Greatest Hits*, Decca 76010.

[35]Bertie May Moses, "To the Pines," Library of Congress Archive of Folk Song, Gordon Recording A-124 (North Carolina MS 182).

[36]Cecil Sharp, *English Folk-Songs from the Southern Appalachians*, edited by Maud Karpeles (London: Oxford University Press, 1932), vol. 2, p. 278. Unfortunately, the corresponding field notebook is missing from Cecil Sharp House, London, so we cannot determine whether the original text was longer.

[37]Riley Puckett, "The Longest Train I Ever Saw," Decca 5523, recorded ca. Sept., 1937, in New York City.

[38]Bronson, *Traditional Tunes*, vol. 2, p. 392. Resemblances may be seen even wider afield, of course, e.g., between the contour of "In the Pines" and some of the tunes presented for Child 250, "Henry Martyn." But considering the multiple correspondences, in a variety of tunes and occasional suggestive stanzas (such as "dove and pine"), the "Goerge Collins" assemblage remains the most useful to cite.

[39]Lee Monroe Presnell, "George Collins," *The Traditional Music of Beech Mountain, North Carolina, I*, Folk-Legacy FSA 22, recorded by Liam Clancy, Diane Hamilton, and Paul Clayton, in July, 1956.

[40]Dick Justice, "One Cold December Day," Brunswick 367, recorded May 21, 1929, in Chicago.

[41]Bascom Lamar Lunsford, "To the Pines," LC AFS 1829 B3, recorded by George W. Hibbitt and William Cabell Greet in 1935 in New York City.

[42]This harmonic structure is reinforced by the vigorous instrumental counterpart to the "Reuben"/"900 Miles" vocal tradition, usually titled "Train 45." See Cohen, *Long Steel Rail*, pp. 504-5, 511-14, 517.

[43]Daw Henson, "I'm Crazy over You," LC AFS 1500 A, recorded by Alan and Elizabeth Lomax, Oct. 11, 1937, at Billy's Branch, Clay Co., Ky. I am grateful

to Mike Seeger for bringing this recording to my attention. Cf. Asa Martin's "On My Way Back Home," transcribed in Judith McCulloh, "What Is 'the Tune'?," in *Discourse in Ethnomusicology: Essays in Honor of George List,* edited by Caroline Card et al. (Bloomington: Ethnomusicology Publications Group, Indiana University, 1978), pp. 94–95.

[44]Howard Odum and Guy B. Johnson, *The Negro and His Songs* (1925; rpt., Hatboro, Pa.: Folklore Associates, 1964), p. 260.

[45]Merle Travis, "Dark as a Dungeon," Capital 48001 (recorded Aug. 8, 1946, in Hollywood), released in album *Folk Songs of the Hills,* Capitol AD 50; Jean Ritchie, "Blue Diamond Mines," *A Time for Singing,* Warner Brothers W 1592.

[46]Bronson, "Interdependence," p. 195.

[47]Maggie Hammons Parker, "The Lonesome Pines," *Shaking Down the Acorns,* Rounder Records 0018, recorded by Dwight Diller, Carl Fleischhauer, and Alan Jabbour, 1970–72, in Pocahontas and Greenbrier counties, W.Va.; Dee Hicks (from Jamestown, Tenn.), "In the Pines," LC AFS LWO 12527, recorded at the Archive of Folk Song's fiftieth anniversary concert, Nov. 16, 1978, in Washington, D.C., and made available through the kindness of Bobby Fulcher and Joe Wilson.

The "Mary Scott" Complex:
Outline of a Diachronic Model

James Porter

Clusters of songs, or song-complexes, that exhibit shared features are of perennial interest to the student of traditional expressive forms. The interpretation of such complexes and their common elements can, however, extend beyond filiation of verbal or melodic structures, for folk songs mirror not only the patterning abilities of a *communitas* and its individual members over space and time, but also the passions, rationalizings, contradictions, and aspirations embedded in the human condition as it copes with living and with change. Examination of the internal properties in related groups of songs ought, therefore, to be balanced by a scrutiny of those who brought them to life and the society that nourished them, as far as this is possible.[1] Consequently, the study of song-clusters in the light of their social import marks a significant step in grasping not just the relationship of texts and tunes in a diachronic sequence but further, the vital synchronic link between the re-creators of the songs and their social environment.[2]

While a legitimate purpose of the scholar is to reveal the nature of traditional variants so that principles of continuity and change, stability and variability may be interpreted within the broader cultural frame, an analytical model with a complementary objective may be proposed.[3] If one is to comprehend the *style* of a society through its common creative effort, the persons who contribute to that effort must command attention. It is a logical step from Bronson's lucid portrait of the mental habits of Anna Brown in recreating ballads to the wider study of those who, at a particular place and time, cumulatively added to the formation of a specific song-complex and a song style in general.[4] The complex designated here as "Mary Scott" provides the basis for outlining, in summary form at present, a diachronic model not only of songs and tunes but also of re-creators, singers and their cultural milieu.

As one examines this group of songs, problems of an historical nature immediately arise: there were in fact two persons named Mary Scott, both of whom had songs composed in their honor; both were connected by family to two famous Walter Scotts; and their virtues as beauties of their respective periods (ca. 1550–1600, ca. 1700–70) in Scotland were celebrated by, among others, two Allan Ramsays. A particular task, then, is to distinguish historical persons within the complex and to view them in the context of their times. Another objective is to identify the musicians, singers, and poets who contributed to, or who touch upon, the song materials and to account for changes of taste in popular styles of music-making. Finally, the nature and evolution of the songs, verses and tunes, need to be analyzed. The resulting elaboration of persons and periods, creators, re-creators and styles, and of the songs themselves can provide a model that emphasizes the organic relationship among these three levels.

Persons and periods

It has frequently been observed that post-medieval Scotland possessed cultural conditions ripe for the making of ballads and songs, the earlier sixteenth century being especially creative.[5] Two centuries later, in the wake of political union with England in 1707, a powerful sense of revival in cultural matters drew attention to a community of ballad lovers that had long been in existence.[6] Two distinct periods, the second half of the sixteenth century and the first seventy years of the eighteenth, form the backdrop for the two figures at the heart of the "Mary Scott" complex.

Who were these two Mary Scotts, and why should they inspire a host of songs, poems, and tunes? The first Mary was the daughter of John Scott (not, apparently, Philip Scott, as both Sir Walter and Stenhouse maintain), of Dryhope in the Border county of Selkirk.[7] The old tower of Dryhope, where she was born in the mid-sixteenth century, is situated near the lower end of St. Mary's Loch, and its ruins are still standing.[8] We know little about her childhood but, having grown into a striking beauty she was married, on March 21, 1567 (not 1576 as another commentator has it), to Walter Scott of Harden, later known as "Auld Watt," who had succeeded his father as laird in 1563.[9] By their marriage contract, Dryhope agreed to keep his daughter for a year and a day after the marriage, in return for which Harden bound himself to give his father-in-law the profits of the first Michaelmas moon.[10]

Walter and Mary Scott had four sons (Sir Walter believed six), one of whom was killed in an affray by rival Scotts and three rather than six daughters.[11] Evidently, it was the gentleness and grace of Harden's spouse that earned her the sobriquet of "The Flower of Yarrow," a title that reverberates through Border literature. A student of local history has conjectured that the name was conceived by a young English captive whom she rescued from the rough hands of Harden's freebooters as they returned from a raid into Cumberland; this prisoner may have been the composer of the original song of "Mary Scott."[12] Another, less genteel legend recounts that when the last bullock brought from English pastures had been consumed, the Flower of Yarrow would place a pair of clean spurs on the table to indicate that her lord and his retainers must ride forth for their next meal.[13]

Life at Harden in those times was undoubtedly harsh, given the semi-feudal character of Border society and the constant strife between the Scotts and their neighbors, whether English or Scottish. The fortress of Harden itself was well suited to this factious world, having a situation superior even to those of Branxholm or Hermitage Castles. One of the darkest and deepest glens shielded it from attack, and this glen seems to have been so frequented by hares that it acquired the name of Hare-dean, afterwards contracted to Harden. Another glen of equal depth converged to form a tongue of land on which the house stood, so close to a precipice that the view from the windows overlooked a depth of some two hundred feet. Just below the castle, the glen facing south admitted the cattle that Auld Watt and his followers would drive from Cumberland. From the castle turrets the reiver, who features prominently in the ballad "Jamie Telfer of the Fair Dodhead" (Child 190) could survey the hills south towards the English border, so that when beacons were lit those at Harden would always be among the first into battle.[14] Mary Scott probably died about 1596-7, for Watt married again in 1598 and lived on until 1629.[15]

The period in which Watt of Harden and his spouse lived was marked by the watershed of the Reformation (1560), the abdication of Mary, Queen of Scots in favor of her infant son James (1567), and continual turmoil between civil and religious factions. But the topography of the Border region, cut off by a belt of hill and muir from the rest of Lowland Scotland, lent it an autonomous political character at times, and Border chieftains could stand together against any outsider, even the King, who is sometimes criticized in the ballads for his actions.[16]

In his study of Border history, John Veitch suggests that the persistence of traditions about Mary Scott is significant quite apart

from her being the wife of a noted Border reiver.[17] It is hardly
surprising that Auld Watt and the Flower of Yarrow should be
commemorated in song when one considers their personal charisma,
the consanguinity of many local families, and the roughshod temper
of the times. At this point one can note the traditionality of the old
song eulogizing Mary that Stenhouse heard in his youth (ca. 1780–
90) by the banks of the Tweed.[18]

Sir Walter Scott refers to Mary in the *Minstrelsy*, adding a comment in a fragment of autobiography written at Ashestiel in 1804:

> My father's grandfather was Walter Scott, well known in Teviotdale
> by the surname of *Beardie*. He was the second son of Walter Scott,
> first laird of Raeburn, who was the third son of Sir William Scott,
> and the grandson of Walter Scott, commonly called in tradition
> *Auld Watt*, of Harden. I am therefore lineally descended from that
> ancient chieftain whose name I have made to ring in many a ditty,
> and from his fair dame, the Flower of Yarrow — no bad genealogy for
> a Border minstrel.[19]

According to Robert Chambers, Scott also spoke of the later, eighteenth-century namesake of Mary (actually Mary Lilias) as "the
Second Flower of Yarrow," observing that she was recognized in the
fashionable circles of the time by the nickname of "Cadie" because
she had once gone to a fancy-dress ball in the costume of a *cadie*
(Fr. *cadet*), or street-porter (Henry Mackenzie, the novelist, offers
a less plausible etymology below).[20] Mary Lilias was born around
the beginning of the century as the second daughter of John Scott
of Harden (which overlooks the valley of Borthwick Water, not the
Yarrow) and grew into a woman of acknowledged beauty, reaching the height of her charms about 1725.[21] Stenhouse links the
second Mary to the first in his *Illustrations*, declaring the latter to
be the ancestor of the former.[22] In her youth Mary Lilias was, with
her elder sister, an excellent singer, and her vocal talents are confirmed by Henry Mackenzie, author of *The Man of Feeling*, who
tells how the ladies of Edinburgh would sing traditional airs at tea
and after supper without any accompaniment:

> The youngest Miss Scott of Harden (called from that circumstance
> *La Cadette*, thence vulgarly corrupted to *Cadie Scott*), sung some of
> these songs with the greatest expression and effect. She was the reign-
> ing beauty of the time, and so much a favorite with the then Duke
> of Hamilton that he had her picture painted . . . and, it was confi-
> dently said, wished to marry her. Why he did not, I never learned.
> I knew her only when above middle age, still a fine, interesting, and
> amiable woman, but her face spoiled with a scorbutic affection;

her voice, however, was as good as ever, and her singing full of taste and pathos. Her *Lochaber no more* (of itself indeed a most tender and expressive song, quite appropriate to the pensive melancholy of the words) bro't tears into her own eyes, and seldom failed of the same effect on her audience.[23]

It is not improbable that "Cadie" Scott (who lived till about 1770) knew the old song about her ancestor and sang it at one of these gatherings in an Edinburgh drawing room. This was a period of cultural renaissance in the city, for at the close of the seventeenth century the church had withdrawn its anathemas against dancing, and a spirit of revival entered public and private music-making. In this age of contrast between Reason and the power of the Reformed Church, between speculative thought and medieval modes of behavior, Allan Ramsay (1686–1758) set about restoring a native literary tradition that had become quite anglicized in the work of poets such as Sir Robert Aytoun (1570–1638) and Drummond of Hawthornden (1585–1649). Operating from the bookshop that he opened in the wake of his successful pastoral *The Gentle Shepherd* (1725), Ramsay began the first circulating library in Britain in 1728 and founded the city's first regular theater in Carrubber's Close (1736). Within the social pattern of convivial clubs that were common at the time, Ramsay met with gentlemen and citizens of the Easy Club, where they would drink claret, discuss literary affairs, and listen to songs.[24] His collection of song texts, *The Tea-Table Miscellany* (1724), met a specific need in catering to gentlewomen, who preferred to stay in Edinburgh rather than the country during the winter, to attend the concerts and other entertainments with the rest of fashionable society, and to cultivate a repertoire of native song. Ramsay's achievement in reviving a "national" song repertoire, while uneven in quality, was substantial, and one of the song texts he reworked to meet changing tastes was "Mary Scott," which was published in his *Poems* of 1721.[25]

Nowhere is the presence of the European Enlightenment in Lowland Scotland symbolized more aptly, however, than in the case of Allan Ramsay (1709–84), the poet's son and portrait painter to George III, whose cultivated manners and adherence to the principle of Reason made him something of a contrast to the liveliness, simplicity, and "uncultivated genius" of his father.[26] Ramsay took the Grand Tour (1736–8), studying in Italy and Paris. Later in Edinburgh (1754) he founded the Select Society, a body of intellectuals that counted among its members David Hume, Adam Smith, Lord Monboddo, the architects John and James Adam, and James Boswell.[27]

FIG. 1 *Allan Ramsay.* Miss Mary Lilias Scott. *Engraving by John Faber (1748).*

Stenhouse asserts that the Duke of Hamilton had Mary Lilias Scott's portrait painted by Ramsay, and a portrait said to be by him is duly praised by Pennant in his *Tour.*[28] But Pennant seems to have confused the work with another, for there is no record of Ramsay's having painted a full-length portrait of Mary Scott "in white satin; a most elegant figure."[29] The 1759 Catalogue of the Duke of Hamilton's collection has a reference to a portrait of Mary Lilias Scott, full-length, by Jeremiah Davison, a Scottish contemporary of Ramsay, which is now in a private collection.[30] Ramsay's picture of the lady, engraved by John Faber in 1748, is bust-length

FIG. 2. *Gerrit van Honthorst. Miss Scott called the Flower of Yarrow (ca. 1628). Private Collection. Reproduced by permission.*

in a feigned oval, the subject facing right and holding a piece of music [fig. 1].

A recent biography of Ramsay reveals that the painter was enamored of Mary Lilias Scott, and began courting her with verses in 1747 while on a visit from London.[31] It can be concluded that, although the romance came to nothing, Ramsay probably executed the lady's portrait in the same year. A portrait of the first Mary Scott, wife of Watt of Harden, by the Dutch artist Gerrit van Honthorst (1590–1656) is extant, though chronology precludes his having painted it from life. Honthorst is known to have worked in

Britain around 1628, and it must have been at this time that he created the picture using a current beauty as his model (another Mary Scott?). No doubt the memory of the Flower of Yarrow, and her song, were still widely celebrated. The subject of this portrait faces left in a feigned oval, the title below reading "Miss Scott called the Flower of Yarrow" [fig. 2].[32]

Creators, re-creators, and styles

A detailed picture of individual musicians and composers in the time of the first Mary Scott is difficult to draw because of the disruptive effects of the Reformation on cultural life and the lingering autonomy of the Border region where many stirring songs were created. But some facts can be sketched in. By the time of Mary Scott's adolescence, for example, Court records describe the musicians at the baptism of Mary Stuart's son James at Stirling (1566): John Hume, the chief minstrel, was the principal of three "lutars," with five "violars" and several woodwind players who are all named.[33] Into the royal employ, which had seen Italians and Frenchmen in its ranks as well as native Scottish musicians, stepped the Piedmontese David Rizzio, whose subsequent rise to favor as confidant of Queen Mary and brutal death at the hands of the jealous Scots lords are well known. Such a charismatic figure could easily become, later, the person to whom misguided antiquarians attributed many anonymous popular songs.[34]

As a young man James VI, who succeeded his mother in 1567, showed considerable interest in music, and by the age of 15 was ordering two pairs of virginals from London.[35] James had four "violars" assigned to him who were, significantly, English rather than Scottish, Italian, or French (Thomas, Robert, James, and William Hudson, probably brothers). It is also recorded that payment was made, at Holyrood in 1596, to "four English violars" who were doubtless visiting performers.[36] The increasing contact with England, which James was anxious to pursue for reasons of succession to the English throne, ran parallel to the harsh edicts passed continuously by the Reformers against both pre-Reformation church music and the secular music of the lower classes in Scotland after 1560.

One of James's court musicians, James Hudson, was a friend of the poet Alexander Montgomerie (?1545–?1615) who, with his contemporaries Alexander Scott (fl. 1548–68) and Mark Alexander Boyd (1563–1601) introduced a breath of Renaissance *dolce stil nuovo* into their verses. But another gifted poet of the time, Alexander Hume (?1557–1609), forsook poetry and music for the cause of religion, confessing in his *Hymns* (1599) that he too had followed

the path of secular poetry but was now setting out to show the correct use of his gifts:

> In Prince's courts, in the housis of great menn, and at the assembleis
> of yong gentlemen and yong damesels, the chief pastime is to sing
> prophaine sonnets and vain ballattis of love, or to rehers some
> fabulos faites of Palmerine, Amadis, or other such like reveries. . . .
> Alas! for pittie, is this the richte use of a Christianes talent?[37]

It is evident that there was plenty of "profane" music about, even
though Hume came to disapprove of it, and some of this recreation,
whether Italian or domestic, may have taken place at Harden.

Pedagogically, the upper classes in Scotland had been well served
by the Sang Schools founded in the fourteenth century. The masters
of these retained a certain prestige, such as "Sir" John Lesley (1526-
96), made master at Aberdeen in 1554. As a prisoner in England
while acting on behalf of Mary Stuart, Lesley came to know the
composer Christopher Tye, whose music may have been played in
Scotland (his *Ascendo* is in the David Melville MS).[38] The important
poet and composer Sir John Fethy (?1480-ca.1570) had introduced
a new technique of playing the organ into Scotland about 1530, and
Fethy is of interest here because of his leasing his emoluments, in
1563, to Walter Scott of Branxholm and Dame Janet Betoun.[39]
The Border region was thus open to gifted poets and composers
from outside it. Other Sang School masters such as John Black at
Aberdeen (d. 1587) and Edward Henryson at Edinburgh (d. 1579)
were fine musicians.[40] At Ayr, again, the master taught scholars
how to sing and play spinet, while the master at Haddington in
1610 was teaching the virginals, lute, and gittern.[41] Despite some
spoliation of the schools in 1559-60, an important statute encouraging the Sang Schools was passed in 1579, which implies that the
Reformers were no longer threatened by the practice of "learned"
music in educated levels of society although they violently dis-
approved of instrumental music in church.

Throughout the country at this time the old professional choir
and organist of the pre-Reformation church were banished, all
vocal praise now issuing from the people as a whole, who would
"sing a psalm together, in a plain tune."[42] The Reformers thus
prescribed a straightforward homophony that was to persist until
1625, when the first harmonized Common Tunes appeared. Of
the new composers for the Reformed Church—John Angus, Andrew
Blackhall, John Buchan, Andrew Kemp, John Black, John Fethy—
one in particular, David Peebles (d. before 1592), managed to effect
the uncomfortable transition from his previous position at the
Abbey of St. Andrews to employment in the arranging of psalm
tunes.[43]

In the year that James acceded to the throne and Mary Scott married Watt of Harden (1567) there was published *The Gude and Godlie Ballatis,* a compendium ostensibly of devotional verses but also containing scurrilous satire and clumsy adaptations of popular songs such as "John Cum Kis Me Now."[44] The authors of this work, the brothers Wedderburn, were attempting to bring religious life more into line with continental models and in particular to establish links with Germany and Lutheran influence. The *Ballatis,* however, were not sanctioned by the Reformers because of the obvious indelicacies they retained, and the collection was superseded by psalmbooks in the Genevan and Calvinist tradition.[45]

Popular song, as seen through the distorting mirror of the *Ballatis,* was to suffer most from the Reformers' bleak view of singing and music-making outside the new religion. The old Corpus Christi pageants had been swept away since 1555, and minstrelsy was looked upon as "low, clandestine, and sinful."[46] By an Act of Parliament (1579) every gentleman and yeoman was bound to possess a psalmbook, an ordinance that would presumably apply to Watt of Harden and his family.[47] In 1560 Edinburgh ordered all "vagabonds, fiddlers, pipers" without masters to depart the city on pain of burning of the cheek, and again in 1579 it held "all minstrels, singers, and tale-tellers" as "idle beggars" unless attached to Lords of Parliament or burghs as their common minstrels.[48] In 1587 the same city issued an edict against "common sangsters," especially those who sang "bawdy and filthy sangs."[49] Women at Aberdeen (1574) were charged with singing "filthy sangs" on Yule Day and Sunday evenings, and at Errol, in 1593, the practice of "caroling" was considered "fornication."[50] Bagpipers, who provided the normal accompaniment for weddings and dances, were particularly singled out for remonstrance, though it is a reflection on the instability of the period that King James could have his pipers play before him when he attended church at Dalkeith.[51] There were very probably pipers at the wedding of Harden and the Flower of Yarrow in 1567.

Out of such turbulent times, then, emerged several contrasting streams of music and poetry. One is expressed in the gentle lyrics of the courtly poets and the songs and lute pieces of the Panmure (seventeenth century) and Rowallan (1612–28) MSS. Another, less sophisticated, style that nevertheless reflected the shifting sensibilities of the period, is embodied in the curiosities of *The Gude and Godlie Ballatis.* Yet another can be traced in the homegrown meters of poets like Sempill of Beltrees (d. 1595), the rustic songs mentioned in *The Complaynt of Scotland* (ca. 1550), and other popular songs of native origin with their dance-like qualities that Sir Richard Maitland (d. 1586) no doubt had in mind when he longed for the old times when "blitheness, dancing, singing, game, and play" were rife in pre-Reformation Scotland.[52]

* * * * * *

While the makers of the older Border songs and ballads are inevitably anonymous, there is a tantalizing account of the possible composer of the old song of "Mary Scott" in John Leyden's *Scenes of Infancy* (1803):

> Tradition relates that, amid the plunder of household furniture hastily carried off by them [the Scotts] in one of their predatory incursions, a child was found enveloped in the heap, who was adopted into the clan, and fostered by Mary Scott, commonly known by the epithet of the *Flower of Yarrow,* who married the celebrated Watt, or Walter, of Harden, about the latter part of the sixteenth century. This child of fortune became afterwards celebrated as a poet, and is said to have composed many of the popular songs of the Border; but tradition has not preserved his name.[53]

Earlier in the same work, Leyden recalls the youth in verse:

> He lived, o'er Yarrow's flower to shed the tear,
> To strew the holly's leaves o'er Harden's bier;
> But none was found, above the minstrel's tomb,
> Emblem of peace, to bid the daisy bloom:
> He, nameless as the race from which he sprung,
> Saved other names, and left his own unsung.[54]

Is this the composer of the old song? It is quite possible that the young man may have made a song in honor of his patroness. It might even have been expected of him if he showed any talent in that direction. From Leyden's verses one can at least suppose that, if he did exist, this shadowy figure outlived both Harden and his spouse, and was also the creator of numerous songs on local persons and events.[55] Whether he is, on the other hand, the first person of the old song ("When I look east my heart grows sair") can only be guessed. And to what sort of relationship to the words refer?[56]

There is a youth mentioned in a stanza of "The Douglas Tragedy" recorded by Veitch from William Welsh, a Peeblesshire cottar and poet ("taking great care," says Veitch, "to authenticate it"), but this probably refers to a period before Mary's marriage to Watt of Harden:

> At Dryhope lived a lady fair,
> The fairest flower in Yarrow;
> And she refused nine whole men
> For a servan' lad in Gala.[57]

Such connections with the often more savage side of traditional
ballad narratives may be at the root of the episode in Mary Scott's
life described in a nineteenth-century journal as taken "from tradition":

> The single story of her life relates to her secret elopement with her
> lover, one of the Douglasses of Blackhouse, who, with his brothers,
> was in the act of escorting her to their tower, when the party were
> intercepted by the Scotts of Dryhope, who had suspected or been
> informed of the plot. The two families being at feud at the time,
> a deadly combat ensued, in which all the brothers on both sides were
> either killed or wounded.[58]

Whether this is authentic or "creative history" adduced from
classic Border ballads is unverifiable. The "old song" of Mary Scott,
which is essentially lyrical rather than part of a ballad narrative,
lived on with its air, at any rate, in rural areas of the Borders during
the eighteenth century even after it was supplanted in urban taste
by the pastiches of Ramsay and others. The existence of three
stanzas of the original song (see below) in the manuscripts of Lady
John Scott (late eighteenth century) and Peter Buchan (1828) suggests a tradition of rural continuity largely ignored or unnoticed
by town society throughout the century.[59]

*   *   *   *   *   *

The beginning of the eighteenth century in Scotland saw far-
reaching changes as the more repressive edicts of the church were
dropped, such as those against dancing, and the Union with England
proceeded, for better or worse (1707). Despite the prorogation of
the Scottish Parliament, Edinburgh continued to be a lively center
of cultural life: in the bustling "lands" (tenements) of the Old Town
straggling down the spine of the High Street from the Castle the
upper classes and their servants mingled and conversed freely and,
in a period critical for their country's identity, educated persons
began to take an intense interest in native song traditions.

Since 1711 the prominent figure in this development, Allan
Ramsay, had been making wigs and producing broadsheets at the
sign of the Mercury in the High Street.[60] Among the gentry, too,
Scots songs were set to old tunes with occasional accompaniment
of the viola da gamba and virginals. At the stately yet simple gatherings that formed the dancing assemblies in Bell's Close, notable
amateur songwriters such as Lady Grisell Baillie (1665–1746), author
of "Werena my heart licht I wad dee" (published in *Orpheus
Caledonius* and much admired by Burns), could be seen with her

daughter, Lady Murray of Stanhope, whose singing of Lord Yester's "Tweedside" so affected her audience that many fell to sobbing.[61]

Other prominent literary ladies of the time were Lady Wardlaw, author of the ballad pastiche "Hardyknute" (1719), and Mrs. Cockburn, born in 1712 as daughter of the Laird of Fairnalie near Tweed and Yarrow, whose "Flowers of the Forest" was probably written in her youth by the Borders although it did not see print until 1765.[62] At Mrs. Cockburn's flat in Blair Street near the Castle everyone was called by their first name. When dancing was the order of the day, furniture would be piled high in the lobby while the fiddler, perched in a cupboard, would alternate his strathspeys and minuets.[63] The tradition of genteel songmaking was to be continued by Jean Elliot (1727–1805), writer of another set of "The Flowers of the Forest," Lady Anne Barnard (1750–1825), author of "Auld Robin Gray," and Lady Nairne (1766–1845). By the 1740s, this was the Edinburgh society in which Mary Lilias Scott was an active participant.

The merchant and professional classes were no less keen practitioners of music and song, as the proliferation of family manuscripts in the first half-century attests. The Thomson (1702), Agnes Hume (1704), Margaret Sinkler (1710), Patrick Cuming (1723), Gairdyn (1729) and Macfarlan (1738–42) manuscripts contain a wealth of Scots tunes arranged for voice or instruments such as treble recorder, violin, or harpsichord.[64] The first of these manuscripts probably belonged to the same Thomson family of which William, compiler of *Orpheus Caledonius*, made such a success at the court of George I in the 1720s.[65]

Music publishing on a regular basis started up in Edinburgh in 1725. Apart from the *Cantus* of John Forbes (1662, 1666, 1682) there was no printed secular music before this date, but three important works appeared in 1726: Lorenzo Bocchi's twelve sonatas for various instruments and a Scots Cantata with words by Ramsay, Stuart's *Musick* for *The Tea-Table Miscellany*, and Thomas Bruce's *Common Tunes*, a psalm book with some ballads added.[66] Publishing was subsequently taken up with enthusiasm by fine printers such as Robert Bremner, who in the later 1750s was busy reissuing the musical collections of Ramsay, McGibbon, and Craig, together with original music and didactic works.[67]

A salient feature of Edinburgh life at this time was the Musical Society, formally constituted in 1728 although it had been functioning under a variety of names since the 1690s and making Steil's Crosskeys Tavern its regular meeting-place. Taverns, for those living in the cramped dwelling-houses of the time, were a focus for social life: Clerihew's, John Dowie's, or Jenny Ha's (where John Gay is reputed to have drunk during his visit to Edinburgh in 1732), were places for both business and entertainment. Even a foreign musician such as Johann Schetky (1740-1824), one of three resident composers of the Musical Society at the height of its fame (the others being Domenico Corri and the Earl of Kellie), found congenial company in the Boar's Club that met at Hogg's Tavern.[68]

At the time of its constitution (1728), the Musical Society had Scots as its main performers (Craig, McGibbon), but these were later succeeded by foreigners who brought with them the fashionable art music of the day: Barsanti, Lampe, Pasquali, Pinto, the Schetkys, Stabilini, Reinagle, and Puppo ("Signor Puppy, First Catgut Scraper," as he is described in a contemporary cartoon).[69] Among the vocal stars were Corri and his wife, and the famous castrato Tenducci (ca. 1735-1790), acquaintance of Mozart and J. C. Bach, whose expressive singing of both Scots and foreign songs fascinated George Thomson:

> I can never forget the pathos and touching effect of his "Gilderoy," "Lochaber no more," "The Braes of Ballenden," "I'll never leave thee," "Roslin Castle." These, with the "Verdi prati" of Handel, "Fair Aurora" from Arne's *Artaxerxes,* and Gluck's "Che faro," were above all praise.[70]

The programs of the Society, which Mary Lilias Scott must have attended, contained native songs as well as music by J. C. Bach, Abel, Stamitz, Vanhall, and later, Haydn and Pleyel. The immense popularity of Scots songs, many of them refashioned by Allan Ramsay, encouraged incomers like Barsanti to make early collections of them (1742). Pasquali wrote a cantata based on "Tweedside" (1755), and by the 1770s J. C. Bach was setting "The Braes o' Ballenden" for voice and chamber ensemble.[71] By 1762, when the new premises of the Society took shape in the elegant St. Cecilia's Hall, the Society was flourishing to the degree that Edinburgh became a European musical center. Glasgow, on the other hand, led a miserable concert existence in the winters of 1743-5, according to "Jupiter" Carlyle:

> There never was but one concert during the two winters I was in Glasgow, and that was given by Walter Scott, Esq. of Harden, who was himself an eminent performer on the violin, and his band of assistants consisted of two dancing-school fiddlers and the town waits.[72]

This Walter Scott, probably a younger brother of Mary Lilias, is doubtless also the one mentioned in the membership list of the Edinburgh Musical Society in 1775.[73] Unlike Glasgow, Edinburgh began to feel itself part of a European artistic community, even though many patrons of the Society volubly expressed their preference for native tunes over the sonatas of Corelli and Handel.[74] Poets were quick to satirize the taste for foreign music, especially Italian.[75]

Church music had become, during the seventeenth century, monodic, orally transmitted, static in repertory, and without definitive texts.[76] Congregational singing in the Presbyterian Church still had no organs or choirs by 1706, and the General Assembly appealed to members to practise singing "scriptural songs in private families."[77] Presbyteries recommended, in 1713, to have such schoolmasters chosen "as are capable of teaching the Common Tunes" since the Sang Schools in which the master had sometimes acted as precentor were moribund as a source of instruction.

The old practice of the precentor's "lining out" the psalms continued, however, till as late as 1830. Bremner remarks that when a precentor was needed, the principal qualifications were "poverty and a loud voice for reading the line."[78] One account relates how John McQuisten, precentor at Greenock, jumped during the service one Sunday from the middle of Psalm 107 into the ballad "Sir Patrick Spens" without noticing the difference.[79] Lady Anne Barnard expressed the educated person's view of psalm-singing in the heterophonic style common in Scottish churches, referring to "the horrid discords with which a Presbyterian congregation assails the ears."[80]

Part-singing began to take over about 1753, and reforms aimed at "improving" the quality of church singing were set in motion. Bremner's *Rudiments of Music* (1756) and *A plan for teaching a croud* (1762) bolstered the reform movement, and by 1800 heterophonic singing was diminishing in the Lowlands though it was to survive, even to the present, in the Highlands.[81] Musicians were imported to meet the new demand for trained choirmasters and organists, and men such as Stephen Clarke from Durham and John Ross of Newcastle played an influential role in both church and secular music.[82] Any links with folk music in congregational singing were coming to an end with the introduction of a new uniformity in choral training.

Individual singers in the population still made an impact at this time, such as the Edinburgh accountant, "Singing" Jamie Balfour. A man of strong Jacobite leanings, he is said to have sung "The Wee Wee German Lairdie," "Awa, Whigs, Awa," and "The Sow's Tail to Geordie" with a good deal of zest.[83] A little later, ballad singers like Anna Brown (1747–1810), daughter of the Professor of Humanity at King's College, Aberdeen and wife of the minister of Falkland in Fife, attracted the attention of antiquarians. Related on her mother's side to the musical Forbeses of Disblair, she learned her ballads in the 1750s when the old oral means of transmission had not yet been powerfully affected by the rise of chap literature.[84]

Both Motherwell and Kinloch pinpoint specific singers in their work
as ballad scholars: in 1826, Motherwell remarked that a copy of
"Gil Morrice" was from "the recitation of Margaret Paterson alias
Widow Michael a very old woman residing at Dovecote ha' Barhead.
She is a native of Banffshire and learned the ballad there in her
infancy . . . It is 70 years since she committed it to memory" (i.e.,
ca. 1756).[85] Mrs. Harris, wife of the minister at Blairgowrie in
Perthshire, learned her ballads from an old nurse, Jannie Scott,
whose store of ballad lore was "inexhaustible," and Mary Barr, one
of Kinloch's informants, retained ballads acquired orally more than
fifty years before.[86] Though some of these singers were exposed to
the street hawker of chap texts, they distinguished between the older
oral songs and later written versions.[87]

In the lower levels of society there was interest in songs and their
makers. Burns, about 1771, heard sung in the streets "There's nae
luck aboot the house," which was popularly ascribed to Jean Adams,
who had died in the Glasgow poorhouse six years earlier.[88] Burns
also took down "O'er the moor amang the heather" from the singing
of Jean Glover, its supposed author, although the title of the air
appears in Bremner's *Reels* (1760), published when Jean Glover was
only two years old. But she may have re-created the song to the taste
of her wandering band of beggars and mountebanks and its audience at fairs and races.[89] Yet another popular song to which Burns
added verses is "Ca' the Yowes," the reputed composer of which was
Isabel (Tibby) Pagan, keeper of a shebeen at Muirkirk in Ayrshire
where she dispensed smuggled whisky to her customers.[90] The
currents of popular and literary songmaking that merged so often
in eighteenth-century Scotland, reaching their high point with
Burns, continued to flow in such authors as Mrs. Grant of Carron
("Roy's Wife o' Aldivalloch"), George Halket ("Logie o' Buchan"),
Rev. John Skinner ("Tullochgorum"), and others: Allan Cunning-
ham, William Nicholson, Hector Macneill, Joanna Baillie, and
Robert Tannahill.[91]

*   *   *   *   *   *

Ramsay fitted his octave verses of "Mary Scott" ("Happy's the
Love That Meets Return") to the air with its second strain as it
appeared in the 1690 edition of *Apollo's Banquet.* But another
pastiche of the old song text that keeps to the quatrains of the
original (though published nearly a half-century later), is "The
Flower of Yarrow," included in Herd's collection of 1769. Herd
probably knew the old song from oral sources but he also printed
a pastoralized *refacimento,* in the final stanza of which the old

burden rubs shoulders with sentiment on contemporary musical taste:

> For ever cease Italian noise;
> Let every string and every voice,
> Sing MARY SCOT without a marrow,
> MARY SCOT the flower of Yarrow.[92]

Herd's cobbling of "The Flower of Yarrow" emerged in later collections though it was never to rival Ramsay's "Mary Scott," which cornered the field. In one such publication it was printed, typically, with Ramsay's poem, Robert Crawford's "Tweedside," and another "Braes o' Yarrow," this time by the folk poet Robert Tannahill (1774-1810).[93] Before the century was out others like John Logan, minister at Leith and of near-Border ancestry, were to add their praise of Yarrow to a lengthening list.[94]

Mary Lilias Scott had, in addition to Ramsay, another contemporary admirer in Robert Crawford (1695-1732), second son of Patrick Crawford of Drumsoy in Renfrewshire and author of the popular ditties "Tweedside" and "The Bush Aboun Traquair." In his much-favored "Tweedside" there is a reference to a lady named Mary, and it is supposed that Mary Lilias Scott is meant.[95] Crawford's verses make for instructive comparison with the older text, sung to the same tune, by Lord Yester (1645-1713), second Marquis of Tweeddale ("When Maggie and I were acquaint"). Despite its less polished surface, the earlier poem has a directness, energy and warmth lacking in Crawford's Augustan lines ("What beauties does Flora disclose"), and these qualities doubtless contributed to the emotional effect of Lady Wardlaw's singing of them.[96] The melody to which both sets of words were sung is traditional: a variant of it is in Leyden's Lyra-Viol MS entitled "Twide Syde" and another, according to Hecht, appears in the Blaikie Lyra-Viol MS as "Doune Tweedside" (also dated ca. 1692).[97] A further version of the tune was adapted by the Florentine composer F. M. Veracini (1690-1768) in his *Sonate Accademiche* of 1774, dedicated to the King of Poland.[98]

A popular versifier of the period, closely associated with the Yarrow region from his best-known composition "The Braes o' Yarrow," was William Hamilton of Bangour (1704-54), the friend of Ramsay. Written in 1724, his poem forges a link with the atmosphere of the older Yarrow ballads in its opening lines; but the feeling of the poem as a whole is self-conscious ("overwrought," in Bronson's words).[99] The air eventually adapted to this song was itself formerly called "The Braes o' Yarrow," and Farquhar Graham believes its ancestor is "The ladys goune," a tune in the Leyden MS.[100] One commentator claims that the song (presumably a select few of Bangour's thirty stanzas to the traditional tune) was often performed at Edinburgh's Crosskeys Inn.[101] Through manuscript copies the words found their way into the houses of the gentry, winning a fashionable popularity.

John Struthers published not only Ramsay's "Mary Scott" but also Bangour's somewhat precious "The Flower of Yarrow" in his *Harp of Caledonia* (1819). Echoes of the old song and the legendary Mary continue to reverberate in its vapid lines:

> Go Yarrow flower, thou shalt be blest,
> To die on beauteous Mary's breast;
> Go Yarrow flower so sweetly smelling,
> Is there on earth so soft a dwelling?[102]

With the change in literary taste as the French Revolution approached Ramsay's, Herd's, Crawford's and Bangour's pastiches were gradually abandoned for the more rhapsodic style of Romanticism. Burns, of course, had fulfilled a trend in vernacular poetry that was not capable of further development on a high level. James Hogg, however, more than Scott or Byron was the "rustic" poetgenius in touch with Nature that taste now sought out, and indeed Hogg impinges upon the celebration of Yarrow and Mary Scott by having created his own "Mary Scott" in "The Queen's Wake" (1813) and other poems. While untutored, Hogg was familiar with the ballad lore of the Border hills, and his mother was a lover of ballads. He himself helped Scott to collect ballad texts, sometimes "rearranging" them as with his Jacobite songs, and in his apostrophizing of nature there are faint echoes of ballad language:

> When they came to St. Mary's Lake,
>   The day-sky glimmered on the dew;
> They hid their horses in the brake,
>   And lurked in heath and bracken cleugh.[103]

The philosopher and essayist John Wilson ("Christopher North," 1785–1854) contributed verses on Yarrow in "Mary Gray's Song," but it was another academic, John Campbell Shairp (1819–85), latterly Principal of United College at the University of St. Andrews from 1868, who rivals Hogg in his intimate knowledge of Teviot, Ettrick, Yarrow, and the Tweed in his poems.[104] It is quite possible that Shairp, born in Linlithgowshire, was drawn to the Borders and especially Yarrow because of his lineage. He was, like Sir Walter Scott, descended from Mary Scott since his great-grandmother, Anne Scott of Harden, was the eldest daughter of John Scott, whose great-grandfather, Sir Gideon Scott of High Chester, was grandson of the Flower of Yarrow. Mary Scott was from Dryhope in Yarrow, and her romantic wooing is referred to in Shairp's poem, "Three Friends in Yarrow."[105] The poems of Shairp are, however, suffused with the spirit and influence of Wordsworth, and mark a period of decline in Scottish poetry before its renaissance in the twentieth century.

Songs and tunes

1. *a.* Long Cold Nights

The traditional singer Jeannie Robertson (1908–75) included a song in her repertoire which she called "Ainst Upon a Time," and this short lyric is linked, through its tune, to the "Mary Scott" complex and the first printed versions of the air: "Long Cold Nights When Winter Froz'em," which was printed in *Comes Amoris* of 1687 and in *Apollo's Banquet* of the same year under the title "Long Cold Nights." The tune may thus be regarded as having kept its identity over the course of two-and-a-half centuries.

The *Comes Amoris* subtitle dubs it "A New Scotch Song" (which may or may not attest to its factual origin), and the words are reprinted in *Compleat Academy of Complements* (1705). A broadside expanding the text to seven stanzas is entitled "The Scotch Lasses Choice," the opening line now ending with the word "frozen." The "pleasant new Scotch tune" printed on the sheet is a badly-garbled version of a quite different tune. A reference in Pepys indicates that the tune "In Cold Nights When Winter's Frozen" was sung to words beginning "All You Ladies That Are Barren."[106] This suggests that the air was used for several texts. The Thomson MS (1702) includes the tune under the name "When Ye Cold Winter Nights were frozen," and the same air further on again as "The Banks of Yaro."[107] This tends to corroborate evidence of its popularity under a variety of names at the turn of the eighteenth century. Of equal significance in the "Yaro" of the latter title is the Border association with "Mary Scott," under which name the tune saw its greatest diffusion during the later seventeenth, entire eighteenth, and early nineteenth centuries.

b. Mary Scott (i)

The air entitled "Mary Scott" appeared in a later edition of *Apollo's Banquet* (1690), replacing its former name of "Long Cold Nights." Playford was probably persuaded to change the title on the basis of some unnamed authority. One may tentatively assume from the evidence that the tune, at least, of "Mary Scott" was known and popular in both England and Scotland in the final decade of the seventeenth century. The words of the old song, however, vanished from favor by 1725. Whitelaw believed them lost, but *Notes & Queries* for 1854 yields a quatrain of the "old song":

> Mary's black, and Mary's white,
> Mary is the king's delight,
> The king's delight, the prince's marrow,
> Mary Scott, the flower of Yarrow![108]

Two textual versions of three stanzas each are included in Lady John Scott's MS (late eighteenth century) and Peter Buchan's MS (1828), the latter being printed later by Charles Mackay in *The Illustrated Book of Scottish Song*:

> O Mary's red, and Mary's white,
>   And Mary she's the king's delight;
>   The king's delight, and the prince's marrow,
>   Mary Scott, the flower of Yarrow.
>
> When I look east, my heart grows sair,
>   But when I look west it's mair and mair;
>   And when I look to the banks of Yarrow,
>   There I mind my winsome marrow.
>
> Now she's gone to Edinburgh town,
>   To buy braw ribbons to tye her gown;
>   She's bought them broad, and laid them narrow,
>   Mary Scott is the flower of Yarrow.[109]

The Lady John Scott MS is, apart from "black" instead of "red" in the first line and a few other minor differences, almost identical; more appositely still, it displays the tune:

MARY SCOTT — THE FLOWER OF YARROW

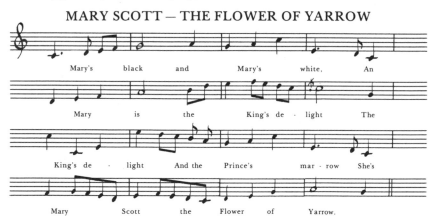

If these two textual variants do indeed embody the words of the "old song of Mary Scott," what is their significance? Was the Flower of Yarrow an early favorite of the reigning monarch, James VI? James acceded to the throne as a one-year-old child a mere three months after the marriage of Mary Scott and Watt of Harden. Does the mention of a visit to Edinburgh and the buying of a gown imply a meeting with the young king some years later, when he was an adolescent and Mary Scott in her thirties? It would not be surprising, in the light of her fame as a beauty, if such a meeting, however innocent, took place, although James Stuart was not particularly noted for his interest in the opposite sex. The birth, in 1594, of Prince Henry might, on the other hand, be a reason for mentioning the king and the prince in the verses. Yet another question arises: who is speaking in the second stanza of the song text?

c. Mary Scott (ii)

The next appearance of the melody first called "Mary Scott" in *Apollo's Banquet* of 1690 occurs under that title in the Agnes Hume MS of 1704, but without a text.[110] A tune book probably belonging to the fiddler George Bowie carries the air (ca. 1705).[111] Untitled again, it surfaces in the Cuming MS (1723), its last appearance before publication in *Orpheus Caledonius* in 1725 and a year or so later in Stuart's *Musick* for *The Tea-Table Miscellany*.[112] With the fuller caption, "Mary Scott's the Flower of Yearow," it was produced in a keyboard arrangement "for the harpsichord or spinett" by Adam Craig,[113] while a similar title graces the melodic variant in the Gairdyn MS of 1729.[114] John Watts included the song, to Ramsay's words (see below, *d*) in his *Musical Miscellany* (1729), and other versions are in Oswald's and McGibbon's collections, the Macfarlan MS (1738–42), Oswald's *Caledonian Pocket Companion* (book 1, 1743, not to be confused with the quite different "The Scott of Yarrow" in book 7), Thumoth's collection (ca. 1745), *Calliope* (1746), Bremner's *Thirty Scots Songs* (1757), Gillespie's (1768), Morison's (1790), and Napier's (1792, where Barthélemon is proclaimed as "composer") collections and others such as *The Caledonian Muse* (1795), Dale's collection of the same year, and Urbani's songs (1799)[115] [fig. 3]. A few additional settings, with the air arranged for flute, exist from the later part of the century. Lady John Scott includes it with the verses of the "Mary Scott" text in her MS.

The tune was firmly wedded to Ramsay's words until the nineteenth century, when the words began to drop from popular esteem. Joshua Campbell prints the air (ca. 1800) as does *The Caledonian Museum* (under the "O Dear Mother" title; see below, 2. *a*) some ten years later.[116]

d. Mary Scott (iii) [Happy's the Love That Meets Return]

Allan Ramsay's recasting of the old song text was printed in his *Poems* (1721). Its pastoral scenario transformed the verses to meet the prevailing taste, though it is probable that Ramsay knew the older text quite well. Chambers supposed that the original was "unfit for ears polite," an assumption guided more by prejudice than by scholarly scepticism.[117] Ramsay may have been consciously echoing the playhouse song beginning "How Happy's the Lover

Fig. 3. "Mary Scot the flower of Yarrow." *Page 64 from* Calliope, *Vol. 1 (1746). Courtesy, The Huntington Library.*

Who After Long Years," with music by Bernard Berenclow, which was included in *Comes Amoris,* vol. 3 (1689), and in *The Banquet of Musick,* book 4 (1690).[118] A half-stanza parody of this song with the opening, "How Happy's That Husband Who After a Few Years," appeared in Durfey's *Pills* (1719–20). Possibly set by Henry Purcell for two-part chorus, it is contained in a British Museum MS of the period.[119]

Ramsay's pastoral verses progressively usurped whatever of the old "Mary Scott" text lingered in educated, urban tradition and continued to be highly popular throughout the eighteenth century. Under both the "Mary Scott" and "Happy's the Love" titles the song was wedded to the old air with its added second strain, and the marriage was so well established by the time of Herd's collection (1769) that Herd's version was no rival. Yet another imitation, with four stanzas to the tune of "Gilderoy," was created by Macmillan in Struthers's *Harp of Caledonia.*[120]

The Ramsay text appeared in tune-less collections such as *The Charmer* (1749) and *The Lark* (1765), occasionally with a subtitle referring to "Mary Scott," as in *The Caledonian Museum* (ca. 1770). The song and the air turn up in John Aitken's *Scots Musical Museum,* published at Philadelphia in 1797.[121] After 1800 the words, though not the tune, diminished in popular favor, and are included in a mere handful of publications such as Struthers's *Harp* and Smith's *Scotish Minstrel* before a last printing in Gow's *Vocal Melodies* (ca. 1835).

2. *a.* O Dear Mother What Shall I Do?

A parallel development of the tune to different words forms a distinctive tributary to the "Mary Scott" complex. In the Sinkler MS of 1710 the air "O Minie" is structurally so close to the "Mary Scott" tune that they must be considered transformations of each other. Watts prints the melody in his *Miscellany,* where "Mary Scott" had previously appeared, but here the air is set to the words of the song "Love Inviting Reason."[122]

The Macfarlan MS, which also houses "Mary Scott," includes the air as "O Dear Mother What Shall I Do?" and a like title graces its appearance in Oswald's *Curious Collection* of the same date (1740).[123] The MS actually has the tune twice, the second time simply as "O Dear Mother" (vol. III). McGibbon's 1746 collection, Oswald in his *Caledonian Pocket Companion* (where it is adorned with variations and a gigue), and Bremner (a guitar arrangement for *Songs in the Gentle Shepherd,* 1759, though Ramsay had written fresh words for the stage pastoral version) all print the melody with this title.[124] Herd and Johnson publish the words, and the words with the air, in their respective collections.[125] The last printings of the tune with this title are in an Advocates' Library MS (late eighteenth century) and *The Caledonian Muse* (ca. 1810).

b. Dinna Think Bonnie Lassie

A later set of words that became popular in the nineteenth century was written by the poetaster Hector Macneill (1746–1818),

author of a number of song texts reflecting his interest in folk versi-
fication.[126] Farquhar Graham, however, quotes lines from the
Poetical Works of Susannah Blamire, a native of Cumberland who
died at Carlisle in 1795, to propose that Macneill in fact had heard
"some part of the song written by her before he began to work it
out on his own plan."[127] It is also possible that Blamire and Macneill
both heard a popular song in existence at the time, and that they
simply adapted the words to their own taste. At any rate, a handful
of collections print the sentimental "Dinna Think" verses with the
"O Dear Mother" tune: *The Scottish Minstrel* (1814), Struthers's
Harp of Caledonia (1819), Smith's *Scotish Minstrel* (1824), and the
Caledonian Repository (1851). Farquhar Graham suggested the
origin of the air as an instrumental piece, citing Stenhouse's opinion
that it is taken from a dance tune, "Clunie's Reel," published by
Angus Cumming of Grantown in his *Collection* of 1780.[128] Curiously,
the earliest copy of the tune in this form is in the Gairdyn MS (ca.
1735) and marked "Highland tune." A later hand (possibly that of
J. Muir Wood) has written "Dinna Think Bonnie Lassie" beneath
the melody.[129] Is this evidence for a Highland origin of the tune?
Gow's later title of "The Braes of Auchtertyre" hints at some Highland participation in the evolution of the "Mary Scott" complex.

3. Carrick's Reel, Clurie's Reel, Carrack's Rant, The Smith's a Gallant Fireman

As "Carrack's Reel" the tune is included in the Gairdyn MS,
which also has it as "Mary Scott's the flower of yearow."[130] Walsh
published it in his *Caledonian Country Dances* (ca. 1740), while
Bremner (ca. 1766) and Gillespie (1768) print the air in their various
collections, the latter entitling it "Garick Reel," perhaps after the
famous actor.[131] In the meantime the tune appears to have become
known as "Clurie's Reel" through Angus Cumming's collection. But
more noteworthy is the caption in *An Evening Amusement* of 1789:
"Clurie's Reel—from Mary Scott."[132] Another fiddle collection,
however, Gow's *Caledonian Repository* (1799), reverses this opinion,
calling "The Braes of Auchtertyre" a strathspey rather than a reel:
"the old Scotch song of Mary Scott is taken from this tune."[133]

In the later eighteenth and early nineteenth centuries the notion
of which tune derived from which was evidently quite confused.
Some of this complication is apparent in Gow's assertion that
"Carrack's Rant" is a descendant of "Mary Scott" and in Stenhouse's
opinion that "The Braes of Auchtertyre" stems from "O Dear
Mother."[134] Variant titles continued to head the melody in its
appearance as a fiddle tune: "Captain Campbell of Carrick's Reel"
(perhaps the original source of the Gairdyn MS attribution, or

possibly grafted on later) in McGlashan's collection of 1795; "Captain Carrick's Reel" in Petrie's *Second Collection* (ca. 1797); "Carrack's Rant" in Urbani and Liston's collection (ca. 1802).[135] It is also printed by Donald Campbell under the Gaelic name of "Caibtein Carraig" in his *Treatise* of 1862.[136] Just how complex the relationship of all these fiddle tunes is may be gathered from Stenhouse's additional declaration that "Carrick's Reel" and "Clurie's Reel" are later variants of "Mary Scott."[137]

The tune's latter-day title of "The Smith's a Gallant Fireman" crops up as early as 1802 in Urbani and Liston's *Selection of Highland Strathspeys*, a few pages after "Carrack's Rant."[138] The connection between "Carrack's Rant" and the later name is made explicit in the *Transactions of the Gaelic Society of Inverness, 1914–19*, where the tune is wed to traditional Gaelic verses.[139] Gavin Greig also contributed a short note bearing on traditional associations of the tune in the Northeast.[140] In yet a further transformation it has been recorded in the Shetland Isles, under the name of "Da Oily Tune," by Patrick Shuldham-Shaw.[141]

4. Fenwick's Lament

A final strand in the texture of the "Mary Scott" complex of songs and tunes can be found in the melody known as "Fenwick's Lament," still played in the Northeast of England. Bruce and Stokoe printed the air with the title, "Sir John Fenwick's the Flower Amang Them."[142] Believing it to be a "gathering tune" from the time of Border chieftains and their summoning of retainers for some foray, the editors associate it with the march of Fenwick's Jacobite friends to support his planned overthrow of William III.

Sir John Fenwick was beheaded on Tower Hill in 1697 after being implicated in the plot to assassinate William. Arrested with others in the summer of 1690, and later in 1696, Fenwick apparently implicated a number of highly placed persons who demanded his death.[143] A fanciful legend recounts how Fenwick's horse, White Sorrel, was confiscated by the Crown; William later fell from the horse and sustained fatal injuries.[144]

Some commentators hold that the tune was composed at the time of Fenwick's execution. Brand's *History of Newcastle* tells how two gentlemen of the county lost their lives, a few years after, for singing it rather thoughtlessly.[145] Citing McGibbon's printing of the air under the title "Mary Scot" (ca. 1740), Bruce and Stokoe suggest that the tune was known earlier in Northumberland.[146] A more illuminating piece of information given by them concerns a John Bell of Gateshead, who wrote to Sir Walter Scott in 1816 asking if he could provide him with evidence on Northumbrian

Jacobite songs, "Fenwick's Lament" among them. Scott replied, saying "I have heard words somewhat similar, alluding probably to some election business —

> They voted twice over, and so they did wrang him,
> They voted twice over, and so did they hang him,
> They voted twice over, and so did they wrang him,
> But Fenwick o' Bywell's the flower among them.

"But you know," Scott adds sagely, "how common it is for new words to be written to any popular tune."[147] The Antiquarian Society of Newcastle offered a reward for a copy of the original song, without success.[148]

The tune appears in the mid-nineteenth century manuscripts of Robert Bewick, son of the famous engraver Thomas Bewick, who played the Northumbrian small pipes. It was seldom cultivated by later bagpipers in Northumbria, although Billy Pigg, the most famous of these in recent times, occasionally performed it. The Folk Revival has brought the air to prominence in the Newcastle area, and it has been recorded under the title of "Fenwick's Lament."[149]

*   *   *   *   *   *

Summary

The "old song" of Mary Scott, words and music, exists in only one redaction, that of the Lady John Scott MS, dated to the late eighteenth century. The verses alone appear in Peter Buchan's MS of 1828. There is no way of knowing whether the words and the melody were composed by the same person or by different hands, nor is it certain that the manuscript version is close to the form of the original song. The song, if indeed it was composed by the young English captive of Harden, may have been made in the period 1594–7, after the birth of Prince Henry (the "prince" of the song text) but before Mary Scott's death and certainly before the departure of King James's court to London in 1603.

The text as it stands, however, reads more like late seventeenth than late sixteenth century, and there may have been some reworking of the words, and the tune also, during the intervening period. It is likely that the song became so well known in the seventeenth century that both words and air were ripe for transformation as tastes began to change at the end of the century, and the "O Dear Mother" tradition may have arisen separately at this time. The Border ambiance doubtless also gave rise to the "Fenwick's Lament" variants at the beginning of the seventeenth century, the Jacobite landowner now being the "flower" of the text. Ramsay and others kept alive the idea of Mary Scott by eulogizing in pastoral lines a contemporary beauty of the same name, though the old song seems to have continued in rural tradition till at least the end of the eighteenth century.

The tune's origin and diffusion are more difficult still to pinpoint: there are hints in the manuscript tradition that although it may have been composed in the Borders it had strong Highland connections (cf. "Highland Tune" of the Gairdyn MS, ca. 1729), most prominently in the medium of a fiddle air; this tradition culminated in the late and still popular "Smith's a Gallant Fireman." The general cast of the tune, however, with its leaping second strain, does not mean that it was filched for the song from an instrumental original. Stylistically it has much in common with the vocal leaps of arrangements in *Orpheus Caledonius* (1725), and the genesis of the tune in this form may belong to the period around 1700. Finally, Jeannie Robertson's lyric song, "Ainst Upon a Time," is a parody of Macneill's "Dinna Think Bonnie Lassie," itself a probable offshoot, in terms of the tune at least, from the early eighteenth-century "O Dear Mother." These hypotheses on the origin and distribution of the song-complex are, in the end, less significant than the way in which the relationship of the songs, tunes, and their makers or re-creators can be explored in their historical context by means of a diachronic model.

NOTES

[1] This idea is outlined by me in two papers, "Prolegomena to a Comparative Study of European Folk Music," *Ethnomusicology*, 21 (1977), 435-51, and "The Turriff Family of Fetterangus: Society, Learning, Creation and Recreation of Traditional Song," *Folk Life*, 16 (1978), 5-26. I must express my thanks to David Murison for reading and commenting on a draft of the present essay; also to Ruzena Wood, Music Section, National Library of Scotland, Charles P. Finlayson, Keeper of Manuscripts, Edinburgh University Library, Michael Anderson, Librarian, Reid Music Library, Edinburgh University, and David Temperley for helpful information.

[2] The terms "diachronic" and "synchronic" have been widely used in anthropology and linguistics since the 1920s. Diachronic studies analyze cultural phenomena across time, synchronic ones at a particular point in time.

[3] The term "model" is employed here much as it is in the social sciences, that is, in the sense of a phenomenon's essential features, abstracted primarily for the purpose of comparison.

[4] See Bertrand Harris Bronson, "Mrs. Brown and the Ballad," *California Folklore Quarterly*, 4 (1945); reprinted in *The Ballad as Song* (Berkeley and Los Angeles: University of California Press, 1969), pp. 64-78.

[5] See Robert Chambers, *The Scottish Songs* (Edinburgh: Ballantyne and Co., 1829), pp. xvi-xvii; Kurt Wittig, *The Scottish Tradition in Literature* (Edinburgh and London: Oliver and Boyd, 1958), pp. 131-50. See also David Buchan, *The*

Ballad and the Folk (London and Boston: Routledge and Kegan Paul, 1972), pp. 40-47.

[6]Bronson, "Mrs. Brown and the Ballad," p. 74.

[7]See Sir James Balfour Paul, Ll.D., *The Scots Peerage*, vol. 7 (Edinburgh: D. Douglas, 1910), pp. 73-74; John Veitch, *The History and Poetry of the Scottish Border*, vol. 2 (Edinburgh: Blackwood, 1893), pp. 206-7. Also Sir Walter Scott, *Minstrelsy of the Scottish Border*, vol. 1 (Kelso: J. Ballantyne, 1802), pp. 92-93; William Stenhouse, *Illustrations of the Lyric Poetry and Music of Scotland* (Edinburgh: Blackwood and Sons, 1853), p. 77. C. G. Cash, however, in his "Notes on Some Yarrow Antiquities," *Proceedings of the Society of Antiquaries of Scotland, 1912-1913*, vol. 47 (1913), pp. 360-63, found initials on a slab in Dryhope Tower ("P.S." and "M.S.") which he believed to be those of Mary Scott's parents Philip and Mary.

[8]See Cash, ibid. In 1592 James VI issued a warrant at Peebles ordering that Dryhope be demolished in punishment for the treason perpetrated by its owner "Walter Scot of Harden." This implies that Mary Scott was an only child, or the last left alive, ownership of Dryhope passing through her to her husband. See T. F. Henderson, *Old-World Scotland: Glimpses of Its Modes & Manners* (London: T. F. Unwin, 1893), p. 104.

[9]Balfour Paul, *The Scots Peerage*, pp. 73-74; also Walter Riddell Carre, *Border Memories* (Edinburgh: J. Thin, 1876), p. 75. For the 1576 date, see Veitch, *History and Poetry*, pp. 206-7, T. F. Henderson's edition of the *Minstrelsy* (1902), vol. 2, pp. 16-17.

[10]Scott, *Minstrelsy*, pp. 92-93.

[11]Balfour Paul, *The Scots Peerage*, pp.73-74; also Scott, *Minstrelsy*, vol. 1, pp. 92-93; Carre, *Border Memories*, pp. 74-75; James Russell, D. D., *Reminiscences of Yarrow*, 2d ed. (Edinburgh: G. Lewis and Son, 1894), p. 258-60.

[12]Russell, *Reminiscences*, ibid.

[13]Balfour Paul, *The Scots Peerage*, pp. 73-74; Carre, *Border Memories*, p. 76.

[14]Carre, *Border Memories*, pp. 74-75; T. F. Henderson ed., *Minstrelsy*, vol. 1, pp. 154-55.

[15]Balfour Paul, *The Scots Peerage*, p. 74.

[16]Wittig, *The Scottish Tradition*, p. 136.

[17]Veitch, *History and Poetry*, vol. 2, pp. 206-7.

[18]Stenhouse, *Illustrations*, p. 77.

[19]See John Gibson Lockhart, *Life of Sir Walter Scott, Bart.* (Edinburgh: Robert Cadell, 1862), vol. 1, p. 8.

[20]Robert Chambers, *Songs of Scotland Prior to Burns* (Edinburgh: W. R. Chambers, 1862), p. 342.

[21]Ibid., also Stenhouse, *Illustrations*, p. 78.

[22]Stenhouse, ibid.

[23]Harold William Thompson ed., *The Anecdotes and Egotisms of Henry Mackenzie: 1745-1831* (London: Oxford University Press, 1927), pp. 79-80; also Stenhouse, *Illustrations*, p. 37.

[24]Henry Grey Graham, *Scottish Men of Letters in the Eighteenth Century* (London: A. & C. Black, 1908), p. 12.

[25]See Wittig, *The Scottish Tradition*, p. 164; David Johnson, *Music and Society in Lowland Scotland in the Eighteenth Century* (London: Oxford University Press, 1972), pp. 130-41.

[26]Alistair Smart, *The Life and Art of Allan Ramsay* (London: Routledge and Kegan Paul, 1952), p. 2.

[27]Ibid., p. 73.

[28]See Thomas Pennant, *Journal of a Tour in Scotland* (1776); also Chambers, *Songs of Scotland*, p. 342; Stenhouse, *Illustrations*, p. 37.

[29]David Laing, *Additional Illustrations to the Scots Musical Museum* (Edinburgh: Blackwood, 1853), p. 115.

[30]Ramsay is unlikely to have painted Mary Scott twice because of the demand on his time, and the bust-length picture may have become confused, in Pennant's mind, with the full-length one by Davison.

[31]Smart, *Life and Art*, p. 57.

[32]I am grateful to His Grace the Duke of Hamilton, R. E. Hutchison, Keeper of the Scottish National Portrait Gallery, and Sara Stevenson, Print Room of the Gallery, for information concerning these portraits.

[33]Henry George Farmer, *A History of Music in Scotland* (London: Hinrichsen, 1947), p. 123.

[34]Ibid., p. 124. William Thompson of *Orpheus Caledonius* and James Oswald both attributed the composition of Scots tunes to Rizzio.

[35]Ibid., p. 127.

[36]Ibid., p. 127.

[37]Ibid., p. 140.

[38]Ibid., p. 86.

[39]See John MacQueen ed., *Ballatis of Luve* (Edinburgh: Edinburgh University Press, 1970), pp. xxx-xxxiii; cf. also Helena Mennie Shire, *Song, Dance and Poetry of the Court of Scotland under James VI* (Cambridge: Cambridge University Press, 1969), pp. 37-38.

[40]See William Dauney, *Ancient Scottish Melodies* (Edinburgh: Edinburgh Printing and Publishing Co., 1838), pp. 138-39.

[41]Farmer, *History*, pp. 138, 195.

[42]Ibid., p. 155.

[43]Ibid., pp. 115, 163.

[44]*The Gude and Godlie Ballatis*, ed. A. F. Mitchell (Edinburgh: Scottish Texts Society, 1897); also Shire, *Song, Dance and Poetry*, pp. 25-33.

[45]Farmer, *History*, p. 153.

[46]Cf. Edward J. Cowan, "Calvinism and the Survival of Folk: or 'Deil Stick da Minister'," in Edward J. Cowan ed., *The People's Past: Scottish Folk, Scottish History* (Edinburgh: Polygon, 1980), pp. 32-57; Chambers, *Songs of Scotland*, passim; Farmer, *History*, p. 130.

[47]Farmer, *History*, p. 131.

[48]Ibid., p. 133.

[49]Ibid., p. 133.

[50]Ibid., p. 131.

[51]Ibid., p. 133.

[52]Ibid., p. 141.

[53]John Leyden, *Scenes of Infancy: Descriptive of Teviotdale* (Edinburgh: J. Ballantyne & Co., 1811), pp. 159-60.

[54]Ibid., pp. 21-22.

[55]Leyden notes, however, a similar tradition among the Clan MacGregor. See *Poems and Ballads by Dr. John Leyden* (Kelso: J. and J. H. Rutherford, 1858), p. 134 n.

[56]See discussion below, pp. 78-79.

[57]Veitch, *History and Poetry*, pp. 194-207; also his *Border Essays* (Edinburgh: Blackwood, 1896), p. 55.

[58]*The Scottish Journal of Topography, Antiquities, Traditions etc.*, vol. 1 (Sept. 1847-Feb. 1848), p. 142. See also James Reed, *The Border Ballads* (London: The Athlone Press, 1973), pp. 136-51.

[59]National Library of Scotland MS 836. "Scotch songs (mostly old) with accompanyments, tunes, and marches, collected by Lady John Scott for the 5th Duke of Buccleugh, including some of her own composition." See f. 25. Cf. also British

Museum Add. 29.408, "Ancient Minstrelsy of the North of Scotland, in its original purity, and Hitherto Unpublished, by Peter Buchan," f. 160.

[60]Grey Graham, *Scottish Men of Letters*, pp. 12–13; also his *Social Life of Scotland in the Eighteenth Century* (London: A. & C. Black, 1906), p. 111.

[61]Grey Graham, *Scottish Men of Letters*, pp. 322–23, 327.

[62]Ibid., p. 322; see also Sarah Tytler and J. L. Watson, *The Songstresses of Scotland* (London: Strahan ; Co., 1871), and Jessie P. Findlay, *The Spindle-Side of Scottish Song* (London: J. M. Dent & Co., 1902).

[63]Grey Graham, *Social Life*, p. 97.

[64]The Agnes Hume, Margaret Sinkler, and Cuming MSS are described by Harry M. Willsher in *Grove's Dictionary of Music & Musicians*, 5th edition (London: Macmillan, 1954), vol. 7, pp. 574–77. The Gairdyn MS (NLS MS Glen 37) was owned by Charles Kirkpatrick Sharpe, though it is not known how he acquired it. He gave it to J. Muir Wood in 1848 and it was gifted, with the Glen Collection, to the National Library in 1927. The Macfarlan MS (NLS MS 2084) is entitled "A Collection of Scotch Airs with the latest variations written for the use of Walter Macfarlan of that Ilk by David Young, 1740."

[65]The Thomson MS is NLS MS 2833–34; MS 2834 has annotations by Davidson Cook.

[66]Farmer, *History*, pp. 292–93.

[67]Ibid.

[68]Robert Chambers, *Traditions of Edinburgh* (Edinburgh: Chambers, 1824; repr. 1947), p. 151; David Fraser Harris, *St. Cecilia's Hall in the Niddry Wynd* (Edinburgh and London: Oliphant, Anderson, and Ferrier, 1911), p. 74.

[69]Fraser Harris, *St. Cecilia's Hall*, p. 61.

[70]Ibid., pp. 111–12.

[71]Johnson, *Music and Society*, p. 142.

[72]Farmer, *History*, p. 314.

[73]Fraser Harris, *St. Cecilia's Hall*, p. 297.

[74]Johnson, *Music and Society*, p. 41.

[75]Among others Ramsay, Fergusson, and Skinner; cf. Johnson, ibid., pp. 192–94.

[76]Ibid., p. 173.

[77]Farmer, *History*, p. 261.

[78]Johnson, *Music and Society*, p. 173.

[79]Ibid.

[80]Quoted in Millar Patrick, *Four Centuries of Scottish Psalmody* (London: Oxford University Press, 1949), p. 143.

[81]See Francis Collinson, *The Traditional and National Music of Scotland* (London: Routledge & Kegan Paul, 1966), pp. 261–64.

[82]Johnson, *Music and Society*, pp. 180–81.

[83]Chambers, *Traditions of Edinburgh*, pp. 141–43.

[84]See Bronson, "Mrs. Brown and the Ballad"; Buchan, *The Ballad and the Folk*, passim.

[85]Buchan, *The Ballad and the Folk*, p. 66.

[86]Ibid., p. 67.

[87]Ibid.

[88]Grey Graham, *Scottish Men of Letters*, p. 352.

[89]Ibid., p. 353.

[90]Ibid., p. 354.

[91]See further Charles Rogers, *The Modern Scottish Minstrel*, 6 vols. (Edinburgh: A. & C. Black, 1855–57).

[92]David Herd, *Ancient and Modern Scottish Songs* (1769, 1776), vol. 2, p. 310.

[93]Printed in *The Goldfinch or New Modern Songster* (Glasgow: J. & M. Robertson, 1780), p. 196.

[94]Logan's poem appeared in Herd; see Appendix, pp. 22–23.

[95]Chambers, *Songs of Scotland,* pp. 341–42; Laing, *Additional Illustrations,* pp. 384–85. Stenhouse and others believed that the Mary referred to was a Mary Stewart of the Castlemilk family, *Illustrations,* p. 36.

[96]See above, n. 60.

[97]See Farquhar Graham, *The Popular Songs and Melodies of Scotland,* rev. J. Muir Wood (London and Glasgow: Bayley, 1908), p. 93.

[98]Ibid.

[99]Bertrand Harris Bronson, *The Singing Tradition of Child's Popular Ballads* (Princeton, N.J.: Princeton University Press, 1976), p. 380.

[100]Farquhar Graham, *The Popular Songs,* p. 43.

[101]Grey Graham, *Scottish Men of Letters,* p. 21.

[102]John Struthers, *The Harp of Caledonia* (Glasgow: Somerville, Fullerton, Blackie, 1819), pp. 318–19.

[103]John Veitch, *The Feeling for Nature in Scottish Poetry* (Edinburgh and London: W. Blackwood and Sons, 1887), p. 234. See also W. S. Crockett, *The Scott Country,* 2d ed. (London: A. & C. Black, 1902), pp. 392–94, 426.

[104]Veitch, *The Feeling for Nature,* pp. 287, 290.

[105]R. Borland, *Yarrow: Its Poets and Poetry,* 2d ed. (Galashiels: Walker, 1908), p. 192.

[106]Claude Simpson, *The British Broadside Ballad and Its Music* (New Brunswick, N.J.: Rutgers University Press, 1966), p. 466.

[107]Thomson MS, ff. 17, 33.

[108]*Notes & Queries* (March 18, 1854), p. 341.

[109]Charles Mackay ed., *The Illustrated Book of Scottish Songs* (London: Illustrated London Library, 1851); see also n. 58 above.

[110]NLS Advocates' Library MS 5.2.17, ff. 1 2.

[111]This manuscript is owned by Francis Collinson; see his *Traditional and National Music,* p. 205.

[112]Alexander Stuart, *Musick for Allan Ramsay's Collection of Scots Songs* (Edinburgh, 1726), part 3, pp. 72–73.

[113]Adam Craig, *A Collection of the Choicest Scots Tunes* (Edinburgh, 1730).

[114]NLS MS Glen 37, 143, f. 3.

[115]John Watts, *The Musical Miscellany* (1729), vol. 2, pp. 140–41; James Oswald, *A Curious Collection of Scots Tunes* (ca. 1740), p. 6; W. McGibbon, *A Collection of Scots Tunes* (1746), p. 9; Macfarlan MS, ff. 214–15; James Oswald, *The Caledonian Pocket Companion,* vol. 1 (ca. 1745), p. 4; Burk Thumoth, *Twelve Scotch, and Twelve Irish Airs with Variations* (ca. 1745), pp. 8–9; *Calliope* (1746), vol. 1, p. 64; Robert Bremner, *Thirty Scots Songs for a Voice and Harpsichord* (1757), pp. 18–19; James Gillespie, *A Collection of the Best and Most Favourite Tunes for the Violin* (1768), p. 85; R. Morison, *A Select Collection of Favourite Scottish Ballads* (1790), pp. 88–89; W. Napier, *A Selection of the Most Favourite Scots Songs* (1792), p. 48; *The Caledonian Muse* (ca. 1795), p. 48; J. Dale, *Collection of 60 Favourite Scotch Songs* (ca. 1795), p. 46; Peter Urbani, *A Selection of Scots Songs* (1799), pp. 1–2.

[116]Joshua Campbell, *A Collection of Favourite Tunes* (ca. 1800), pp. 40–41; *The Caledonian Museum* (ca. 1810), pp. 44.

[117]Chambers, *Songs of Scotland,* p. 341.

[118]Simpson, *The British Broadside Ballad,* p. 317.

[117]BM Add. 33234 [37].

[120]Struthers, *Harp,* vol. 3, pp. 42–43.

[121]I am grateful to Paul Wells for this information.

[122]Watts, *Musical Miscellany,* vol. 5 (1731), pp. 156–59.

[123]Macfarlan MS, vol. 2, f. 262; Oswald, *Curious Collection,* p. 28 of "Musick."

[124]McGibbon, *A Collection of Scots Tunes,* p. 34; Oswald, *Companion,* vol. 6 (ca. 1751), p. 10; Robert Bremner, *The Songs in the Gentle Shepherd* (1759), p. 4.

[125]See Herd, *Scottish Songs,* vol. 3 (1776), pp. 192–93, and James Johnson, *The Scots Musical Museum,* vol. 3 (1790), p. 245; both are to the words of Ramsay's "O dear Peggy, love's beguiling," written for *The Gentle Shepherd.*

[126]See Farquhar Graham, *The Songs of Scotland* (Edinburgh: Bayley, 1861), vol. 3, Appendix, p. 165; also *The Popular Songs,* p. 271.

[127]Farquhar Graham, *The Songs of Scotland,* ibid.

[128]See *The Scottish Minstrel, A Valuable Selection of Popular Songs* (1814), pp. 86–89; Struthers, *Harp,* vol. 1, pp. 29–30; R. A. Smith, *The Scotish Minstrel,* vol. 5 (1824), p. 34; *Caledonian Repository* (1851), 2d series, part 1, p. 4; Angus Cumming, *A Collection of Strathspey, or Old Highland Reels* (Edinburgh, 1780). p. 19.

[129]Gairdyn MS, f. 91 (48).

[130]Ibid., f. 3.

[131]J. Walsh, *Caledonian Country Dances* (ca. 1740), vol. 3, pp. 74–75; Robert Bremner, *A Collection of Scots Reels or Country Dances* (ca. 1765), pp. 94–95; Gillespie, *A Collection . . .* (1768), p. 103.

[132]*An Evening Amusement,* p. 167.

[133]Niel Gow, *Complete Repository of Original Scots Slow Strathspeys and Dances* (1799), p. 20.

[134]Ibid., p. 3; Stenhouse, *Illustrations,* p. 222.

[135]Alexander McGlashan, *A Collection of Strathspey Reels* (1795), p. 9; Robert Petrie, *A Second Collection of Strathspey Reels etc.* (ca. 1797), p. 18; *Urbani and Liston's Selection of Highland Strathspey Reels, Dances, etc.* (ca. 1802), p. 7.

[136]Donald Campbell, *A Treatise on the Language, Poetry, and Music of the Highland Clans* (Edinburgh: D. R. Collie & Son, 1862), p. 8.

[137]Stenhouse, *Illustrations,* p. 78.

[138]*Urbani and Liston's Selection,* p. 18.

[139]*Transactions of the Gaelic Society of Inverness, Vol. 29 (1914–19),* (1922), p. 89.

[140]Gavin Greig, *Folk-Song of the North-East* (Hatboro, Penn.: Folklore Associates, 1963), 73.

[141]From a copy of Patrick Shuldham-Shaw's MS tunes collected in Shetland and given by him to the present author. "This tune is said to be one of Freddie Stickle's compositions and is meant to be representative of the boiling of Fish Livers for oil." Dated 12/ii/47. See further Patrick Shuldham-Shaw, "A Shetland Fiddler and His Repertoire," *Journal of the English Folk Dance and Song Society,* vol. 9, no. 3 (1962), pp. 129–47.

[142]Rev. J. Bruce and J. Stokoe, *Northumbrian Minstrelsy* (Newcastle-upon-Tyne: Society of Antiquaries, 1882; repr. Hatboro, Penn.: Folklore Associates, 1965), p. 158.

[143]See George Hilton Jones, *The Main Stream of Jacobitism* (Cambridge, Mass.: Harvard University Press, 1954), p. 48.

[144]Alistair Anderson, personal communication, 1976.

[145]Bruce and Stokoe, *Minstrelsy,* p. 158.

[146]Ibid.

[147]Ibid., p. 159.

[148]Alistair Anderson, personal communication, 1976.

[149]*Cut and Dry Dolly* (Topic 12TS 278).

Appendix

"Mary Scott": Chronological List of Sources

1687	"Long Cold Nights," J. Playford, *Apollo's Banquet*, 5th ed., vol. 3, no. 3.
1687	"Long Cold Nights When Winter Froz'em," *Comes Amoris*, vol. 1, p. 37.
1690	"Mary Scot," J. Playford, *Apollo's Banquet*, 6th ed.
1702	"When ye Cold winter nights were frozen," *James Thomson MS* (National Library of Scotland MS 2833), f. 17.
1702	"The Banks of Yaro," *James Thomson MS*, f. 33.
1704	"Mary Scott," *Agnes Hume MS* (National Library of Scotland MS 5.2.17), ff. 1–2.
ca. 1705	"Mary Scott of Yarrow," *George Bowie MS* (F. Collinson coll.).
1710	"O Minie," *Margaret Sinkler MS* (National Library of Scotland MS 3296), f. 19.
1723	Untitled, *Patrick Cuming MS* (National Library of Scotland MS 1667), ff. 10–11.
1725	"Mary Scot," W. Thomson, *Orpheus Caledonius*, pp. 38–39.
ca. 1726	"Mary Scot," A Stuart, *Musick for Allan Ramsay's Collection of Scots Songs*, pp. 72–73.
1729	"Mary Scot," J. Watts, *The Musical Miscellany*, vol. 2, pp. 140–41.
ca. 1729	"Mary Scot's the flower of yearow," *Gairdyn MS* (National Library of Scotland MS Glen 143), f. 3.
ca. 1729	"Highland tune" ["Dinna think bonnie lassie"], *Gairdyn MS*, f. 91.
ca. 1729	"Caricks Reel," *Gairdyn MS*, ff. 100–101.
1730	"Mary Scott's the Flower of Yearow," A. Craig, *A Collection of the Choicest Scots Tunes*, p. 33.
1731	"O dear Mother!", J. Watts, *The Musical Miscellany*, vol. 5, pp. 156–59.
1740	"O dear Mother what shall I do," *Walter Macfarlan MS* (National Library of Scotland MS 2084), vol. II, f. 262.
ca. 1740	"Mary Scott," *National Library of Scotland Adv. MS 5.2.22*.
ca. 1740	"Carricks Reel," J. Walsh, *Caledonian Country Dances*, pp. 74–75.
ca. 1740	"Mary Scott," J. Oswald, *A Curious Collection of Scots Tunes*, p. 6.
ca. 1740	"O Dear Mother what shall I doe," W. McGibbon, *A 2nd Collection of Scots Tunes*, p. 34.

1742	"Mary Scot," W. McGibbon, *Scots Tunes*, p. 9.
ca. 1743	"O Dear Mother," *Macfarlan MS*, vol. III, f. 100.
ca. 1743	"Mary Scott," *Macfarlan MS*, vol. III, ff. 214–15.
1744	"Mary Scott," J. Oswald, *A Collection of Curious Scots Tunes* (Second Collection), pp. 12–13.
ca. 1745	"Mary Scott," J. Oswald, *The Caledonian Pocket Companion*, vol. 1, p. 4.
ca. 1745	"Mary Scot," B. Thumoth, *Twelve Scotch, and Twelve Irish Airs with Variations*, pp. 8–9.
1746	"Mary Scot the flower of Yarrow," *Calliope*, vol. 1, p. 64.
1749	"Happy's the love," J. Yair, *The Charmer*, p. 33.
ca. 1751	"O dear mother what shall I do," J. Oswald, *Caledonian Pocket Companion*, vol. 7, p. 10.
ca. 1759	"Mary Scott," R. Bremner, *Thirty Scots Songs*, pp. 18–19.
ca. 1759	"O Dear Mother etc.—Jenny sings to Peggy," R. Bremner, *The Songs in the Gentle Shepherd*, p. 4.
1765	"Happy's the love which meets return," W. Gordon, *Lark*, pp. 61–62.
ca. 1765–1790	"Mary Scott," *National Library of Scotland MS 3346*.
ca. 1765	"Carrick Reel," R. Bremner, *A Collection of Scots Reels or Country Dances*, pp. 94–95.
1768	"Mary Scott," J. Gillespie, *A Collection of the Best and Most Favourite Tunes for the Violin*, p. 85.
1768	"Garick Reel," J. Gillespie, *Collection*, p. 103.
ca. 1770	"The Braes of Auchtertyre a Reell," *National Library of Scotland MS 3378*.
ca. 1770	"Happy the love that meets return," *The Caledonian Museum or The Beauties of Scottish Harmony*, p. 89.
1776	"Mary Scott," D. Herd, *Ancient and Modern Scottish Songs, Heroic Ballads, etc.*, vol. 1, pp. 260–62.
1776	"O Dear Mother what shall I do?" Herd, *Scottish Songs*, vol. 3, pp. 192–93.
ca. 1780	"O Dear Mother what shall I do," *Trotter MS* (Edinburgh Public Library Special Collection M 435).
1780	"Cluries Reell," A. Cumming, *A Collection of Strathspey or Old Highland Reels*, p. 19.
1785	"O dear Minny," *Riddell MS* (National Library of Scotland MS 2086).
ca. 1789	"Cluries Reel—from Mary Scott," *An Evening Amusement*, p. 167.
1790	"O dear mother, what shall I do?" J. Johnson, *The Scots Musical Museum*, no. 236.
1790	"Mary Scot," R. Morison, *A Select Collection of Favourite Scotish Ballads*, vol. 4, pp. 88–89.

1792	"Mary Scott," W. Napier, *A Selection of the most favourite Scots Songs*, p. 48.
1795	"Captain Campbell of Carrick's Reel," A. McGlashan, *A Collection of Strathspey Reels*, p. 9.
ca. 1795	"Mary Scot," *The Caledonian Muse*, p. 48.
ca. 1795	"Mary Scot," J. Dale, *Collection of 60 Favourite Scotch Songs*, p. 46.
1795-98	"O Dear Mother," *School of Scottish Studies MS 2.*
ca. 1797	"Capt. Carrick's Reel," R. Petrie, *A Second Collection of Strathspey Reels etc.*, p. 18.
ca. 1799	"Mary Scott," P. Urbani, *A Selection of Scots Songs*, pp. 1-2.
Late 18th century	"Braes of Auchtertyre," *School of Scottish Studies MS 5.*
Late 18th century	"How sweet the Love that meets return," *British Museum Add. 25071.1.*
Late 18th century	"Mary Scott," *National Library of Scotland Adv. MS 5.2.22.*
Late 18th century	"O dear Minnie what shall I doe," *National Library of Scotland Adv. MS 5.2.25.*
Late 18th century	"Mary Scott—The Flower of Yarrow," *Lady John Scott MS*, f. 25.
ca. 1800	"Mary Scott," J. Campbell, *A Collection of Favourite Tunes*, pp. 40-41.
ca. 1802	"The Smiths a Gallant Fire-man," *Urbani & Liston's Selection of Highland Strathspeys, Reels, Dances etc.*, p. 18.
ca. 1802	"Carracks Rant," *Urbani & Liston's Selection*, p. 7.
ca. 1810	"Carracks Rant, a Strathspey," *A Complete Repository of Old and New Scotch Strathspeys, Reels, & Jigs*, p. 10.
ca. 1810	"Mary Scott the Flower of Yarrow," *The Caledonian Museum containing a favorite collection of Ancient and Modern Scots Tunes*, p. 44.
ca. 1810	"O dear mother what shall I do," *The Caledonian Museum* vol. 2, p. 38.
1814	"Dinna think, bonnie lassie," *The Scottish Minstrel: A Valuable Selection of Popular Songs*, pp. 86-87.
1819	"Dinna think, bonnie lassie," J. Struthers, *The Harp of Caledonia*, vol. 1, pp. 29-30.
1839	"Mary Scot," J. Struthers, *Harp*, vol. 1, p. 351.
1821-24	"Mary Scott," R. A. Smith, *The Scotish Minstrel*, vol. 3, p. 1.
1828	"Mary Scott," *Peter Buchan MS* (British Museum Add. 29.408.409).
ca. 1830	"Braes of Auchtertyre," *McLaren MS* (Aberdeen University Library MS 2424).

ca. 1830   "Carrick's Rant," *McLaren MS.*

ca. 1835   "Mary Scot the Flower of Yarrow," *Gow's Vocal Melodies of Scotland* (part 2), p. 1.

1851   "Dinna think bonnie lassie I'm gaun to leave you," *Caledonian Repository* (2d series, part 1), p. 4.

1854   "Mary Scott, the Flower of Yarrow," *Notes & Queries* (March 18), p. 341 n.

1861   "Mary Scot" ("Happy's the Love that Meets return"), G. F. Graham, *Songs of Scotland*, pp. 102-3.

1861   "O Dinna Think, Bonnie Lassie" ("Clunie's Reel"), Graham, *Songs of Scotland,* pp. 6-7.

1862   "Caibtein Carraig," D. Campbell, *A Treatise on the Language, Poetry, and Music of the Highland Clans,* p. 8.

1922   "Carrick's Rant" ("The Smith's a Gallant Fireman"), *Transactions of the Gaelic Society of Inverness XXIX (1914–19),* p. 89.

Part 3:
Folk Music and the Visual Arts

A Folk Music Exhibition

Archie Green

When the words *music* and *art* join in everyday speech, speakers can dig themselves into semantic traps. Common sense signals that these dual terms, by definition, cover discrete expression. We look at art or listen to music, and categorize each structurally, referring a seascape or a chantey back ultimately to the mode of reception— seeing or hearing. Also, we perceive art as opposite to music in that the former lives in physical space (a canvas, a carving), while the latter (a song, a symphony) must be reborn time after time in performance. However, by moving from the arena of sensory perception to that of personal enactment, we begin to treat music and art as parallels. Even without a technical notion of genesis, we understand dimly that the muses bubble from one spring, linked in a chain at their source.

Folklorists, especially, bind diverse forms and events under the large rubric *artistic behavior:* trickster tale, sand painting, harvest festival, rain prayer, fiddle tune, initiation prank, victory dance, barn sign, woven amulet. Frequently, academicians employ the tag *art* to encompass all creative endeavor (including music). More commonly, visual artists define their field by tool used, and break quickly into sub-genres such as lithography or photography. At times, avant-garde critics attempt to restrict *fine art* to special kinds of sophisticated or experimental constructs. These triple meanings compound when the words *folk* and *art* combine to describe indigenous culture as primitive, naive, untutored, idiosyncratic, or visionary.

Accepting the premise that visual art and performed music stem from related impulses and explicate similar experience, I have long puzzled over the inattention to art history by ballad scholars in the United States. Why have we walked such lonely roads? Do we erect barriers to keep seeing and hearing in separate lanes, or out of timidity in straying too far from the familiar? Some time ago, without credentials, I began to look at paintings and graphics in which

97

the subject was American folk music.[1] Like some colleagues, I used
folk society and *folk music* as limiting terms: people enclaved by
continuous social activity; songs and instrumentals deep in tradition. Conscious that others had extended or shredded these narrow
bounds, nevertheless, I sought fiddlers and bluesmen who were
portrayed on the village green or at the levee camp, and not in the
concert hall. My search itself was shaped by early reading, which
had convinced me that the platonic folk musician was brother to
the itinerant walker in the night or sister to the lonely watcher
of departing trains.

Here, in appreciation of Bertrand Bronson's contribution to
ballad study, I offer a brief overview of folk music depictions, pictures in an exhibition yet to be mounted. Those who serve appren-
ticeships in the ballad quest have been torn often by the bramble
bush. If one sets out singlemindedly to seek a given illustration for a
song narrative, he too may be torn. A few years away from Berkeley,
I read Professor Bronson's article on Captain Kidd's song progeny
(1942) and for nearly four decades I have been unable to hear either
"Sam Hall" or "Wondrous Love" without seeing in mind's eye a
theater. Its stanzaic stage, in turn, is peopled by pirates, chimney
sweeps, and evangelical worshippers. However, I have found but
few ballad drawings of the heroes and villains who strode Kidd's
decks or watched Hall's hanging. This negative reference reminds us
that no available checklist of folksong in art exists; nor a museum
catalogue covering a folk music exhibition; nor a coffee-table anthology ready for desultory browsing. To assume a unilinear cord
from songs about Captain Kidd to pictures of his song-family members is to approach the bramble bush.

Where then do we open our search and does it resemble ballad
collecting? How do we reach out to pioneer scholars who have
opened the field of musical iconography?[2] During two centuries of
American nationhood, and the colonial experience before, many
artists have been pulled to folk music, in all its configurations.
Their work, now scattered in gallery, library, archive or studio
takes in woodcut, pencil sketch, watercolor, etching, lithograph,
oil painting, and wall mural. Multiple formats include: broadside,
sheet music cover, pocket songster, concert poster, record album
jacket, anthology illustration. No governing thread—conceptual,
affective, mechanical—ties this panoply together. No clarion call
pulled artists at the poles of American experience to singular appreciation of folksong. A few artists were skilled musicians, others
approached music only as auditors, many were paid to ballyhoo
show business, some never used the word *folk* in their daily speech,
still others eventually came to believe in folksong as a kind of balm,
or even a call to arms.

I know of no facile approach to the cultural meeting ground where folksong and visual depiction intersect. Hence, for this essay, I have built a make-believe exhibit room out of ten panels, each making a statement about folk life. Within a museum, conventionally, one views a canvas or engraving and bobs to a wall-card for background information. We expect historian, curator, or critic to touch in print something of the painting's intrinsic meaning, revealed by craft dynamics. Ideally, we also ask the catalogue writer to hint at philosophic stance, his own and that of the artist under consideration.

Old portraits of folk musicians, today, may seem sentimental or gauche, while narrative paintings covering ballad events may seem anecdotal or hortatory. From the vantage point of modernity, vast reservoirs of previous art, optimistic and representational, is out of favor within the academy. One critic, for example, stigmatizes as "drab," "harsh," and "spiritually vacant" the work of those "new romantic realists" who fashioned regional art (including numerous folk themes) in the 1930s. Another, defying polemical cliches of radicalism, sees this same decade as artistically anachronistic, if not reactionary. Ideological banners do flutter quietly in the air of museum rooms.[3]

Better than most critics in the 1930s, Constance Rourke struggled to draw together populist planks and anti-fascist appeals, genteel sentiment and robust folk fiber. While working with Holger Cahill for the New Deal's Index of American Design, she asserted that painters of genre in the Age of Jackson and of the American scene in Franklin Delano Roosevelt's years thought it fully appropriate to limn rustic fiddlers, banjo pickers, and dust bowl balladeers, as well as to explicate their moods.[4] We know that artists within recent schools — abstract, non-objective, minimalist, introspective — have not been inspired similarly by "Sourwood Mountain" or the "Cherry Tree Carol." We must accept the reality that art separated by a few decades can be an ice age apart in its reception. Accordingly, we enter our imaginary room prepared to enjoy sight and sound under many lights, and to ask questions about chosen selections.

*   *   *   *   *   *

1. Anonymous. The Harp Player, 1684. In *Cambridge Ephemeris* . . . Massachusetts Historical Society [fig. 1].

The printing of books in Britain's American colonies began at Stephen Daye's press, Cambridge, with the *Bay Psalm Book* (1640). Highly dependent upon European standards, colonial printers struggled both to develop craft skill and to assimilate New World

FɪG. 1. *Anonymous.* The Harp Player (*1684*). *Woodcut. In* Cambridge Ephemeris
. . . *By permission of Massachusetts Historical Society.*

experience. It was not until about 1667 that the printing of pictures began in Massachusetts, with art specifically intended for broadsides, proclamations, maps, seals, tracts, pamphlets, and chapbooks.[5] Of these types, folklorists know best the many elegiac broadsides with their heavy mourning borders arched at the top to suggest tombstones, or with stock cuts of death's-head, hourglass, spade, and death holding scythe. Grim ballads of criminal execution, and their warnings and farewells, similarly held coffins, gallows, or dead carts. Memorable for attempting to relate illustration to poetic text is the vessel (incorrectly pictured as a galley) which heads "Words of Consolation . . ." following Isaac Stetson's drowning by falling from a sloop's deck at the North River's mouth, November 7, 1718.[6]

Previously, in 1684, Samuel Green published an almanac embellished with a cut of a harp player, the first American musician in art, if we accept King David as a New England Puritan. Sinclair Hamilton suggests that this work by an unknown, self-taught wood engraver ranks as "our first imaginative book illustration."[7] Cuts such as these of the harp player are American incunabula — scarce, "primitive," and valued for pointing the way, as well as for their contrast with overseas models. Richard Holman points out that *The Harp Player* was decorative rather than didactic, for it did not "elucidate anything in the almanac," and, further, "this woodcut seems to be a purely lyrical outburst, an unusual thing at any time, in seventeenth-century Boston and Cambridge."[8] Presently, we are uncertain whether the cut was intended specifically for this almanac.

Facts about the Cambridge musician are scant; I am drawn to him because he raises key questions for the discipline of folklore. Although the word *folk* is as ancient as the English language itself, we look to the nineteenth century for combinations of *folk* and *lore, ballad,* or *song.* Yet long before *folksong* fell into lexicographical nets, Renaissance artists had engraved or painted musicians at court, in their homes, and among the peasantry. Albrecht Dürer's *The Bagpiper* (1514) represents a whole class of itinerant musicians set apart from courtly life.[9] We do not know when an American painter first categorized folk musicians similarly set apart. Can we assert flatly that the Cambridge harpist, staring ahead for three centuries, is a folk musician? Not only do we puzzle over our harp player's place in colonial society, but we ask questions in aesthetics. Why do terms such as *quaint* or *crude* come to mind when we examine colonial prints? These code words for folk art imply individuals, self-educated and lacking in formal skills of perspective and balance. Can we not invert conventional judgment and suggest that the craftsman who conceived the Cambridge musician worked in a manner satisfactory to himself and to his audience? Must the folk artist be placed always on the lowest rung of a ladder reaching to norms high above? To remove this metaphoric ladder is to see folk artists in terms of positive self-image and their ability to create within traditional patterns.

Did not limners and carvers in folk society treasure their creative formulas, judging them to be direct and understandable? While oral historians gather stories from the "inarticulate," surely folklorists can learn how rank-and-filers viewed their work as well as that of well-placed peers. Tom Armstrong has suggested wisely that folk art should not be separated from fine art, but rather treated "within the same hierarchy of criteria" used for all artistic judgment.[10] To examine with responsibility a single work of art is to test hoary assumptions and to plow new ground. Hence, the Cambridge harp player (whether he is King David or not, and whether he holds in mind a psalm tune or perhaps a shepherd dance) poses a host of unanswered questions—some of which echo throughout this essay.

2. Samuel Jennings. *Liberty Displaying the Arts and Sciences,* 1792. A. Oil on canvas, Library Company of Philadelphia. B. Oil on linen, Winterthur Museum [figs. 2, 3].

Founded in 1731 by Benjamin Franklin, the Library Company of Philadelphia emerged after the Revolution as a bright center of learning, making it necessary in 1789 to plan a new building. Samuel Jennings, who had moved a few years before from Philadelphia to London to study art, conceived an allegorical painting for the Library and offered his planned gift, via correspondence, to the Company directors.[11] Jennings desired three mythological subjects: Clio, Calliope, and Minerva. The Library committee, by return letter, countered and suggested politely the goddess Liberty, "with her cap and proper Insignia." She was to survey a series of objects symbolizing art and science (including a gilded lyre, a palette and brushes, a telescope, a geographer's globe), while holding underfoot a broken chain. The directors also requested for the background, "A Groupe of Negroes sitting on the Earth, or in some attitude expressive of Ease & Joy."

Many of the directors, and architect William Thornton, were members of the Society of Friends, and active abolitionists. The broken chain of slavery, hence, symbolized their cherished hopes for the future. Jennings, happy with the assignment, displayed the finished painting at the Royal Academy, and shipped it by the Pigou to Philadelphia in 1792. This painting became an expatriate's gift to his native land. Also, hoping to gain some compensation from his work, Jennings made a replica on linen (now at Winterthur), from which he intended to have engravings struck for sale (if accomplished, no copies of this have survived).

Fig. 2. *Samuel Jennings*. Liberty Displaying the Arts and Sciences (*1792*). *Oil on linen. Courtesy, The Henry Francis du Pont Winterthur Museum.*

Robert C. Jones, who studied this painting carefully, has noted its technical imperfections but historical significance, for it is one of the first American allegories to integrate patriotism, abolitionism, and intellectual endeavor. The Library Company's directors clearly felt that the Old World's achievements would flower best in the New World when all men, black and white, were free. Colonial representations of Negroes had usually pictured them attending masters. By contrast, Jennings portrayed a self-contained group of individuals, of various ages and both sexes, under their own laurel-wreathed liberty pole.

Within this group of slaves, I am especially attracted to the blind banjo player and his lead boy, for I know of no previous painting of this subject in the United States. Dena Epstein has dated early references to the banjo: *banza* (1678), Martinique; *bangil* (1708), Barbados; *banjer* (1754), Maryland. Sir Hans Sloane, a physician in Jamaica during 1687, saw and heard a gourd-like banjo, the strum-strum, which was included as an illustration in *A Voyage to the Islands . . .* (1707).[12] Perhaps an artist, following Sloane, showed the banjo in living performance. Unless such a cut or sketch surfaces, we credit Jennings for a first depiction.

FIG. 3. *Detail from Samuel Jennings,* Liberty Displaying the Arts and Sciences *(1792). Oil on canvas. Courtesy, Library Company of Philadelphia.*

Jones believes that Jennings was familiar with Negro life from his Philadelphia youth, and possibly from observation in London. We can only speculate whether or not he actually heard a black street musician before moving to England. Regardless, Jennings treats a folk musician with dignity—a conception foreign to most artists who were drawn to stage minstrelsy in the 1830s and beyond. It is refreshing today to look back two centuries and see a figure we can place under the rubric *folk* in a non-cloying, non-stereotypical mold.

3. James Goodwyn Clonney. A. *Militia Training*, 1841. Oil on canvas, Pennsylvania Academy of the Fine Arts. B. *Fiddler*, ca. 1839–1841. Wash on paper, Museum of Fine Arts, Boston [figs. 4,5].

Folklorists use the word *genre* literally to categorize items in expressive culture; figuratively we drop ballads and blues or moccasins and madstones into discrete bins. By contrast, art historians hear the word *genre* as meaning a scene in daily life. Hermann Williams's definition of such a painting is "an everyday activity of ordinary people, painted in a realistic manner. The artist must be contemporary with the scene depicted."[13] Williams places the beginning of American genre in colonial times, when some frontier families could afford painted overmantels or wall paintings which complemented ancestral portraits. Artists of early social history saw farmhands at their chores, loafers in taverns, and artisans at work or play. I do not know who first heard a fiddler and was impelled to place him on canvas, but I cite as possibilities John Lewis Krimmel's *Quilting Frolic* (1813) and *Fourth of July Celebration in Center Square, Philadelphia* (1819). The domestic scene holds a black musician, and Independence Day, a white musician.[14]

FIG. 4. *James Goodwyn Clonney.* Militia Training *(1841). Oil on canvas. Courtesy, Pennsylvania Academy of the Fine Arts.*

Fig. 5. *James Goodwyn Clonney.* Fiddler (*ca. 1839–1841*). *Wash on paper.*
Courtesy, Museum of Fine Arts, Boston.

The two best known American genre painters are William Sidney Mount (1807–1868), and George Caleb Bingham (1811–1879). The former devoted himself to depicting bucolic life on Long Island, and the latter to Missouri politics and river work. Today, we recognize Mount and Bingham as conscious Jacksonians, not only in their paintings of the common man, but also in directing their work to a populist aesthetic. The continuing appeal of Currier & Ives prints attests to the longevity in these values.

Mount and Bingham each painted folk musicians, but for our exhibition I select a canvas and a drawing by their contemporary, James Goodwyn Clonney (1812–1867). Lucretia Giese has marshalled the known details of his life: birth in England, youthful emigration to Philadelphia for work in a lithographic firm, further work in New York City, removal to Cooperstown, death at Binghamton.[15] Fortunately, some of his drawings made as preliminary studies for oil paintings are found in museums. Clonney sketched constantly prior to transferring figures to canvas; his drawings are tight and accurate, infused by anecdotal humor short of caricature. In this sense, he worked in a tested Dutch tradition known to many practitioners of American genre.

Clonney's *Militia Training* is an ambitious canvas, stressing not the militiamen in the background, but rather the celebrants in the foreground, who include an elderly white fiddler and young black dancer. The original title *Fourth of July* marked the importance of our major patriotic holiday; Clonney's choice of revellers conveyed the citizenry's strength in "breaking down" the Fourth into a folk event (the title *Militia Training* appeared when the painting was engraved for reproduction in *The Gift*, 1843, to illustrate a story by that name). Under a clear empty sky, the artist melded landscape and genre, dwarfing his figures—a scale unusual to paintings focussed on minute and constant human activity. Recent scholarship in folklore uses such activity to situate musical performance socially. Accordingly, we see two contexts for Clonney's fiddler: the large and festive militia day; the specific action of one musician paired with a dancing youth. Today, we can only guess at their tune by triangulation: date, ca. 1839; place, rural New York; dancer's step, clog or jig. Just as we must use our imagination to project musical notation beyond the page in order "to see" a bowing arm or supple wrist, we must turn inward from Clonney's fiddler, on paper and canvas, if we wish "to hear" his tune. Even the most gifted artist can carry us only to the threshold of audition.

4. Thomas Eakins. *Cowboy Singing*, 1890. Watercolor on paper, Metropolitan Museum of Art, New York [fig. 6].

In the decade after the Civil War, cowboys replaced herders and drovers in driving Texas longhorns north to market. Before 1900

Fig. 6. *Thomas Eakins.* Cowboy Singing *(1890). Watercolor on paper. Courtesy, The Metropolitan Museum of Art, Fletcher Fund, 1925.*

the working cowboy, boosted by tent showmen and dime novelists, had become a demigod on the plains; and in this century, film makers and rodeo promoters have added gaudy symbolism to the hero's load. Part of the training for present-day ballad scholars is the study of cowboy lore, and an acquaintanceship with John Lomax's career. The latter's fascination with this material, itself, helped define American folksong.

Within the corpus of Western art, representational to romantic, Thomas Eakins's *Cowboy Singing* demands elucidation. His works are well known; I cite three key sources: Goodrich, Hoopes, Hendricks.[16] During the summer of 1887, Eakins visited the B–T Ranch near Dickinson in the Dakota Badlands, using the open country to overcome a period of despondency. The artist delighted in observing cowboy life, and bought a white horse Billy and a brown Indian pony Baldy, riding every day. He also heard the ranch hands singing, accompanying themselves with banjo and mouth-organ. At the B–T he made sketches and photographs for future use. Returning to Philadelphia, Eakins rode from the station in full cowboy regalia, mounted on Baldy, leading Billy. For several years he used these equine models for painting and sculpture.

Between 1888 and 1892, Eakins's students posed for him in the worn buckskins and sombrero which he had carried back from the Badlands. His student Franklin L. Schenck, who played the guitar, is now memorialized as a dreamy, red-bearded figure in Eakins's *The Bohemian*. For *Cowboy Singing*, Schenck appears as a banjo player in watercolor and again in oil. Additionally, he appears with guitar in *Home Ranch*. One of Eakins's children recalled a Christmas holiday in which Schenck told the youngsters improbable wolf tales, later singing Gounod's "Ave Maria," "with Papa and Mama at the organ and piano."[17] This memory of the bohemian at ease with Gounod underscores the tangle of detail which surrounds even the most straightforward portrait of an American folk musician.

Eakins heard the banjo played in cow camps. To pose the unwordly Schenck as a cowboy was a step removed from reality, yet it served to bring to new viewers in the 1890s a sense of uncompromising realism. Before the turn of the century, illustrators of pulp fiction and Wild West Show poster painters had already exaggerated greatly the cowboy image. Eakins, of course, often at great cost to his career, sought the truth behind such popular mythology. *Cowboy Singing* has been reproduced frequently in this century. It fits closely the poetry in the anthologies of Lomax and his fellow collectors; it gives us a stainless standard against which to judge Hollywood's legion of singing cowboys. As I look at Eakins's banjo player again in 1982, however, I am conscious that Schenck's "grandchildren" continue to enjoy buckaroo togs. Many new "cowboys," unlike Eakins returning to his Philadelphia art studio, only ride the range from film to recording studio. These rhinestone dudes exist in rodeo motel and honkytonk. We shall continue to see them making music within art for decades to come.

5. Miguel Covarrubias. *Blues Singer*, 1927. In *Negro Drawings* [fig. 7].

In the century from Jim Crow's debut on the minstrel stage to the appearance of race record advertisements in the Negro press, commercial artists have had considerable scope in developing nega-

Fig. 7. *Miguel Covarrubias*. Blues Singer (*1927*). *In* Negro Drawings. *Courtesy, Alfred A. Knopf, New York.*

tive stereotypes of black musicians. Jim Crow, the shuffling clown, and Zip Coon, the hustling dandy, were both prominent on sheet music covers throughout the 1830s. Their grimacing descendants in the 1920s displayed banjos and guitars on flyers and record catalogues by Okeh and sister firms. This burnt-cork portraiture, comic and exaggerated, represented unreflective mainstream images of plantation mores, as well as tentative understanding of black/white expressive interaction.[18] Jim Crow paraded as brother to the Mike Fink of backwoods legend and the Davy Crockett of Almanac fame, while Zip Coon preened as a black-faced Yankee-Doodle.

In strong contrast to the cardboard manikin derivative of minstrel stage and recording studio, a number of American artists saw the Negro musician as an idealistic figure. After abolitionist teachers had collected slave songs in the Civil War decade, and after others had helped Fisk University students bring spirituals to world audiences, it became appropriate to treat black folk musicians in glowing terms. Two painters, white and black, make the point: Richard Norris Brooke, near Warrenton, Virginia, painted *A Pastoral Visit* (1881) in which a preacher lunches with a Negro family in its cottage. In the foreground, father's banjo lies on a stool; we sense that it is integral to community, put aside momentarily in honor of the guest. Henry Tanner, one of Thomas Eakins's best students, painted *The Banjo Lesson* (1893) in which a serene elder holds on his lap a lad, as tall as the banjo he fingers. Tanner offers more than a musical lesson, when we see enacted continuities in folk society.[19]

It is not difficult to array art depicting black music along a scale, pejorative to ameliorative; it is difficult within this array to select a particular piece in order to probe an artist's understanding of folksong. Can a single canvas or engraving explicate large questions: what is the American stamp within Afro-American music? Did slaves in the United States inhabit a cultural cyclotron which disintegrated African experience? Did black music become a survival tool, a cluster point for endurance? Which forms were obviously "folk" within the corpus of black song?

Miguel Covarrubias, born in Mexico in 1904, came to New York during 1923 to continue his education.[20] An early friend in the city, Carl Van Vechten—novelist, photographer, music critic, and trumpeter of Negritude—introduced the young artist to dazzling figures of the Harlem Renaissance, including Langston Hughes. For the ultra-sophisticated *Vanity Fair*, Covarrubias began a series of caricatures of Manhattan's literati and cognoscenti. His first parody appeared in January 1924 and, at year's end, the magazine featured eight of his drawings on "The New Negro" from the realm of entertainment. In 1927 Alfred Knopf published *Negro Drawings*, touching chiefly music and dance. This book complemented illustrations by Covarrubias for black composers and collectors, W. C. Handy and Zora Neale Hurston.

Covarrubias's 1927 collection contained *Blues Singer,* a sculptured line drawing of a powerful woman, arms aloft. To my knowledge, it is the first work by a fine artist to be named *blues* (beyond sheet music or record ad.). In the 1920s only a few white collectors, such as Dorothy Scarborough, had heard any folk blues in rural settings.[21] Most other enthusiasts came upon this form as an extension of jazz within city clubs or theater concerts. The academic debate on the dichotomous terms, *city/country blues,* has been endless. Central to framing differences is our understanding that many cultural arbiters, upon first hearing blues, judged this music "from the lips of harlots" to be degenerate or perverted. Among black intellectuals, W. E. B. Du Bois treasured spirituals, but treated vernacular song as debased. In contrast, James Weldon Johnson heard ragtime, jazz, and blues as intrinsically exciting, setting norms to which white musicians would forever aspire.[22]

I see Covarrubias's *Blues Singer* as a visual passport back to the period when Harlem creators struggled to chart their course. Black poets, novelists, and painters were torn between exuberant folkways, novel abstractions, African decorative motifs, and social polemics. Covarrubias, perhaps because he was a foreigner in Manhattan, and perhaps because he accepted the ideals of the Mexican revolution, was predisposed to favor folk culture. It is true that the speakeasy musicians he heard and drew were several steps removed from cotton field or baptismal river, yet he assumed that in the America beyond Harlem all black musicians seemed paradigmatically "folk." Without an instrument, without props, with no hint at setting, Covarrubias's *Blues Singer* is, nevertheless, emblematic of Afro-American folksong. She is at once charwoman and streetwalker, Ma Rainey and Bessie Smith. The artist asks each viewer to meet this enigmatic singer on her platform, to puzzle at her role, to name her song.

6. Anonymous. *Sacramental Scene in a Western Forest,* 1854. In
   Old Redstone . . . by Joseph Smith [fig. 8].

Is it useful to include in a folk music gathering a work which depicts neither instrument, musician, nor singer? To reply positively suggests at once either a scene of performance, or a literal song text happening. In special attention to intimate domestic settings, many folklorists have distanced themselves from large crowds, civic institutions, and creedal movements. Notwithstanding these framing devices, we recognize the spiritual folksong as a major contribution out of American life, and we know that it was born in western camp meetings at the nineteenth century's opening.

Fig. 8. *Anonymous.* Sacramental Scene in a Western Forest (*1854*). *In* Old Redstone . . . *by Joseph Smith.*

Listeners frequently assume spirituals to be exclusively black. However, white and black worshippers, buoyed by belief in personal salvation, came together on the frontier to shape a dynamic body of hymnody still vital in the United States. The re-creation of religious folksong seems endless, for the rhetoric of the King James Bible cleaves to song. Old tunes are recycled constantly, and faith is renewed within each generation. Historians place the spiritual's genesis about 1801 within the Great Revival at Cane Ridge, Bourbon County, Kentucky.[23] Some of the tension poured into Cane Ridge song continues to be heard in urban storefront churches, black and white, throughout America. It is to these dilapidated sanctuaries that scholars ought to turn when the shell of other ballad communities — linguistic, occupational, regional — erodes.

Nearly all writers on folk or rural hymnody have searched hymnals and other ephemeral songsters for pictures of camp meetings. The two earliest reproductions which I have seen date to 1830 at the Blackwood and Haverstraw grounds.[24] Many artists centered upon stump or shed pulpits from which preachers exhorted crowds, alternatively passive or frenzied, and their prints featured tents used for camping during extended services. The Sacred Harp couplet, "I pitch my tent on this camp ground/And give old Satan another round," could well have served as a caption for most engravings in frontier hymnals.

Sacramental Scene in a Western Forest does not show tents, nor are the worshippers caught in a moment of ecstasy. However, this illustration with a foreground sentinel, long rifle at rest, suggests a time before camp meetings were secure from marauding Indians. I cannot identify the artist, nor guess the engraving's date prior to its publication in Joseph Smith's *Old Redstone. . .* , although a clue may be present in the name of the lithographer, P. S. Duval, Philadelphia.[25] The Redstone Presbytery, formed in 1781, took its name from a creek entering the Monongahela below Brownsville. However, during early years this new association ministered to settlers in land claimed by Pennsylvania and Virginia "west of the mountains." Although Smith offers no clue to precise location, John Boles, upon reproducing the illustration in 1972, identified it as "one of the first Kentucky camp meetings, circa 1801."

Folksong enthusiasts hear a wide variety of styles and songs when *camp meeting spiritual* becomes an identifying rubric: the congregational singing, heterophonic and asynchronous, of Old Regular Baptists in mountain communities; the polished offerings of Paul Robeson and Marian Anderson on concert LPs; black Primitive Baptists lining out long-meter hymns; modern gospel effusions, jazz- and rock-based, which are tied by archaic title or theme to devotional purity. Ideally, these multiple forms need be assimilated in order to understand the full growth of America's camp meeting tradition. The forest canopy we see in *Old Redstone . . .* continues to shelter limitless song.

7. James Wells Champney/William Ludlow Sheppard. *The Dance Hall—Denison, Texas.* In *Scribner's Monthly* (July, 1873) and *The Great South* by Edward King (1875) [fig. 9].

We are uncomfortable in the juxtaposition of sacred and profane expression, for we learn early that they occupy polar realms. Occasionally, a medieval illustrator brought untamed satyrs and nymphs to religious works, either by direct personification, or allegorical disguise. The imaginative impulse which led to a dragon with a monk's head, or a friar with a beast's posterior, seems in the United States to have been channelled into political cartooning. Perhaps the force of puritanism or that of scientific empiricism thwarted the creative energies of artists who viewed churchly behavior. While searching for folk music settings, I have felt free to move from wilderness camp meeting to minstrel stage, riverboat salon, gin mill, juke joint, and honkytonk. A Denison, Texas saloon—a scant four months after this raw town "sprang into existence"—exemplifies folksong's sinful abode.

Following the Civil War, national magazines of wide circulation sent reporters and artists to all reaches of the old Confederacy. The South was perceived as both exotic and beckoning, or backwards and terrifying—nearly powerful enough to have severed the bond of union. During the 1870s these magazines gradually shifted from harsh disapproval of the enemy to accommodation to Recon-

Fɪɢ. 9. *James Wells Champney/William Ludlow Sheppard.* The Dance Hall —
Denison, Texas. *In* Scribner's Monthly *(July, 1873) and* The Great South, *by*
Edward King *(1875)*.

struction, with editorial policy cast in mediatory roles. *Scribner's*
star reporter Edward King (1848–1896) had already covered the
Franco-Prussian War, and had witnessed the Paris Commune. On
his Southern trip, King covered 25,000 miles, using private railway
car, steamer, stagecoach, and horseback. His findings, in fifteen
monthly instalments, appeared during 1873–74, and a year later
these articles were rearranged and expanded into a lavish tome,
The Great South.[26]

King's companion J. Wells Champney sketched in pencil, dis-
patching his drawings back to *Scribner's* in New York for wood
engraving at a then-modern plant. Today, with instant photo-
journalism and daily TV newscasts, we marvel at the quickness of
artists and artisans, a century ago, in presenting travel pictures
within months of completing field trips. Champney apprenticed as
a Boston wood engraver, served in the Civil War, and studied genre
painting in France before accepting a commission to work with
Edward King. Although Champney was credited on the title page
of *The Great South* as the book's sole artist, in many areas *Scribner's*
employed local contributors to supplement his work. In some
instances his sketches were reworked by staff artists or engravers in
New York.

I have added the name William Ludlow Sheppard to the Denison saloon illustration because his initials appear in the lower left-hand corner of the engraving. Also, he signed "W L Sheppard after Champ" to a preceding gambling house scene, *Playing Keno.* Seemingly, Sheppard saw Texas through Champney's eyes. The former, born in Richmond, Virginia, is remembered for illustrations of Negroes "done with a sympathetic truthfulness to nature" as well as for Confederate statuary in his native city.[27]

A few lines by reporter King carry us back to Denison: "Every third building in the place was a drinking saloon with gambling appurtenances, filled after nightfall with a depraved, adventurous crowd, whose profanity was appalling, whose aspect was hideous. Men drunk and sober danced to rude music in the poorly-lighted saloons, and did not lack female partners."[28] *The Great South* was a dynamic work, pulsing to the notion of economic progress, but its author was not blind to reality. While King stressed vulgarity and indecency in Denison, Champney caught a fiddler and guitarist in the shadows. Nineteenth-century string band depictions are rare, indeed; this one is the earliest I have encountered which has included a guitar. Can we speculate that a Mexican *vaquero* had carried his instrument north on a cattle drive? In retrospect, King might have contributed to our knowledge of frontier music, folk and popular, if he had noted a few song titles heard in Denison, or touched on the identity of the performers. We are left, today, to guess at the "rude music" Champney and Sheppard portrayed. Our task is to reconstruct the spirited steps of their dancers, and to turn elsewhere for collaborative detail.

8. Thomas Hart Benton. *Coming 'Round the Mountain,* 1931. In
   The Lithographs of Thomas Hart Benton, by Creekmore Fath
   (1979) [fig. 10].

A canon in ballad scholarship is the separation of narrative from lyric song. Many artists sensed this distinction when turning to specific songs for titles of their works, at times touching mood and at times detailing event. Ballad walls are easily breached when we formulate notions of decay and disintegration, seek the emotional core hidden within sequential stories, or subject narrative to structural and semiotic analysis. Often, in description of lyric folksong, we turn to the subtle language of impressionistic painting — color, tone, texture, ambience.

In 1931, Thomas Hart Benton completed his first lithograph to use a song title, *Coming 'Round the Mountain.*[29] Previously, in the *American Songbag,* Carl Sandburg had included a full text and tune to "She'll be Comin' Round the Mountain," relating it back to the Negro spiritual "When the Chariot Comes." Newman Ivey White similarly tied "She'll . . ." to the "Old Ship of Zion," well-

Fig. 10. *Thomas Hart Benton.* Coming 'Round the Mountain (*1931*). *In* The Lithographs of Thomas Hart Benton, *by Creekmore Fath. Reproduced by permission.*

known in black and white camp-meeting tradition.[30] Benton, acquainted with folksong scholarship, was not impelled, in a drawing, to place a given item in a text-tune genealogical frame. Instead he focussed on the kind of music which resonated in mind when a gallery viewer or print collector saw a mountain trio perform.

I return here to the ever-present difficulty in the visual depiction of music. A museum visitor who has heard "Coming 'Round the

Mountain" can conjure up its music upon seeing Benton's print. But if the song is unknown, the drawing itself must elicit sounds associated with old time music (alternately labelled *mountain, country, western, hillbilly,* and *bluegrass*). In my judgment, this lithograph is an outstanding representation of an American lyric folksong. Benton's accordionist and guitarist sing as well as play; we are left guessing whether or not the fiddler also sings. The tall mountain woman responds to music with stylized dance; her partner is ambiguous, for he may be dancer or singer. Almost out of the framed action, he may be also the spectator everyman. The iconic pine tree, log cabin, and hayrick speak directly to rurality. In the distance a young woman wildly drives careening horses into our consciousness and out of the picture's bounds. A serene rooster in the right foreground clues us to Benton's knowledge of this song's humor.

Few American artists were as knowledgeable about folksong as Benton. One senses that he grew up originally nourished by a George Caleb Bingham political painting, for Tom carried Missouri Senator Thomas Hart Benton's populist convictions as a badge of honor. On walking trips in the Ozarks during the 1920s, Benton began to sketch mountain musicians and gospel singers and to commit their vital tunes to memory. In Greenwich Village during the early 1930s, he formed a hillbilly band bringing folksong to urban and radical audiences; Charles Seeger long praised Tom for opening fresh paths to old music during these years.[31] One of Benton's most widely reproduced canvasses is *The Ballad of the Jealous Lover of Lone Green Valley,* in which he combines two sets of actors: girl fatally stabbed by lover, knife in hand; three musicians around a table jug.[32] Although recent critics have narrowed Benton into the corner of romantic realism (or Regionalism), he saw himself as an explicator of large myth (folklore) and stern history, hardly separating these twins.

Ultimately, any work of art must be satisfactory in intrinsic terms to an individual viewer, no matter how much baggage he or she brings to perception. Do Benton's musicians and dancers compose a ring which compels entrance on our part? Does his trio carry enough imaginative power to represent folk musicians beyond the Ozarks? Is the young woman driving horses a puzzle if we cannot read the lithograph's title? To answer these and similar questions about *Coming 'Round the Mountain* is to trust sensory perception, at best complemented by knowledge gleaned from cultural history.

9. John Held, Jr. *Frankie and Johnny Were Lovers,* 1930. Linoleum block print in *The Saga of Frankie & Johnny* [fig. 11].

No critic has named the first American artist to conceive a cycle of linked pictures keyed to the unfolding story within a particular

FIG. 11. *John Held, Jr.* Frankie and Johnny Were Lovers (*1930*). *Linoleum block print, in* The Saga of Frankie & Johnny. *Reproduced by permission.*

ballad. A good candidate is John Held, Jr. (1889–1958). In a long series of wry pen-and-ink drawings for *Life, Judge,* and *College Humor,* he helped define "The Jazz Age" as well as erect markers for its impudent youth. Editors today who wish to illuminate "The Roaring Twenties" turn inevitably to his cartoons of razor-thin flappers with bobbed hair and scanty dresses and to saxophone-tooting, coonskin-coated sheiks. Surprisingly, although Held's name is forever linked to jazz, he never portrayed it in downhome settings. Rather, he placed this music in fraternity/sorority revels, while pallid combos accompanied few dancers but many "neckers." This artist's jazz slipped away from rhythmic, improvisational expression to hedonistic conduct, code-breaking, and public sensuality.

Held actually commented on two musical eras: Jazz Age, Gilded Age.[33] For the latter period, he employed a "woodcut" technique in linoleum blockprints or pen drawings on scratchboard. Using this antique style, pegged to subject matter of the century's end, he portrayed his flappers' grandparents as heroines (buxom, bustled, wasp-waisted) and heroes (elegant, cynical, dandified). These burlesque engravings were neither nostalgic nor acid; they were formal and always explicable. Held offered many "old-time" comic items in its initial years to *The New Yorker,* some of which were used again in three of Frank Shay's hilarious folksong books.[34]

Held's picture book, *The Saga of Frankie & Johnny,* literally divides an American ballad into twenty-three segments—a full page linocut for each stanza. Additionally, it holds sly cameos such as those of a piano player, pistol, beer bottle, bed, and gallows. The stanza cut illustrated here introduces the ballad's principal characters before the familiar plot unfolds. In a short preface the author indicates that as a youth he had learned the piece from "a colored piano player, who was called 'Professor' in a parlor house" in Salt Lake City.[35]

Some professors suggest that "Frankie and Johnny" stemmed from a murder in a St. Louis bordello, 1899, while others advance earlier dates.[36] Regardless of time of origin, this ballad has continued to move back and forth from popular to folk domicile. Carl Weinhardt has provided an excellent commentary on Held's apprenticeship in engraving and newspaper cartooning. However, we need additional data for Held's inspiration—well before 1930—while turning a folksong into a picture series analogous to cartoon comic strips or framed film stills. We need considerable attention to the work of his fellow artists who also fell back upon folk material absorbed in childhood. As knowledge in this area deepens, we shall find Held's "woodcut" ruffles and flourishes appropriate to Gilded Age brothel or grog shop, to songlore born within their steaming walls, and to our complex discipline folklore.

10. Palmer Hayden. *When John Henry Was a Baby,* 1940–1946.
National Collection of Fine Arts, Smithsonian Institution [fig. 12].

Our exhibition opened with biblical hero King David; it closes with ballad hero John Henry. We assert readily that this legendary black worker—swinging his hammer, defying the steam drill, and dying tragically—is America's olympian folksong figure. During 1870–72, Chesapeake & Ohio crews completed a tunnel through a West Virginia spur of the Allegheny Mountains. In 1909, Louise Rand Bascom submitted a "John Henry" fragment to the *Journal of American Folklore* and, in following years, additional bits surfaced. Louis W. Chappell and Guy B. Johnson, separately, wrote important books on John Henry.[37] I have been intrigued by John-

FIG. 12. *Palmer Hayden.* When John Henry Was a Baby (*1940–1952*). *Courtesy, National Collection of Fine Arts, Smithsonian Institution and Mrs. Miriam Hayden.*

son's anecdote from a Tar Heel laborer, who told about John Henry carved in solid rock at the Big Bend's portal. This imaginative leap projects a lowly tunnel stiff into a stone monument, which memorializes not only his life and death but also the power within folksong.[38]

A now-unknown illustrator, Eben Given, first depicted John Henry in *Here's Audacity,* a book for young readers on heroes, aged and newly-minted.[39] In the half-century since Given presented John Henry as a dignified factory worker, the latter has dominated the visual landscape of folksong. He is seen more clearly and more often than Barbary Allen, Brave Wolfe, Jesse James, Stagolee, or Captain Kidd. John Henry cavorts in juvenile literature, where he drives drill bits, operates pneumatic hammers, mauls railroad spikes, and brandishes stevedore hooks. Two fine artists, J. J. Lankes and Fred Becker, have also touched John Henry, the former with woodcuts for Roark Bradford's novel *John Henry* (1931), the latter with nine prints from WPA Federal Art Project years 1935–39. Becker extends Lankes's bucolic representations to abstract form and surreal statement.[40]

Palmer Hayden (1890–1973) has offered the most ambitious series by any American artist on a discrete folksong. Born in Widewater, Virginia, he served in World War 1, after which he located in New York City. Working as a janitor he studied first at Cooper Union and later, with the help of friends, in Paris. Home again in New York, he turned consciously to "race" themes as well as to "naive" techniques in folk art. *The Legend of John Henry* includes a dozen vivid canvasses completed in the years 1940–1946. During January, 1947, Hayden exhibited the set initially at the Argent Gallery, New York. For this showing, Hayden stated that he had heard the John Henry ballad "when a boy in my early teens at home in Virginia. As I grew older, I came to realize the deeper significance of the story . . ."[41]

We cannot show all Hayden's *John Henry* oils, but his twelve titles together form a ballad precis. I have selected *When John Henry Was a Baby* as a concluding piece to our visual overview of folk music. In this canvas, John clutches a mallet and points out to his mother an enacted vision at the tunnel mouth. Significantly, a mule-drawn cart dominates one track, a locomotive engine the other. John Henry must have been double-visioned as well as double-jointed. He knew to his bones his own mule-like strength; he knew also that he could never beat the steam drill nor deny modernity.

Hayden uses, in this canvas, decorative chickens in the yard, sunflowers, and a coonskin on the cabin wall as symbols of country life. Also, they are limned in a manner which fits the style of many folk artists who cherished John Henry's story. Hayden's painting itself seems to say, "I, too, am folk." No folklorist interviewed Palmer Hayden before his death to probe his own affection for "John Henry" or, more importantly, for his views on the problems inherent in transcending musical/literary statement by visual construct. His achievement is a challenge for ballad scholars and art historians for years to come.

*   *   *   *   *   *

The first music printed in the New World, a Latin *Ordinarium*, dates back to 1556, Mexico City; the first in Massachusetts to 1698 — a crude *Bay Psalm Book* (ninth edition) with diamond-shaped notes cut in wood.[42] In 1770, Paul Revere designed and skillfully engraved in copper an unusual frontispiece for William Billings's *The New England Psalm-Singer,* showing seven elders seated at a round table with singing-books before them.[43] This picture, encircled by an oval staff holding a six-part canon, well represents colonial music illustration. Before the Revolution, psalmody slowly gave way to wordly song: patriotic airs, dance manuals, reprints of European classics. Within this body of secular material, newly-composed items which were individually printed (such as the "Liberty Song," 1768) appeared; these anticipated the rise of widespread sheet music publication in the early United States.[44] We look especially to sheet music covers for colorful illustrations of dramatic song subjects.

In time, commercial artists hired by music publishers turned to other forms: pocket songster, heavily bordered broadside, piano folio, song anthology and, eventually, sound recording album. Victorian editors in Britain commissioned leading illustrators to embellish folk collections, some intended for children. Technically, these books often intermingled literary and musical ballads. The most unusual American volume of this sort which I have encountered is John Williamson Palmer's *Folk Songs,* published by Scribner in 1856. This garland of refined poetry, "flowers of lyric tenderness and beauty," held pictures by a score of then-prominent artists based in New York, including Felix O. C. Darley and Thomas Nast. I am at a loss to fathom what Palmer meant in selecting his title, for few of the poems included were sung at any time, and only one or two of these had any life in tradition.

After Francis James Child's *The English and Scottish Popular Ballads* (1882–98) was abridged to a one-volume school text (1904) by Helen Child Sargent and George Lyman Kittredge, editors could visualize illustrations in some way faithful to norms shaped in field and archive by serious collectors. We need a pictorial volume pulled from published anthology and LP record jacket in order to document the latitude in public reception to traditional material. We shall benefit by study of iconographic devices now standard in folksong illustrations. However, for our imaginary museum journey, I have overlooked folksong collections and recordings in favor of artistic material of other intent.

Casting an essay for Bertrand Bronson in the form of a desired exhibition, I am conscious of narrow focus. I have chosen no Child ballads or their carriers. Nor have I used any of the fine ethnographic depictions of native American musicians by George Catlin and his co-workers in the West. None of the many immigrant performers who have turned the folksong kaleidoscope are here: where is the Cajun triangle beater, the Rio Grande *corridisto,* the steel milltowns' *tamburitza* band? In selecting naturalistic works of art, I have put aside rebels and innovators who also touched folk culture. For example, Stuart Davis, while still a student, frequented black saloons in Newark where "you could hear a tin-pan-alley tune turned into real music for the cost of a five-cent beer." His watercolor, *Negro Dance Hall* (1912), anticipated a lifetime of modern paintings in which he caught the hot and cool spirit of jazz without using music for direct subject.[45] It has been difficult for me, in this commentary, to neglect Davis (and equally difficult to exclude art linked to folksong by giants such as John Sloan or Ben Shahn). Surely, we can project future explication for material other than that selected here.

Finally, I have leaned deliberately, in the ten works reproduced— from psalm singer to steel driver—towards positive notions which shore folk society. In more than a thousand years of usage, the word *folk* has been stretched to convey diametric opposites: wholesome beings; those less than whole. *Folk* is simultaneously a label for all dwellers in a tribe or clan, and for some dwellers set apart or enclaved within a nation. One has but to display a few sheet music covers from the minstrel stage to see musicians as grotesques. One can turn to recent "revival" portraiture to see "folksingers" as sugary paper dolls. I have not, in the span of two hands, encompassed all American folk music, nor balanced neatly poles of centrality and marginality, hope and despair. To note lanes untrod is to appeal for friends within our discipline to take up exploratory challenges. Folk music and visual art do intersect. We need bright signposts as we move ahead.[46]

NOTES

[1] My findings on graphics have appeared regularly in the *John Edwards Memorial Foundation Quarterly* from 1967 to date.

[2] For example, see Emanuel Winternitz, *Musical Instruments and Their Symbolism in Western Art* (New Haven: Yale University Press, 1979).

[3] For recent criticism, see Sam Hunter, *American Art of the Twentieth Century* (New York: Abrams, 1972), pp. 124-62, and David C. Driskell, *Two Centuries of Black American Art* (Los Angeles: County Museum of Art, 1976), pp. 63-68. For participant views, see Francis V. O'Connor, *The New Deal Art Projects: An Anthology of Memoirs* (Washington: Smithsonian Institution, 1972), and *Art for the Millions* (Greenwich: New York Graphic Society, 1973).

[4] Constance Rourke, *American Humor* (New York: Harcourt, Brace, 1931); *The Roots of American Culture and Other Essays* (New York: Harcourt, Brace, 1942).

[5] For an exemplary work, see Elizabeth C. Reilly, *A Dictionary of Colonial American Printers' Ornaments and Illustrations* (Worcester: American Antiquarian Society, 1975).

[6] Ola Elizabeth Winslow, *American Broadside Verse* (New Haven: Yale University Press, 1930), plate 16. For other facsimiles, see Georgia B. Bumgardner, *American Broadsides* (Barre: Imprint Society, 1971).

[7] Sinclair Hamilton, *Early American Book Illustrators and Wood Engravers, 1670-1870* (Princeton: Princeton University Library, 1958), p. xxv; *Cambridge Ephemeris* . . . described, p. 4; King David reproduced, plate 4.

[8] Richard B. Holman, "Seventeenth Century American Prints," in *Prints in and of America to 1850,* ed. John D. Morse (Winterthur: Winterthur Museum, 1970), pp. 23-52.

[9] For reproductions of musicians in various settings, see Sidney Beck and Elizabeth E. Roth, *Music in Prints* (New York: New York Public Library, 1956); Francois Lesure, *Music and Art in Society* (University Park: Pennsylvania State University Press, 1968); Anil de Silva and others, *Man Through His Art: Music* (Greenwich: New York Graphic Society, 1964).

[10] Tom Armstrong, "The Innocent Eye: American Folk Sculpture," in *200 Years of American Sculpture* (New York: Whitney Museum of American Art, 1976),

pp. 74–111. See also Kenneth L. Ames, *Beyond Necessity: Art in the Folk Tradition* (Winterthur: Winterthur Museum, 1977).

[11]Details from Robert C. Jones, "Liberty Displaying the Arts and Sciences: A Philadelphia Allegory by Samuel Jennings," *Winterthur Portfolio*, 2 (1965), 84–105.

[12]Dena J. Epstein, *Sinful Tunes and Spirituals* (Urbana: University of Illinois Press, 1977), pp. 359–62; Sloane strum-strum reproduced, p. 15.

[13]Hermann Warner Williams, Jr., *Mirror to the American Past* (Greenwich: New York Graphic Society, 1973), pp. 16–19. See also Joshua C. Taylor, *America as Art* (Washington: National Collection of Fine Arts, Smithsonian Institution, 1976).

[14]Krimmel's paintings in Williams, *Mirror to the American Past*, color plate III and figure 22. For related art, see Patricia Hills, *The Painters' America* (New York: Praeger, 1974), and Donelson F. Hoopes and Nancy Wall Moure, *American Narrative Painting* (Los Angeles: County Museum of Art, 1974).

[15]Lucretia H. Giese, "James Goodwin Clonney (1812–1867): American Genre Painter," *American Art Journal*, 11 (October, 1979), 4–31. See also *M. and M. Karolik Collection of American Paintings, 1815–1865* (Cambridge: Harvard University Press, 1949).

[16]Lloyd Goodrich, *Thomas Eakins* (New York: Whitney Museum of American Art, 1933); Donelson F. Hoopes, *Eakins Watercolors* (New York: Watson-Guptill, 1971); Gordon Hendricks, *The Life and Work of Thomas Eakins* (New York: Grossman, 1974). "Cowboy Singing" in Hoopes, *Eakins Watercolors*, color plate 30.

[17]Schenk's portrait in Hendricks, *The Life and Work of Thomas Eakins*, plate 37; see also figs. 180, 181, 183, 185, 223; "Ave Maria," p. 195.

[18]For challenging studies, see Robert C. Toll, *Blacking Up: The Minstrel Show in Nineteenth Century America* (New York: Oxford University Press, 1974); Hans Nathan, *Dan Emmett and the Rise of Early Negro Minstrelsy* (Norman: University of Oklahoma Press, 1962).

[19]Brooke, figure 207 in Williams, *Mirror to the American Past;* Tanner, figure 36 in Driskell, *Two Centuries of Black American Art.* For an overview, see Elsa Honig Fine, *The Afro-American Artist* (New York: Holt, Rinehart and Winston, 1973).

[20]No adequate English-language study is available. My "Miguel Covarrubias' Jazz and Blues Musicians," *JEMF Quarterly*, Issue 48 (Winter, 1977), 183–95, lists his illustrations for folklore books. For example, see William C. Handy, *Blues: An Anthology* (New York: Boni, 1926); Zora Neale Thurston, *Mules and Men* (New York: Lippincott, 1935). For the Harlem period, see Bruce Kellner, *Carl Van Vechten and the Irreverent Decades* (Norman: University of Oklahoma Press, 1968).

[21]Dorothy Scarborough, "The 'Blues' as Folk-Songs," in *Publications of the Texas Folk-Lore Society*, no. 2 (Austin: The Society, 1923), pp. 52–66. For a recent study, see Jeff Todd Titon, *Early Downhome Blues* (Urbana: University of Illinois Press, 1977).

[22]The tension among black intellectuals over vernacular music remains largely unexplored. For leads, see Eugene Levy, *James Weldon Johnson: Black Leader, Black Voice* (Chicago: University of Chicago Press, 1973); Langston Hughes, *The Big Sea* (New York: Knopf, 1940); W. E. B. Du Bois, "The Sorrow Songs," in *The Souls of Black Folk* (Chicago: McClurg, 1903), pp. 250–64. For a setting in which differences surfaced, see Nathan Huggins, *Harlem Renaissance* (New York: Oxford University Press, 1971).

[23]John B. Boles, *The Great Revival, 1787–1805* (Lexington: University Press of Kentucky, 1972). See also thesis by Richard Hulan, *Camp-Meeting Spiritual Folksongs* (Austin: University of Texas, 1978). For extension, see Don Yoder, *Pennsylvania Spirituals* (Lancaster: Pennsylvania Folklife Society, 1961).

²⁴Blackwood pictured in George Pullen Jackson, *Down-East Spirituals and Others* (New York: Augustin, 1939), p. 210; Haverstraw in Richard Hulan, "Folk Hymns: The Cane Ridge Legacy," in program guide, *Festival of American Folklife* (Washington: Smithsonian Institution, 1973), p. 19.

²⁵Joseph Smith, *Old Redstone: or Historical Sketches of Western Presbyterianism, Its Early Ministers, Its Perilous Times, and Its First Records* (Philadelphia: Lippincott, Grambo, 1854), facing p. 310.

²⁶Edward King, *The Great South: A Record of Journeys* (Hartford: American Publishing Company, 1875). Reissued in England with additional illustrations, *The Southern States of North America* (London: Blackie & Son, 1875). American edition of 1879 reprinted with introduction by W. Magruder Drake and Robert R. Jones (Baton Rouge: Louisiana State University Press, 1972).

²⁷Hilson Gallery, Deerfield Academy. *James Wells Champney, 1843–1903* (Deerfield: The Academy, 1965); William Ludlow Sheppard, 1833–1912, in Sinclair Hamilton, *Early American Book Illustrators*, pp. 205–7.

²⁸King, *The Great South*, p. 177.

²⁹Creekmore Fath, *The Lithographs of Thomas Hart Benton* (Austin: University of Texas Press, 1979). See also my "Thomas Hart Benton's Folk Musicians," *JEMF Quarterly*, issue 42 (Summer, 1976), 74–90.

³⁰Carl Sandburg, *The American Songbag* (New York: Harcourt, Brace, 1927), p. 372; Newman Ivey White, *American Negro Folk-Songs* (Cambridge: Harvard University Press, 1928), pp. 93–97.

³¹For Seeger and Benton interaction, see Richard Reuss, "Folk Music and Social Conscience: The Musical Odyssey of Charles Seeger," *Western Folklore*, 38 (1979), 221–38, and my "Charles Louis Seeger (1886–1979)," *Journal of American Folklore*, 92 (1979), 391–99.

³²"Jealous Lover" in Matthew Baigell, *Thomas Hart Benton* (New York: Abrams, 1974), color plate 124. See also Ray Lawless, "Thomas Hart Benton's Jealous Lover and Its Musical Background," *Register of the Museum of Art*, University of Kansas, 2 (June, 1961), 32–39.

³³For further references, see my "John Held, Jr.: Jazz Age and Gilded Age," *JEMF Quarterly*, issue 49 (Spring, 1978), 23–37. The best overview is "Introduction" by Carl J. Weinhardt in *The Most of John Held, Jr.* (Brattleboro: Stephen Greene, 1972).

³⁴Frank Shay, *My Pious Friends and Drunken Companions* (New York: Macauley, 1927); *More Friends* (1928); *Drawn From the Wood* (1929).

³⁵John Held, Jr., *The Saga of Frankie & Johnny* (New York: McKee, 1930).

³⁶For an excellent headnote, see Vance Randolph, *Ozark Folksongs*, vol. 2 (Columbia: State Historical Society of Missouri, 1948), pp. 125–27.

³⁷Louise Rand Bascom, "Ballads and Songs of Western North Carolina," *JAF*, 22 (1909), 249. Guy B. Johnson, *John Henry: Tracking Down a Negro Legend* (Chapel Hill: University of North Carolina Press, 1929); Louis W. Chappell, *John Henry: A Folk-Lore Study* (Jena, Germany: Biedermann, 1933). For John Henry bibliography and discography, see Norm Cohen, *Long Steel Rail: The Railroad in American Folksong* (Urbana: University of Illinois Press, 1980).

³⁸Big Bend anecdote first used in Howard W. Odum and Guy B. Johnson, *Negro Workaday Songs* (Chapel Hill: University of North Carolina Press, 1926), p. 240.

³⁹Frank Shay, *Here's Audacity: American Legendary Heroes* (New York: Macauley, 1930), p. 246. See also my "John Henry Depicted," *JEMF Quarterly*, issue 51 (Autumn, 1978), 126–43.

⁴⁰Roark Bradford, *John Henry* (New York: Harper, 1931). For author and illustrator, see "Roark Bradford, 1896–1948" in Robert Bain and others, *Southern Writers: A Biographical Dictionary* (Baton Rouge: Louisiana State University

Press, 1979), pp. 44–45, and "J. J. Lankes" in Carl Zigrosser, *The Artist in America* (New York: Knopf, 1942), pp. 180–91. For Becker, see my "Fred Becker's John Henry," *JEMF Quarterly*, issue 53 (Spring, 1979), 30–37.

[41]Recollection in catalogue, *Palmer Hayden: The John Henry Series* . . . (Nashville: Fisk University Art Gallery, 1970). See also *The Legend of John Henry* (Pittsburgh: Fine Arts Gallery of the University of Pittsburgh, 1969). For details see my "Palmer Hayden's John Henry Series," *JEMF Quarterly*, issue 60 (Winter, 1980), 199–213.

[42]*The Printed Note: 500 Years of Music Printing and Engraving* (Toledo: Museum of Art, 1957).

[43]Clarence S. Brigham, *Paul Revere's Engravings* (New York: Atheneum, 1969), plate 25.

[44]Harry Dichter and Elliott Shapiro, *Early American Sheet Music* (New York: Bowker, 1941); David Tatham, *The Lure of the Striped Pig: The Illustration of Popular Music in America, 1820–1870* (Barre: Imprint Society, 1973).

[45]"Negro Dance Hall" in Diane Kelder, *Stuart Davis* (New York: Praeger, 1971), facing p. 116. Music quotation from James Johnson Sweeny, *Stuart Davis* (New York: Museum of Modern Art, 1945), p. 8. See also John Lucas, "The Fine Art Jive of Stuart Davis," *Arts*, 31 (September, 1957), 32–37.

[46]Over the years, in the *JEMF Quarterly*, I have named friends who have shared material for my studies of folk music and art. Here, I thank Harlan Daniel for criticism of an initial draft of this essay.

Part 4:
Individual Singers and Creators

Analyzing the Revival: the Influence of Jeannie Robertson

Herschel Gower

Jeannie Robertson was discovered in 1953 by Hamish Henderson and was at once acclaimed by Alan Lomax as "a monumental figure in twentieth-century folksong."[1] In *Folk Revival,* published four years after her death in 1975, Fred Woods called her "the acknowledged Queen of traditional singers."[2] When Jeannie first encountered the world beyond the Travellers' campfire or left the crumbling, cold-water flat in the Gallowgate, Aberdeen, she made no excursions into self-pity as she talked about her early life as a Traveller child and a wayfaring hawker selling from door to door.[3] She also liked to talk about how she learned songs from her mother, Maria Stewart, a singer admired among the Travelling folk, and how she took pride in the singing and piping of her relatives in the Croall, Stewart, and Robertson clans. Jeannie recalled her own apprenticeship that began at age six by the blazing campfires at night. Her recorded reminiscences date from that spring afternoon when the Scottish folksong scholar Hamish Henderson knocked on Jeannie's door at 21 Causeway End and she sang into the microphone of his tape recorder for the first time. Henderson was quick to see that the dark-eyed, heavy woman of 45 — with hair so black that it cast blue highlights — was one of Scotland's greatest bearers of tradition. Maurice Fleming has noted that the tapes made during the next decade on which Jeannie gives "vivid accounts of her experiences, all told in her splendid, vigorous tongue [are] almost certainly the longest record of spoken Scots in existence."[4]

Before her discovery and until the time of her death in 1975, Jeannie was such a commanding figure and beloved matriarch in the Scottish Revival that her full influence is hardly to be calculated. It is no more possible to take a yardstick and measure Burns's stature as a popular poet than to take a tape measure and determine Jeannie's

breadth of influence as a singer. Not only did she receive and inter-
pret a great legacy of traditional song that had shifted to the Travellers from the population at large, she presented what she had
inherited in such a way that even before Henderson arrived she had
earned, like her mother and grandmother, the approval of "her
ain folk."

Soon after her discovery Jeannie became a national figure in Scotland through appearances before societies, folk clubs, and on radio
and occasionally television. By 1960 she had drawn the attention of
ballad scholars from around the world, including Bertrand Bronson, who began publishing her songs in volume 3 of *The Traditional
Tunes of the Child Ballads* (Professor Bronson heard her sing in
person at least once: one morning at 11 o'clock Jeannie was presented in an Edinburgh Festival program sponsored by the Saltire
Society at Gladstone's Land, 1967, and he was in the audience). In
the course of the twenty years that marked her life as a public singer,
Jeannie mothered a whole generation of revivalists who were searching for a strong leader and a solid traditional base.

Jeannie proved to be that leader with authority, and the first base
was her house in the Gallowgate; they then followed her to the
prefab at 22 Montgomery Road, and finally to the council house
at 90 Hilton Road, Woodside, Aberdeen. These houses she shared
with her husband Donald Higgins, her brother-in-law Isaac, her
daughter Lizzie, and finally such young singers as Ray Fisher and
Andy Hunter and the many others who came to listen and learn.
"God forgive me," Jeannie would say to callers, "I never put naebody
awa' frae my door in my life—let him be rich or poor." Thus the
hospitable matriarch was a bearer of tradition in the fullest and
most complete sense: in performances she shared what she had
received; she passed the songs on by teaching them to a new generation face-to-face; she inspired her "bairns" to use their own talents
to revitalize and reshape the Scots tradition of song. During a period
of Revival, she was the chief cornerstone.[5]

We know all too well how scholars, critics, collectors, editors, and
singers are sometimes at odds about how to handle a folk legacy or
a substantial body of traditional materials. The various attitudes,
compromises, and shortcomings of practitioners since the turn of
the century have been briefly noted by Woods in the first chapter
of *Folk Revival*.[6] Theorists in folklore have so often disagreed about
such problems as transcription, notation, and interpretation that it
is hardly necessary to review their arguments here. Instead, we can
begin with the notion that a traditional singer, the inheritor of a
body of words and music fostered and handed down by his society
and accepted by his cultural milieu, wakes up one morning with a
sudden recognition of the value of the legacy. He may be jolted
into this awareness by the outside world: the knock on his door by

a professional folklorist with tape recorder; hearing his songs in different versions sung on radio or records by other singers; chancing upon his songs in print. Few traditional singers these days are exempt from confrontations with the outside world and none is, in turn, entirely free from its influences.

Whatever the causes that bring about the conscious discovery, the *dedicated* traditionalist will try to take stock and make the most of his legacy. But how does he go about making the most of it? What relevant responsibilities must he assume? How long is he expected to bear the burden of tradition, folk custom, and the "pure" art itself? How far should he go to preserve and keep viable a tradition that is either threatened or fast on the decline? In other words, how much tradition is the tradition-bearer called upon to go on bearing?

Although these questions have been rather bluntly presented, we shall move on to Jeannie Robertson's tapes, for they are rich in autobiographical detail and we can search them for some possible answers. We shall also make use of interviews with younger singers who talk about the Scots tradition in song and their relationship to it and who give a variety of testimonials about Jeannie as mentor and tradition-bearer.[7]

Jeannie liked to narrate, with embellishments, the details leading up to her discovery in 1953. It is a story she did not seem to tire of telling:

> I heard Hamish Henderson and Alan Lomax on the wireless [the year before] speakin' aboot auld sangs. But I never seed 'em. We never seed folks like that. I was puttin' oot the supper when I heard them discussin' the sangs. So I said to Donald and Isaac: "If those men only kent to come up to Cassie End, I cud give 'em a guid few auld sangs."

The conversation on the radio indicated to Jeannie for the first time that the British Broadcasting Corporation and its listeners might like to hear the songs of a Traveller's child, hawker, babysitter, and housewife. The next year Henderson was in the Castlegate of Aberdeen asking tradesmen and Travellers in the stalls about the singers among them. It was a well-known trader by the name of Bobby Hutchison who directed him to Jeannie in the Gallowgate. Jeannie had spent that day keeping her sister-in-law's two children and they had gotten on her nerves to such an extent that she tried to put Henderson off. She wanted to "fa' doon to my bed" and rest before singing.

> But after the older bairn had sung several of his Auntie Jeannie's sangs, Hamish stayed on to tea and I sung for him steady till two o'clock in the morning. I never got my rest—nae rest that day, you see. And that's the God's truth if I never rise from this chair.

Like all major collectors, Henderson was willing to remain "in the field" and keep fresh tapes on the recorder as long as his subjects were willing to sing. In the following months he was responsible for many ceilidhs in the little tenement, standing the crowd to refreshments as the recordings went on. New singers, pipers, fiddlers, and instrumentalists would appear as Jeannie's house became a center for trading songs and lore. The two worlds had met at "Cassie End."

Besides singing hundreds of lyric songs, scores of broadside and twenty or more Child ballads, Jeannie recited for Henderson a poem called "Cruel Fate" which she said "Robert Burns had written to his Jean when he was planning to go to the West Indies." She had found the words first in what she called "a Burns auld, auld song book — a big auld song book, lang, lang ago, when I was jeest a lassiekie. But there was no air attached till it. So therefore I put a hauntin' kind o' air till it mysel'." Then she sang "Cruel Fate" with the tune she had devised for it. Though there were slight variations, the words were essentially those of Burns as printed in Volume 2 of *The Scots Musical Museum,* with the note that they are to be sung to the tune "The Northern Lass." Thus the printed word had moved Jeannie as a "lassiekie" to respond with her own tune.[8] She had memorized the print and had gone on to create something of her own beyond it.

Although essentially not a student of song books and the printed word, Jeannie would occasionally resort to them to fill in forgotten verses or those she had failed to learn from her mother. She had also been attracted in her early years to the gramophone and had learned a few Harry Lauder songs, some half-dozen Music Hall pieces, and a handful of sentimental ballads from America. But neither print nor the gramophone altered the basic repertoire that she had received orally from family and friends. Nor did modernism in the guises of Tin Pan Alley, jazz, Hollywood movies, or the London musicals of the 20s and 30s change her singing style, which she had adapted from her mother's:

> I sing verra like my mither, but she hudnae sae high a voice as what I have. She was a guid singer and a *true* singer, bit nae sae high — down lower. Yes, ma mither sung a lot o' sangs — three times mair fit I can mind. Three times mair.

Still a child during World War I, Jeannie remembered that Maria spent sleepless nights worrying about her second husband James Higgins and her two sons who were away bearing arms:

> Her and her brother used to set up till aboot two in the mornin' and sing the auld sangs together, and I used to listen. I started to learn them at that time. The auld sangs went frae mooth tae mooth in these days.

Here Jeannie is noting, of course, that the songs her mother and uncle sang were not only a cultural ornament for the family but served a practical function. Because they were oral and in practice communal, the songs amounted to an ordered act, a literal, vocal response to the confusion of the world.

One is inclined to wonder if Maria's emotional intensity or the heroic style of the Travellers could ever have been achieved away from the campsites in the Scottish glens. Yet Jeannie at her own fireside maintained both the intensity and the style. She could project the epic style of her forebears when she sang at concerts, in clubs, and before the microphone. "When I sing a big battle song like 'The Battle o' Harlaw,' I see every sword giein' clash for clash," she insisted.

It was finally style that marked Jeannie most as a great traditional singer, whether one heard her first in person or on a sound recording. As a musical journalist, Fred Woods has described what most laymen hear and find immediately arresting: "a voice of *power* and *purity* such as has been given to few other folksingers."[9] But what were the stylistic techniques that brought such wide acclaim? Andy Hunter of Glasgow studied at Aberdeen University so that he could be near Jeannie and Donald and learn about singing and piping from them on weekends. As a young man of twenty he absorbed Jeannie's style, taking up the pipes also under Donald's and Isaac's tutelage. He then began to write his own Scots songs while working on an honors degree in French. Hunter points out the abilities Jeannie had as an interpretive singer, and how she could sing a story that would hold a modern audience for as long as fifteen minutes. Hunter was a careful student of her techniques:

> Besides believing in the "truth" of the narrative, she knew how to dramatize the action and dialogue. She would place emphasis on certain phrases and thus alter the pace—slow it down or heighten it — and avoid the monotony of a steady, predictable beat. In other words, she tricked her listeners into going along with her narrative by changing tempo. And she caught all the foot-tappers out—as many as two or three times in a single stanza.[10]

If the foot-tappers were caught off guard, so were the accompanists. Most of them gave up and let Jeannie maintain her own rhythmic patterns. Norman Buchan, formerly a school-teacher in Glasgow and now a Labour M. P. in the House of Commons, recalled an incident when Jeannie was staying with his family and recording some of the songs for her first LP. It was suggested that guitar embellishment would make the record commercially more attractive. Norman and his wife Janey knew the guitarist Josh MacCrae and invited him to the next session. An admirer of Jeannie and sympathetic to the task in hand, MacCrae and his guitar were nevertheless a distraction. As Buchan described the episode:

> Jeannie was an individualist and not used to accompaniment. Things did not go well. But the problem was finally solved "backstage" when the producer put Josh in the cupboard with a mike and earphones and closed the door on him while Jeannie sang outside, unfettered. It was literally background accompaniment, with Josh playing only an interval filler here and there.[11]

Finally, as regards Jeannie's style and the hold she had on listeners because of it, I quote James Porter, who has spent several years studying Jeannie's songs:

> A great traditional singer manifests perhaps a greater degree of difference in actual style from his or her peers than do art-singers, by virtue of the unfettered nature of the material. One might therefore note the following characteristic traits in Jeannie Robertson's style: (1) an expansiveness of delivery that is nevertheless tightly controlled in the length of phrases; (2) fluidity of rhythm, which appears in two distinct forms—as an externalized pulse or quasi-regular tempo; and as an evasive, complex, internal pulse which makes heavy demands on the listener's rhythmic sense; (3) an idiomatic enunciation, with speech-rhythms and dialectal peculiarities native to the North-East of Scotland; (4) a wealth—in this closely associated with (1) and (3)—of expansive *portamenti* and *appoggiature;* (5) a pervasive finesse in phrasing that is the hall mark of a unique musicality; and (6) a powerful sense of drama and characterization.

Not only has Porter pinpointed the elements that characterize Jeannie's style, he has published meticulous notations that reflect its intricacies and subtleties.[12]

Although only outlined above, the repertoire that Jeannie Robertson recorded has been rightly acclaimed as one of the most extensive of the century. She became aware of its importance almost at once, as evidenced by her many recordings for the School of Scottish Studies and her long interviews with Henderson. We go back to the question of "handling" tradition and "insuring" its continuity. How much could she do, as an individual, to preserve and bequeath? How guarded should she be? How open? What kind of formal protection was there in the matter of copyright laws, legal contracts, fees and royalties? Then the inevitable: was there any money to be had from it? Travellers are traders, swappers, bargainers.

The house at Causeway End became a school for young singers, collectors, scholars, and social anthropologists because Jeannie's generosity kept the door open. Accompanied by my friend Russell Hart from Harvard, I went to call on Jeannie one evening in September 1953. The house, its atmosphere, and the ceilidh which was put on for us that evening is remembered as a distinctive cultural moment. We entered directly from the street into a small front bedroom—the large bed to the right filling half the room, and Isaac's pipes sprawled on the bed. We moved straight ahead with the bed on our right to the kitchen. The sink was in the far left corner of a room about 10' by 12'—one light bulb hanging from the ceiling center—the stove on the left wall. A window on the back wall was open at the top. I remember this, because at midnight Isaac was persuaded to get his pipes and play, and he did, and I eyed the open window wondering who in that crowded neighborhood could sleep.

Jeannie stood at the back left corner, her right hand on the sink as she sang. Who else sang? Wee Willie, I think. And then there were long, ardent, and for us very sophisticated debates about which tune fitted "Gypsy Laddie" best. Call these "aesthetic" if you will. But they were alternating with Jeannie's careful accounts of the people of the stories: "The Gypsy Laddie" was *known,* and Jeannie had spoken to people who had been familiar with the family long ago. They were authenticated in the way James Hogg authenticated his tales—he had a real if indirect link with the persons involved, and he *knew the places.* Specific place always has unique authority in Scottish lore; it gives "truth."

But Jeannie had a splendid mobility of attitude too. She could have no sense of "historic" time—so that "long ago" included half a century and five centuries without distinction. Yet she could always tease and trick collectors. I remember the sly way she had of recalling how she handled "Aalun" Lomax, how superbly patronizing she could be in speaking of him and Hamish Henderson and others. Then the marvellous trick of singing us a song she thought we might not have heard—and afterwards admitting that she had composed it the day before while doing the washing-up. That is the Burns analogy: fierce loyalty to authentic tradition, and at the same time passing off her own as traditional songs—yet not realizing that they were authentic because it was she who made them.

The evening was a true ceilidh—most people contributed their song, their playing, or their part to the debate. Jeannie stood solidly planted in the corner or leaning on the mantel: the matriarch, in control, sipping a half teacup of whisky throughout the evening. We also recalled the Buchan fiddler with no teeth; yet how he could play! And the wee man, dressed in dirty working clothes, who was the soul of dignity and concerned hospitality. Finally, Hart and I both came away thinking that the evening was arranged for our visit, and that these people had not all been together for several months. The city and city lives kept them apart. We were thus present for a rare and vital renourishing of tradition—and not just song, but story and debate as well. As we walked back through the great grey streets of Aberdeen at 1 a.m. we knew that this was, indeed, one of the unique nights of our life because never have song and story had such force as for the group with whom we sat.[13]

Although the Travellers sometimes lapsed into Cant that evening and told jokes in a dialect neither Hart nor I could decipher, they were obviously flattered by our interest in their songs. They were remarkably open as well as curious about us. In a country where legal whisky is so heavily taxed that it is beyond the reach of the working man, our contributions in that line were almost reverently accepted. Nor were we armed with tape recorders to make away with their songs, however much we would have liked a record of the evening. They thought they could trust us, and they could, and after all we had come "a lang mile" to get there.

We knew then that Jeannie's first use of the legacy was keeping it alive in her own home, among her own folk, and among appreciative visitors. Second, she had agreed to let the tapes made by Henderson become part of her first LP. These eventually brought her festival, club, radio, and a few television appearances. She began to meet other traditional singers on such occasions as these and the Scottish Revival was well on its way by the end of the 1950s.[14]

In performance, Jeannie's classic (or "big") ballads were delivered magnificently. She was particularly successful with "Son Davit" (Child 13, "Edward") and was not beyond learning more, especially when audiences kept asking for the obvious—"Lord Randal." Yet she learned it only when she found a version that she liked or which met her standards:

> When I was a bairn an air caught my fancy first. I learned the air first, and I think if you get the air o' a sang, the words are nae ill to learn. The words or the idea would come second. You know how long it took me to learn "Lord Donald"? It's the longest sang I've got. I learned it from a chap in one night's time. But it wisnae only because o' the air wi' it. It appealed to me as a guid story.[15]

Thus when in her fifties she added to her repertoire, putting together complete versions from fragments, and came to talk about Professor Child and the "big ballads."

Andy Hunter recalls that she often had more than one tune for a ballad and would make a conscious choice about which to sing:

> She had two tunes for "Little Matty Groves"—a big one and a short, thumpy one. Once at a festival when someone requested her to sing "Matty" at the opening of the program before she was warmed up, she said, "Dammit, I'll no' start off with my big tune first and be here five minutes longer!" So she sang the short one first. That's how she built up a program to a climax. The big guns came last when she was all warmed up and the audience completely with her, expectant.

Students in Scotland's first folk club, stimulated by teachers like Norman Buchan, Maurice Blythman, and Ewan MacColl, invited Jeannie to come to Glasgow in the autumn of 1953 to sing at a ceilidh they were staging. They passed the songs around, still the mark of a good evening, everyone contributing his piece. Among the members were two young singers, Ray Fisher and Andy Hunter, who were being educated in the city, although Hunter had worked in a farming community in Dumbartonshire during school holidays. Both had talent and had been struck by Jeannie's voice on the tapes played to them earlier by Hamish Henderson. Ray Fisher retains a vivid description of her first meeting with Jeannie and what it ultimately led to in her own career:

> Norman Buchan was trying to show Jeannie and the other older singers what was happening in Glasgow at the time and he asked me to sing. Very sheepishly, I sang "Jeannie My Dear, Will You Marry Me?" Jeannie Robertson came up to me afterwards and she said to me, "That's one of my songies you're singing," she says, "and you're no' takin' it oot richt," she says . . . and I said, "Ooh." To "tak' it oot" means to vary the emphasis and timing; thus the implication was that I was not singing it right, and she proceeded to illustrate her proper fashion. And Jeannie sang the entire song after I'd sung it . . . talk about up-staging! Nevertheless, as a result of that she said, "I think you'd better come to Aberdeen," and I went and stayed with her for about six weeks. I learned a tremendous amount about Jeannie's songs, her singing, and Jeannie herself.[16]

With her readiness to "come out to people," Jeannie broke the barriers between rural and urban, traditional and revival, and was able to awaken enthusiasm and understanding. She made urban singers like Ray and her brother Archie feel at home with the tradition. This was the beginning of a collaboration and a lasting teacher-pupil relationship. Ray learned a fragment from Jeannie called "Ainst Upon a Time" that had only three verses; soon Ray had composed five others to fill in the story and make the narrative coherent. Then they both began to sing the expanded version and the whole was later published.[17] What was handed down as a lyric had now been transformed into a ballad with the development of the narrative line, and the traditional idiom had been maintained as a result of the collaboration.[18] By that time Jeannie had watched her pupil come a long way—from a teenage singer of American skiffle music like "The Wreck of the Old 97" and the songs of Lonnie Donnegan to a reaffirmation of Scots song.

Those who heard Ray Fisher sing under Jeannie's influence would say to her: "Yes, that's one of Jeannie's songs. I recognize it not only because I know Jeannie sings it, but by the way you are singing it. You have learned it from Jeannie Robertson." The impact of Jeannie —repertoire, style, and personality—was enormous. "Yes," Ray would reply, "you mimic because you admire. Any student will take guidelines from the master." But those who hear Ray Fisher today agree that she has put her own mark on the materials.

> You adapt and find a bit of yourself instead of just a reproduction of the original. I cannot forget Jeannie's singing, but I sing the songs my way now. Jeannie was such a proficient artist that she communicated the material, the sensitivity and the understanding she had. I would like to think I retain some of this in my singing . . . but I am not a traditional singer; I am a singer of traditional songs. I interpret what traditional singers have done, the difference being that the traditional singers have their songs handed down within the family.[18]

Ray has thus used her talents to study a tradition, adapt it, and go her own way as an individual performer. She is as much an individualist as Jeannie would have wanted one of her own children to be.

As a matter of fact, Jeannie's first child and only son, James ("Jeemsie") Higgins, appears often in the taped memoirs, for he was a boy with promise as a singer. It is clear that Jeannie never fully recovered from his death at the age of eight. She would say about him, "he came into this world on a mornin' o' strong sun and dieit in the Christmas week lyin' blind wi' meningitis — wis eight year and seven month — and wis buriet the day before Hogmanay. He wis big fir his age and ivir sae bonnie — till the last he wis ivir sae bonnie." Lizzie Higgins, only 15 months younger than her brother, later spoke of the mother-son relationship in terms of the music. Donald was a fine piper, widely acknowledged and respected. When Jeemsie was born Donald looked at his son's fingers for the sign of a good piper. According to Lizzie:

> . . . the clanspeople looked at their newborn baby boys to see if they had the mark of great pipers. My father had the two misshaped crookit crannies, and the misshapen second fingers as well·. . . . It's a rare gift o' God.[19]

But her brother's fingers were straight and Jeemsie took not so much to the pipes as to the songs.

> My brother . . . he always asked for — "The Gallowa' Hills" . . . 'e wouldn't go to sleep without his ballad sung . . . [later] they didn't have to preach on my brither to sing . . . He was a bonnie singer. He sung like Jeannie. Traditional ballad, classical ballad style though he was only a wee boy . . . An' I'd be staundin' back, I was always the shy one, like.[20]

Over the years Lizzie, having been constantly exposed to her family's songs — Donald was also a fine singer — nevertheless acquired a repertoire that she is not too shy to sing today. Until she was seven she was competing with her brother. For the next two decades she was in competition with her mother. But as those close to Lizzie know, she is now, at age 50, a superb singer with a style of her own.

Jean Redpath, Lizzie's contemporary, is another of the younger singers who can look back to the beginning of her career and acknowledge the profound influence of Jeannie Robertson. In 1959 she was studying English at the University of Edinburgh, had sung "respectable music like Brahms as a child," and was not singing at all till she heard Hamish Henderson lecture on Scottish folksong and play some of Jeannie's tapes. Those sessions called up songs Redpath had heard as a child in Fife. Then Jeannie appeared at the students' folk club. Jean Redpath met the woman behind the voice and was greatly taken with her:

> She was always in command. Her age and personal maturity were two of the factors. If she had been a woman in her twenties or thirties, it would probably not have been as easy—the command—but she was mature, she knew exactly who she was. She was very sure of the material she was dealing with. It never occurred to her to apologize for speaking broad Scots. That generation is probably the last that will ever feel that way. As a result I think they had an edge on us in their ability to present the material without ever analyzing it, without wondering whether it had any "application." It had a very immediate and direct application for them, and that's why it comes over so powerfully.[21]

Jean Redpath studied Jeannie's tapes and records and listened to her at ceilidhs when no one moved a hair during a long ballad. She regrets never having gone to Aberdeen, as did Ray Fisher and Andy Hunter, to study with Jeannie at home. However, her career has taken her throughout Britain and often to the United States for lecture recitals, recording sessions, and university fellowships. Besides many albums, she has recorded all the songs of Robert Burns. In her perception of stylistic differences between Jeannie's and Lizzie's singing, Jean Redpath found that mother and daughter revealed significant personal attitudes to the songs:

> I will go so far as to call Jeannie the Queen of Tragedy and Lizzie the Mistress of the Poignant. Jeannie came in at a very high frequency and hit all the tragic chords. Lizzie will move me to tears faster. It's the poignancy. With Lizzie there's more of the personal, I suppose. It's a matter of levels. Each style has something emotionally moving to recommend it.[22]

Perhaps another way of comparing the two styles is to say that Lizzie's is in large measure derived from her interest in and inclination towards the pipes. The melodies are often close to her father's pipe tunes and she believes "pipes is one of the most beautiful music a person can listen till. They're soulful in a lament . . . they bring your soul out o' ye. The pipin' and the singin' in my voice becomes as one."[23] Lizzie's accounts of family history point to Jeannie's expectation that Jeemsie would learn the old songs—that she would teach them to him as Maria had taught her. Another such opportunity would come many years later in the person of young Andy Hunter, who has already been quoted and who in many respects filled the role of the son Jeannie and Donald had lost.

Although born in Glasgow, Hunter experienced a semi-rural environment as a boy: "In the country I was provided with a ready, discerning audience at barn dances, Hogmanay parties, and ceilidhs. The older people knew bothy ballads. My grandfather was a good Scots speaker using Ayrshire dialect and wrote poems celebrating local events." His grandfather was a great admirer of Burns's lyrics and his father was a trained singer. Andy inherited a good voice from both but little in the way of traditional song. The Glasgow folk clubs sparked his interest, particularly with the appearances of traditionalists like Jeannie, Jimmie McBeath, and the Stewarts of Blair. After finishing school, Hunter went as an apprentice into an accountant's office because he was not sure at the time that he was interested in a university degree. But after a lot of self-searching, he decided to apply for admission to Aberdeen because it was the most Scottish of the four major universities, and having already visited Jeannie and Donald, he would use his spare time studying Scottish tradition among the folk who had somehow retained the old ways and traditions longest. He explains his dual education in this way:

> Jeannie's people had a basic understanding of life which I hadn't met, an understanding of human nature, of people, and this came through in the songs, the stories, and the music which went on in the prefab in Hayton. These people would communicate instantaneously knowledge of other human beings which, as I said, I hadn't been able to find anywhere else. Jeannie taught me as a young singer to translate some of this into my singing and into my music. And if she has left me with anything it's this magnificent gift of recognizing authentic music, folk music, and recognizing the human qualities in it.[24]

Hunter said that although he never actually lived with Donald and Jeannie, "for four years I was never out of the house." The adopted son got to know the members of the Traveller community, caught on to Cant, learned about their daily lives, their codes, their ways of trading, dealing—all this in addition to their songs. He went with them to ceilidhs, was accepted as a promising piper and singer, and was encouraged to sing his own songs to a ready audience. "By the way," Andy reminds us, "Bobby Hutchison, a prosperous Traveller, bought me the first set of quality pipes I was ever to own.

Bobby very generously made me this gift as I was a penniless student with very little means."

In 1964 Hunter accompanied Donald, Isaac, "Wee Froggie" (Jeannie's nephew), and others of the clan to the Braemar Games, which include a competition for pipers, an event Travellers habitually throng to. The night before there was an incident at a bar in Aboyne. Out of the incident, which Hunter observed at close hand, he made a ballad which he entitled "Aboyne Games" and which he later sang to the great approval of Jeannie. It seems that Isaac Higgins, Jeannie's brother-in-law, well known as a piper and a recognized authority on the Scottish bagpipe, was asked by one Alec McPhee to judge the quality of McPhee's pipe chanter when they met in a bar. Isaac began to try it out, obliging McPhee and trying to form an opinion. But there were Stewarts from Lumphanan in the pub as well and they had not only competed in the games that day, they had lost. As a result they were badly disgruntled, retreating to the bar when the rain continued; nor did the drinking let up. We take up Hunter's ballad text here:

The Stewarts are a fighting clan, Prince Charlie's sons and true,
Wi' the Prince's smile, and the Prince's guile, and the Prince's
    pouted mou'.
Weel kent roon aa the countryside for lads tae drink and fecht
Oh they never think twice or tak advice as tae wha is in richt.

Wan o them, the faither, took the chanter in his hand
An' said it wisnae worth a damn, the warst in aa the land.
But Alec McPhee he cudna see his chanter handled thus
And he asked of him quite civilly if he wid stop his fuss.

But the Stewarts three, they grabbed McPhee while the laddie stood
    his ground,
And splattered their blood aroon the wa's as their faces he did pound.
But they cracked his heid doon aff the bar and left him on the floor.
Aye, and in their fear they grabbed their gear and ran ootside the
    door.

But my friend he took the laddie's pipes and gied the drones a tune
An' through the rain the bagpipe's strain wis heard intil the room.
Alec McPhee he joined us then, his bluid aa doon his face,
An he played us "John MacFadyen" and he marched it pace for pace.

Next day the Clan McPhee were tellt, and they cam' frae near far,
And thirty stout and stalwart lads assembled at Braemar.
But the Stewarts did not turn up that day so terrible wis their fear,
The first time they had missed the games for fully fifty year.[25]

When Andy first sang "Aboyne Games" to Jeannie, Donald, and Isaac (Isaac being "my friend" of the narrative), the ballad was greeted with much laughter. Jeannie even went so far as to urge Andy to go to Lumphanan to sing it to the branch of Stewarts who had failed to show up at the Braemar Games when the McPhees were out in numbers to settle with them (once tempers were cooled off it was an incident they could all laugh about). The point here is that a ballad had been created, words and music were put together as a result of a fight over the quality of a set of pipes. The ballad ends with sage advice:

> But noo my sang is ended, and I'll hiv ye bear in mind,
> The Stewarts are not all like this; there's plenty guid and kind.
> But drink gings roon a bodie's heid in gills and quarts and pints,
> But drunk or sober, never misca anither gadgie's pipes.

Whatever you do, never "misca" or belittle another man's pipes. That's breaking the code; it's a violation of manners. The situation called for a simple Scottish response like "Ach, they're nae aa bad." And there the matter might have rested. What remains with Andy Hunter is the image of the bleeding, battered Alec McPhee standing outside the pub after closing hours playing his beloved pipes in the pouring rain after the Stewarts had fled. The last note was his, bloody though he was.

From Jeannie and the Travellers in Aberdeen young Andy also learned that Jeannie's people were known as the summer walkers, those who had homes and a roof over their heads in winter, who carried on their trades in town and went forth to sell and camp and enjoy the countryside in spring and summer. Hunter learned from them a variant of the chivalric code. A Traveller like a medieval knight must avenge a wrong. Jeannie's mother felt she had been insulted by a woman called 'The Terror of the North' and it was necessary to do physical battle with the woman only two days after Maria had given birth to her fourth child. Travellers fought not only with "scaldies," or non-Travellers, but with yokels, country people, and also with their own kind when the code was violated. Honor and revenge were understood and upheld.

Donald Higgins died of cancer on July 25, 1971, after a long and painful illness. That same year Jeannie suffered three strokes and was left with considerable impairment of speech. She did not sing again in public. When collectors brought their machines to her door, she talked about her songs and hummed an occasional tune. Lizzie usually supplied answers to the questions when her mother's memory faltered. As always, the household was hospitable. Isaac would rise silently, disappear for a while, then return with tea and sandwiches.

Among those who called regularly was young Stanley Robertson, Jeannie's nephew, the son of her older brother Willie. He remembered his aunt when he was a boy at the campsites along Deeside: "She was always dressed in a red cardigan with a brooch at the neck.

She had beautiful black hair which she wore high, with ringlets coming down over her forehead. She was a very attractive, Gypsy-like woman." As Stanley grew older and became more committed to music, the greater was his admiration for his aunt. He came to know also what he calls "her awesome side," for he learned she could be critical and demanding:

> If I was asking her for a ballad—asking her to teach me something—she was very, very strict—very very hard. "All right, laddie, I'll learn you this song, but I want you to sing it right, sing it proper, and sing it real." If you did not sing it *exactly* as she told you, you were in trouble. She would say, "Noo, listen again and listen careful." By the time she was through she'd put you through.

It was during the final year of her life that the relationship between nephew and aunt grew closer, the mutual respect stronger, the ties of blood and song greater than ever:

> Her last song she taught me was called "The Moon Shone on my Bed Last Night." She was very ill. This was about six or seven weeks before she died. I went by her house on a cold day—it was January—and she said I want to teach you this song. Her speech was very erratic and her health was very bad. Her legs and arms were very sore because of the gangrene. The song begins:
>
> > The moon shone on my bed last night
> > No rest then could I find . . .
>
> I think she knew it would not be very long before the end, but she never gave up teaching, however ill and weak she was.[26]

After many weeks of suffering Jeannie died of complications resulting from chronic diabetes on March 14, 1975. Hamish Henderson and John MacQueen, Director of the School of Scottish Studies, notified her friends abroad by cable and her clansmen laid her to rest with honor and affection. Among the mourners were her "bairns": her daughter Lizzie, her nephew Stanley, Andy Hunter, Ray Fisher, Arthur Argo, and of course Hamish Henderson. A few hours before she died Andy Hunter sat at her bedside and told her what a tribute Lizzie's record, *Princess of the Thistle,* was to her. Jeannie replied firmly, some of the old sparkle left: "And I still have sangs mysel' for them to tak doon. Many mair, Andy."

*   *   *   *   *   *

This essay began with words of praise for Jeannie Robertson—with terms like "monumental" and "heroic" and "queen of folksong." Then we asked how she was able to extend the tradition and pass on her songs to another generation. The many testimonials show how she went about it, how she expressed her "critical" values, how she extended her legacy.

In one of the many sessions with Hamish Henderson, Jeannie looked back to a conversation with her mother and a talk they had had about the songs:

> Ma mither said t' me before she died: "Sing my songs tae everybody," she says, "I want the warld t' hear them." I wisnae gotten [known] at that time. I says, "What wey am I gaen t' let the warld hear them, mither? I'm askit t' sing at nae place, but the hoose here. Or maybe amang wir ain people." Funny idea, she had, and she said, "Will ye sing my songs, min', Jeannie?" she says. And I promised her that day. I said, "I'll sing them to the best o' my ability—whenever anybody requires t' hear them."

And Jeannie kept that promise—not only to the past but to the future. In her 67 years of singing, talking, tutoring, entertaining, haranguing, sometimes playing games with collectors and scholars, but finally embodying the tradition, she became not only "Scotland's Jeannie" but "the world's Jeannie." Her bairns remain firm in their expressions of kinship and devotion.

NOTES

[1] Letter to Hamish Henderson, December 31, 1953.

[2] *Folk Revival: The Rediscovery of a National Music* (Poole [Dorset]: Blandford Press, 1979), p. 26.

[3] David Murison, Aberdonian and former Editor of the *Scottish National Dictionary*, remembers a young Jeannie with pack in the streets of Aberdeen. Personal communication.

[4] *Scots Magazine*, April 1965.

[5] Jeannie Robertson and her songs are treated in four articles published by Herschel Gower and James Porter in *Scottish Studies*, vols. 12 (1968), 113-26 (by Herschel Gower); 14 (1970), 35-58; 16 (1972), 139-59; 21 (1977), 55-103. A book-length study of her life and songs is now in preparation. Her nephew, Stanley Robertson, is quick to point out that "the folk revival does not affect the Travellers because we had always kept alive these songs. The revival was among non-Travellers." Personal communication.

[6] Woods, *Folk Revival*, ibid.

[7] Quotations from Jeannie Robertson are taken from taped interviews made by Hamish Henderson for the School of Scottish Studies, others by James Porter and Herschel Gower, and some are from unrecorded conversations from 1955 to 1973.

[8] The tune is reprinted in "Jeannie Robertson: Portrait of a Traditional Singer," *Scottish Studies*, 12 (1969), 120.

[9] Woods, *Folk Revival*, ibid.

[10] Interview, Edinburgh, June 27, 1979. Hunter illustrates these techniques admirably by singing two songs Jeannie had taught him: "New Chapelle" and "Twa Recruitin' Sergeants."

[11] Interview with Norman Buchan, M.P., Glasgow, June 24, 1979.

[12] *Scottish Studies*, 14 (1970), 37-38. See also *Scottish Studies*, 21 (1977), 55-103.

[13] Russell Hart and Herschel Gower, recollections, January 12, 1979.

[14]She was 48 when the first LP was issued. It, along with the dozen records which followed, brought scant returns in royalties. Her club appearances netted her fees that were usually low. After ten years she began, quite rightly, to feel exploited. Through the efforts of Norman Buchan she was awarded the M.B.E. on the occasion of her sixtieth birthday by the Queen and received it at Buckingham Palace. The Scottish Home Service of the BBC honored her in June of that year with a program, "Oor Jeannie," produced by Arthur Argo (great-grandson of the folksong collector Gavin Greig), who was also responsible for many of her folk club engagements.

[15]*Scottish Studies,* 12 (1968), 121.

[16]Ray Fisher, "A Tremendous Sort of Feeling: An Interview by Howard Glasser, October 3, 1973, Assonet, Massachusetts," *Sing Out,* 22, 6 (1974), 2–8.

[17]*Chapbook,* 3, 1 (1966).

[18]Cf. Hamish Henderson's liner notes to *The Muckle Sangs: Classic Scots Ballads* (Scottish Tradition 5: Tangent TGNM 119/D, 1975), 5. Henderson points out how Jeannie used the tune of the bothy song, "The Rovin' Ploughboy," as that for the text of "The Gypsy Laddie," received orally from her own folk, thus transforming a bothy lyric song which had already drawn verbal elements from "The Gypsy Laddie" back into a ballad. The point is, of course, that traditional singers have a fluid conception of song recreation and of the generic forms that scholars demarcate as "ballad" and "lyric."

[19]Fisher, "A Tremendous Sort of Feeling," 2–3.

[20]Stephanie Smith, "A Study of Lizzie Higgins as a Transitional Figure in the Oral Tradition of Northeast Scotland" (M. Litt. Thesis, University of Edinburgh, 1975), p. 22.

[21]Ibid., pp. 22–24.

[22]Interview with Jean Redpath; Edinburgh, December 27, 1978.

[23]Smith, "A Study of Lizzie Higgins," p. 53.

[24]Interview with Andy Hunter, June 27, 1979.

[25]The full text of "Aboyne Games," including music, with several of Hunter's other original songs, appeared in *Chapbook,* 5, 2 (1968). Hunter was a regular contributor to this journal and wrote a brief but important essay on songwriting in modern Scotland. His version of "King Fareweel" is included in *A Collection of Scots Songs* (Edinburgh: School of Scottish Studies, 1972), p. 5. His "Baron James McPhate" is printed in Norman Buchan's *101 Scottish Songs* (Glasgow: Collins, 1962).

[26]Letter from Stanley Robertson to Herschel Gower, July 17, 1979.

Joe Smith: The Poet as Outlaw

Edward D. Ives

Satirical songs are frequently condemned to death by their own vitality. Composed as they are for local audiences thoroughly familiar with their subject matter, they capitalize on that familiarity by being oblique and elliptical rather than direct and narrative and by being full of allusions to local jokes, legends, characters and places, all of which make them immediately and uproariously understandable to those in the know but often almost incomprehensible to outsiders. Furthermore, as soon as the events themselves become old hat, the songs about them tend to become old hat too. Years later, in response to questionings by a junketing folklorist, they may be recalled either by elderly singers who just never were given to forgetting songs of any kind or by community members of an antiquarian turn of mind for whom such songs are reminiscent of old times (frequently, of course, the antiquarian and the singer turn out to be one and the same person). This kind of accidental immortality is about the best such songs can hope for. More commonly they are amiably forgotten, or rather they are replaced by new and more current satires, but folklorists may find occasional fragments of an older satire along with persistent reports that there *was* a song about this-or-that, that so-and-so had made it up, and that "it was a corker."[1]

For the folklorist, then, the continuity in tradition of individual satirical songs is of peripheral interest; his central concern should be with the continuing tradition of their composition. What were they made up about? Why? How were they composed? What functions did they serve? And, finally, who made them up? It is to this final question that I have devoted much of my energy, partly for the scholarly reason that it largely subsumes the other questions, but partly also, I am sure, because I am fascinated by the problems of writing common-man biography.

What I have found in the twenty or more years that I have devoted to the study of satirical song in Maine and the Maritime

Provinces of Canada is that while within any given area many
people tried their hand at songmaking, the names of one or two
always stand out — men (never women) who were "always making
'em up."[2] On the east end of Prince Edward Island, for example,
there was Lawrence Doyle, but people also recalled Hugh Lauch-
lan MacDonald, Dan Somers, and Tom Lewis. Along New Brunswick's Miramichi River, there is pretty general agreement that the
legendary Larry Gorman was in a class by himself, though others
like Frank O'Hara and John and George Calhoun were known to
be able to make up good songs when the occasion demanded.
But no-one on the Miramichi came closer to Gorman's reputation
than Joe Smith, "The Roving Joe," of Renous.

*"Joe Smith?" said eighty-five year old Mark Hambrook of
Renous in response to my question. *"Joe Smith? I camped with him
and worked with him and knowed him year in and year out. Every
winter we worked together . . . Joe Smith? He was well-known everywhere."[3] As I continued my field work, I found that Hambrook was
right: everyone knew of him and knew that he was a poet, but typically no-one remembered more than fragments or reports of his
songs. Then one afternoon Nick Underhill of Northwest Bridge sang
three of them for me.

Nick, a well-beloved performer at the Miramichi Folksong Festivals from 1958 through 1968, *was* that combination of singer and
antiquary I spoke of earlier. He had learned many songs as a young
man working in the woods, but as the Festivals went on he began
seeking out new ones, filling out those he remembered imperfectly,
and otherwise improving the items in his repertoire by polishing up
rhymes and even changing the sense of a song if he thought that
would make it more acceptable to Festival audiences. For these
reasons, it is hard to say how much of "A Winter on Renous" is
Joe Smith's work, how much Nick's. Nick had sung it for Louise
Manny, and she had played his singing of it on one of her Sunday
afternoon radio programs on CKMR, Newcastle, New Brunswick.[4]
Several people upriver laughed about Nick's version, claiming it was
all wrong or that he had combined "a bit of this song and a bit of
that one" to make it. I made the usual allowances for such claims,
but Nick finally admitted to me (insisting that I turn the tape
recorder off first) that he had not learned the song all at once but
had put it together from bits and pieces a friend (who had known
Smith and had the song from him) was able to recall. Although he
made no attempt to explain or modify such obscure references in
the song as the one to the mules in stanza 8, he did change lines
3 and 4 in stanza 11 from their original,

> "I spent a winter on Renous and I still don't love
>   their ways,

> There'll be no rest in the land of the blest, for
> his sons and Morgan Hayes,"

to their present complimentary form out of consideration for any Hayeses who might still be around. Further, "A Winter on Renous" mightily resembles Larry Gorman's "The Winter of Seventy-Three," a song Nick had known well for a long time, and in fact he sang both songs to the same tune.[5] In short, there may be as much Nick Underhill as Joe Smith in this song. Nevertheless, I give it here as Nick sang it.

Nick's singing style—as any Festival attendee of those times could attest—was extremely idiosyncratic. Its chief characteristic was his dwelling on high notes for anywhere from three to eight extra beats, the length varying from stanza to stanza—and even in the same stanza from singing to singing. Nick also sang rather slowly, taking rests and breaths at various places, and in the lower reaches of his register his pitch tended to be imprecise. All of these things make his singing difficult to represent in any standard notation. Too careful fidelity would result in a transcription that only a few specialists could read, while a skeleton or "average" of the stanza-to-stanza variations would give the reader no sense of the song as Nick sang it. The compromise I have adopted is to present a "sample stanza" reduced to its underlying meter, but the reader should understand that Nick treats meter very freely, and notes he dwelled on I have marked with an asterisk.

A WINTER ON RENOUS[6]

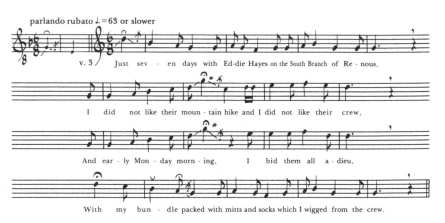

1. On the ninth day of October in the year of nineteen-four,
   That day I left old Indiantown as I oft-times did before;
   I did not like the country, and I did not love their ways,
   For to spend the winter on Renous with the sons of Morgan Hayes.

2. Of this happy crew I'll tell to you is Eddie, George and Mike;
   They had no mercy on a man but to work him day and night.

With big Ephraim Kirk I went to work and they sent me for to
    chop,
And my mind being bent on rambling and with them could not
    stop.

3. Just seven days with Eddie Hayes on the South Branch of Renous,
   I did not like their mountain hike, and I did not like their crew;
   And early Monday morning, I bid them all adieu,
   With my bundle packed with mitts and socks which I wigged
       from the crew.

4. It just being a fortnight after and at the break of day,
   When down to Morgan Hayes's I carelessly did stray;
   Two men sat at the table I had saw the day before;
   Their given names I will explain was Bill and Tommy Poore.

5. A good breakfast it being served and we all walked out the lane;
   It being my intention for to try the woods again,
   As we sat jolly smoking up at the Devil's Back,
   About two miles from Thomas Colepaugh's where we had
       another snack.

6. When I arrived at Hayes's camp I knew the place in style;
   'Twas there I talked to Eddie Hayes, likewise to Charlie Doyle.
   "Where is your crew a-working?" I said I would like to know;
   "High up on yonder mountain there's a place for Roving Joe."

7. It's high up on the mountain the sun don't shine so bright,
   Where the beast of prey do hold by day and roam by will at night.
   Quite early in the morning about the hour of five,
   The cook would call, "Come one and all, that's if you're still
       alive!"
   The provisions they were rather shy and the molasses was all
       done,
   And the crew commenced to wonder why the toter didn't come. [7]

8. Then between six and seven we would be on our way,
   The tall black spruce to chop and sluice and those lofty pines to
       slay.
   We would hear them shout, "The mules are out," and they would
       swing back the door,
   And the bushes loaded with the drops like they were the day
       before.

9. John Hayes he being our teamster, he drove the landing team —
   A mare that came from Napan and Stella was her name.
   And a big red mare and her ribs shone bare, as you will
       understand,
   She was drove by Johnny Bolster, a true-born Irishman.

10. Morris Doyle he was our yardman, a boy both stout and strong;
    His parents died and left him, I will mention in my song.
    He left his home quite young to roam, but he knew the
        woodsman's ways

And would always try to deck them high for the sons of Morgan
Hayes.

11. I'm the Roving Joe youse all do know, it's time and I'll say adieu,
     In praise of our cook and team-es-ters, likewise their jolly crew.
     I spent a winter on Renous, and now I love their ways;
     In the land of the blest there is peace and rest for his sons and
     Morgan Hayes.

12. So it's now I'm going to end my song, and I've done the best I
     could.
     When working for this happy crew while in the lumberwoods,
     The winter it has passed and gone and their spring drive has
     come through,
     It being forty days with Edward Hayes on the South Branch of
     Renous.

The second song Nick sang for me, "Charming Laura Brown,"
is straight local satire, a song Joe is supposed to have made up on a
neighbor couple. The grant map shows a William Turner living
about two miles up the Dungarvon River from where it joins the
Renous, and Laura Brown was from Breadalbane Settlement about
four miles into the woods in back of Blackville.[8] "He just made that
up to tease poor Laura," said Mrs. Dan McEvoy of Pineville. "Both
she and Turner were a little odd." And while some of the local
allusions are now lost, the song can still stand as an example of the
kind of outright character assasination local satires could indulge in.

CHARMING LAURA BROWN[9]

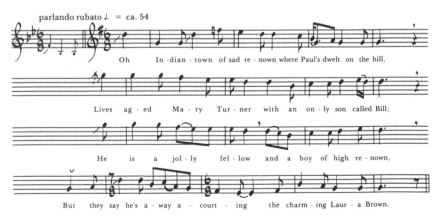

1. Oh Indiantown of sad renown where Paul's dwelt on the hill,
    Lives aged Mary Turner with an only son called Bill;
    He is a jolly fellow and a boy of high renown,
    But they say he's away a-courting the charming Laura Brown.

2. She sleeps in every morning, and at noon she will get up;
    Then a-growling and a-grumbling she will break a china cup.

They give her education and they done the best they could,
But she being wild and wayward and she done but little good.

3. Now William's gone a-courting, the neighbors they do say;
He used to drive a red horse but now he drives a grey.
"I'll go down to Father Murdoch's to the place of high renown;
I will marry but I will not tarry with the charming Laura Brown."

4. She is cross-eyed and she's lazy and is always on the road,
And lives in on the [Lina] road all in a small abode;
There with her brother Israel, and she never was to town,
But young William Turner he cuts a swell for his charming
Laura Brown.

5. They have joined their hands in wedlock bands, I am about to
say,
And live up on Dungarvon about six miles away.
They have one son called Johnny who is noted as a clown,
And would romp all day all in the hay like charming Laura
Brown.

6. So now my friends I will attend and my pencil lay away;
I have wrote those simple verses I made up the other day.
Renous River and Dungarvon, those two rivers does combine,
Stands the home of William Turner sheltered in a bunch of pine.

Nick said he learned Joe's "The Belles of Renous" somewhere in
the early 1920s in a lumbercamp on Dungarvon River from one
Dinny Cormier. Cormier had known Smith, Nick said, and claimed
this was the poet's own favorite among his songs. In it he pits the
local girls from his home area, Dungarvon and Pineville, against the
silly and effete young things from eight miles down-river in rather
more metropolitan Renous.

THE BELLES OF RENOUS[10]

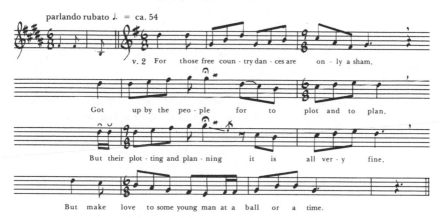

v. 2 For those free coun - try dan - ces are on - ly a sham,
Got up by the peo - ple for to plot and to plan,
But their plot - ting and plan - ning it is all ver - y fine,
But make love to some young man at a ball or a time.

1. Come all you good people who live at your ease,
Give up your night travellings and going to sprees;

Stay home with your mother, don't cause her to fret,
And do not mix up with the downriver set.

2. For these free country dances are only a sham,
   Got up by the people for to plot and to plan,
   But their plotting and planning it is all very fine,
   But make love to some young man at a ball or a time.

3. The posters are out and the word goes around;
   Come one and come all where your welcome is found.
   Then they flock from all quarters from ten miles around,
   And they [make all things jingle] in a quiet little town.

4. The girls of Dungarvon are bound for to shine;
   There's the Munns and the Tuckers and the Spoony O'Briens.
   Then horses and carriages will come to their call,
   For to take them and bring them safe home from the ball.

5. The girls of Renous they are hard for to suit;
   A man dressed in homespun they'd call him a brute.
   But a dude from the city with a cutaway coat
   And a high-standing collar near cutting his throat;
   Not a cent in his pocket his fare for to pay,
   And has not been shaved for many a day.[11]

6. The girls of Dungarvon are sly as a fox
   And many a time they have laid in their stocks,
   But for dancing or singing there's none can outshine
   The Dungarvon girls at a ball or a time.

7. When those girls get to forty they do not lament,
   Nor think of the days they have foolishly spent;
   With cheeks like the cherries and their hair done in curls,
   It is easily to know they're not Dungarvon girls.

8. Now come all you good peoples who live at your ease,
   With hearts light and gay and going to sprees,
   Now you belles from Renous when to sporting do go,
   Take a tip from a friend which they call Roving Joe.

These three songs show Joe Smith to have been a competent
craftsman in the art of satirical song, but his reputation went far
beyond that. "He was really meant for a goddamned poet," said
Grant Forsyth. "He was always at it. Even when he'd be working
he'd be making up songs. All of a sudden he'd laugh and you'd know
he'd thought of something for a song."[12] As Nick Underhill had
heard it, *"He was always around among the boys and he was making up verses and singing for them, and he was liked awful well in a
crew." Everyone knew him to be a songmaker, it seems, and a
damned good one. "Larry Gorman was a corker," said Alec Underhill, "but he wasn't one damn bit better than Joe." That, along the
Miramichi, is high praise indeed. We are left with two problems:

first, given his reputation, why were Joe's songs not better remembered; second, given the facts that his songs were not better remembered and that those that have survived are in no way astonishing productions, how do we account for his rather considerable fame among Miramichi woodsmen and watermen?

The first problem is only half a problem, since, as has already been pointed out, satirical songs tend not to outlive their topicality, but even so we might have expected Joe's songs to have survived better. I can offer three reasons why they did not. First, most of his songs were not so much full-scale songs as they were occasional rhymes and verses. As we have seen, a couple of informants even wondered whether Nick Underhill might not have created "A Winter on Renous" by stringing together verses from here and there, and while I doubt that that is exactly what he did, such questioning suggests that people thought of Joe less as a songmaker than as an occasional versifier. Second, many of Joe's songs were supposed to have been obscene, and it may be that singers chose not to learn them for that reason. Everett Price suggested as much to me one day. Earlier in the interview he had said that most of Joe's "songs" were just little rhymes, and I was questioning him again about that:

> *Well, the most of them [*were*]. Oh, he made some songs, but at the time when I heard Smith's stuff there was nobody cared much about learning it. . . . You know, it was stuff they couldn't—didn't like to sing before women and people, respected people, and they didn't bother with it much. But there was some that was pretty rough. Oh, the old singers, you know, was pretty careful about that. They was very careful. You know that they had their songs classed? There was rough songs made too. But you know that they might learn a couple of them for to sing for the boys out on the drive somewhere, but they never mixed them among their old [*songs*]. Their old songs was a story, you see. They told a story to a tune.

Price may have been right, but it is also possible that Joe's songs did in fact survive but that I was simply unable to collect them *because* they were obscene. That would not be an unusual experience at all for a collector of songs. It may be, then, that obscenity did contribute to the scarcity—real or illusory—of Joe's songs, but I think a third reason suggested to me by Mrs. Dan McEvoy of Pineville was much more important. "Joe didn't want people to learn his songs," she said. "He wanted to sing them, and if he thought you were beginning to get onto one he'd change it." To sum up, then, his songs may not have survived well because they were less songs than occasional verses, were frequently obscene, and were considered by their author to be his private property. If what we had to solve was only half a problem to begin with, we have certainly more than half solved it.

For the second problem, that of Joe Smith's local fame, I can offer two solutions. To begin with, Joe, like Larry Gorman, was his own best press agent.[13] Larry called himself "The Man Who Makes the Songs," Joe Smith was "The Roving Joe," and both worked their names into their songs. In addition, just as there were a number of cante-fables — short, funny stories with a verse for the clincher — that had Larry Gorman for their protagonist, there were several about Joe Smith, and since, as I suggested, Gorman told these stories about himself, I imagine Smith did the same thing.[14] They were perfect vehicles for showing oneself to be a dangerously quick and witty versifier.

Joe's press agentry certainly helped his legend along, but its main strength lay in the many kinds of folk hero he was. Joe Smith was not only a poet; he was also a strong man, a trickster, and an outlaw, and we can best see how these different aspects of his character combined by seeing them in the context of his biography.

According to his baptism record — and other records bear it out reasonably well — Joe was born June 11, 1872, the come-by-chance son of Mary Ann Sullivan and a man by the name of William Harris, but his mother did not keep him.[15] According to Grant Forsyth, he first lived with a family of Underhills but they had to let him go because they had too many children of their own around, whereupon the family of James Smith agreed to bring Joe up, and he took their name. Sure enough, the 1881 Census shows James Smith, 72, born in England, Anglican, occupation "shoemaker," and his wife Susanna, born in Scotland and a Baptist, with four children (three daughters and a son) between the ages of 18 and 27; with them is Joseph, aged 9, "attending school," and specifically not listed as a son. The grant map shows a James Smith living about three miles out of Blackville on the road to Renous, and tradition has it that this is where Joe was brought up. The railroad crossing there is still known as Smith's Crossing.

Tradition also has it that Joe was hard used as a child, and a between-the-lines reading of the Census suggests that that could have been so, a young Irish lad in with an elderly English shoemaker and his grown family! Evidently Joe stayed with them until he was about twelve, went up to Doaktown to live with Jimmy Sims, the blacksmith, then came back downriver and worked on the boom. He lived with another family for a while, but finally they turned him out, and the fifteen-year-old Joe turned up in Barnettville at Jim Underhill's place. Jim's son Alec, who considered himself Joe's best friend, told me the story this way:

> I was working out in the fields one day, when Joe came along. "Alec," he said, "they threw me out down there, and I'm broke and

got no place to stay at all." Father ran an operation in the woods, and I asked him would he hire Joe, and he did. Joe stayed with us for five or six years. Mother was always awful good to him.

Physically, he became a tremendous man. "Not that he was so tall," said Grant Forsyth. "He was no more than five-foot-ten, but just big. Why he had an arm on him as big around as your leg, and a broad deep chest like I don't know when I've seen one as big." Everett Price said he looked something like a bear on his hind legs. But Joe wasn't just big; he had strength to match his size, and agility that was equal to both. And he loved to show all three off. "He was always cutting up somehow," Johnny Tucker told me:

> He could do all kinds of acrobatics—cartwheels, hand-springs, stuff like that. He had one trick he called the "salmon leap," where he'd spring up in the air from lying flat on the ground. And he was great at log-rolling. I only remember one man throwing him off once, and then Joe sprang right off the bottom back onto the log and threw the other guy off anyhow. And a beautiful skater. He'd skate a circle so fast he could lean way over and pick up a handful of scrapings from the ice with one hand, then reverse the circle and gather it up the same way with his other hand! He was a great trout fisherman too. He'd wade more water than any other two men. Sometimes he'd go right out up to his armpits in that cold water and fish for hours. Never saw another man could do it!

"He didn't care for nothing," another man told me. "He'd go into the woods and travel and work all day with nothing but dry bread and black tea to go on, but he'd take it and laugh and you'd never hear him say it was a poor meal." And there was not much he could not do in the woods or on the drives. Tucker remembered another little incident:

> He was working up Renous one time. He was chopping and he had a man by the name of Kelly swamping for him, and this Kelly was an ugly sort with a big shock of white hair, so they used to plague him by calling him Dandylion. Well this Kelly was bucking up a big spruce Joe had felled, and Joe saw he wasn't doing too well and said, "Here, I'll take an end of that saw." Well, they worked along, but Joe was so much stronger and faster than Kelly that poor Kelly was always falling behind. "Look out there, Dandylion," Joe said, "look out I don't just pull you right through the cut." Kelly got so sore he all but walked off the job.

Small wonder, then, that in this culture where sheer physical strength and stamina were of daily importance Joe became well known, especially when he obviously delighted in displaying his abilities. He even dressed the part. "Joe used to like to look rough and dress rough too," said Mrs. Dan McEvoy. "He'd go around with several days' beard and one pant leg cut off short, one long. He'd be pretty raggedy, but he didn't care. That's the way he wanted it." Small wonder too that his show-off strength led to fights, but evidently Joe was constantly equal to any such challenge. "God, he was an awful man to fight," I was told. "He could jump up and kick the head right off you!" Yet Joe also seems to have known where to draw the line. "Don't think that Joe was a pick-fight or a bully," said Grant Forsyth, "because that wasn't true," and Forsyth illustrated Joe's restraint with the following story:

I remember Joe and me and a bunch of others were on our way into the woods one fall and we stopped off at Paul Kingston's [a well-known way station for woodsmen] for the night. Joe was cutting up and we were all having a lot of fun when a fella named McEvoy got mad and tried to pick a fight with him. Joe kept putting him off in as good-natured a way as he could, but McEvoy just kept pestering him. "No sir, Smith," he'd say, "you can be hurt just like any other man, and I'm the lad that's going to do it!" Well, Joe took all he could. Then he turned to a friend and said, "Fetch me one of them salt cod from out in the dingle, will you?" Then he grabbed McEvoy, hauled down his pants and put him across his knee and whaled hell out of him with that codfish! Everybody was laughing, and after it was all over, "I didn't want to do that," Joe told him. "We all come to Paul's to have fun, not fight, but you asked for it!"

Everyone agrees that Joe was wonderful company, and that he was frequently given to elaborate pranks. Alec Underhill recalled one:

Joe was staying with a man by the name of Jewett one time, and he took it into his head to bedevil the man. So he rigged up a bottle on the end of a rope and let it down through a hole he'd cut upstairs so that the bottle was inside the wall right next to Jewett's bed. Then Joe'd make it rattle at night, and it scared the poor man half to death.

Grant Forsyth recalled another:

His father-in-law, "Spoony" O'Brien had been losing grain and didn't know who to suspect. He told Joe, and Joe said he'd solve it for him. So that night Joe filled a sack with grain and poked a hole in it and carried it out of Spoony's barn over to Tucker's place, which left a trail of grain right into Tucker's barn. Next morning O'Brien found the trail and roared over to Joe's to tell him that Tucker was the thief. "Oh, don't be too quick about it," Joe protested, but O'Brien went right over to Tucker's and the two had quite a scrap. Joe just did it, of course, to see the two old guys fight.

In this context, Joe's songmaking can be seen simply as another kind of prank, another way to bedevil or tease someone. Grant Forsyth gave me a beautiful example of that:

There was a peddler by the name of Ben Betts from Doaktown, and Joe had it in for him for some reason. One day he met him on the street and started making up this song on him. It was really a rough one, too, and when Joe'd come to the end of a verse he'd fart (he could do that, just fart whenever he wanted to). Well this Betts stood it as long as he could, then he got back up on his wagon and left. Joe ran right alongside the horse and wagon, keeping the song going, singing and farting. Then he gave one last fart and jumped a fence and disappeared.

We have already seen that Joe could make up monicker songs, those chronicles of a winter's work in which the songmaker would name members of the crew and get off a combination of compliments and nasty digs. It was a perfect form for Joe. "A Winter on Renous" (assuming it is more Joe's than it is Nick's, and I do assume that) is a splendid example of the form, and I have reports of two others. The first was recited for me by Al Keating of Strathadam, N.B. He had mentioned a piece Joe made about Sinclairs, a famous Miramichi lumbering family, and I was asking him about it again. *"Oh yeah," he said:

> Old Bob Swim, you all know him,
> Who robbed the [off-bound] shores,
> Who robbed poor orphans of their homes,
> Turned widows out of doors.
> High-collared Jim, you all know him—

and then Eddie Sinclair, he said . . . he called Eddie Sinclair the "King of the Miramichi" and then he said,

> Tim Lynch and Dan they are at hand,
> A verse for them I'll make,
> For I know the Devil will have their bones
> And throw them in the lake;
> In the lake that'll burn forever
> 'Til that eternal day. . . .

And he come from way up in Blackville right down, clean down here to Nelson over here, South Nelson. And all the fellows that lumbered, he got all their names in.

And Grant Forsyth remembered one Joe made on a crew he had worked in with Joe one winter:

It was about all the men in the crew. They were all in there, and there were some stanzas on me that had to do with a "bronco" I was supposed to have used to plow a garden, and there was also something about me jumping on a great big French girl. He said I was from "The Island," which I'm not, and Joe knew it, and that stuff about the French girl was just a lie too. Joe just put that stuff in to be funny.

Did people ever get angry, I wondered, when Joe made a song on them? *"No, no, no," said Al Keating, "'twas no'one'd get sore, because he didn't care for no-one . . . he didn't care." Mrs. Dan McEvoy put it a little differently. "Yes, some of them would get mad when he'd cut them pretty bad," she said. "But it was no use getting sore about it, because if you did he'd just make it worse yet. And he didn't care what anyone thought!" The point seems to be that Joe's physical invincibility made his songs something that his victims had to suffer, while everyone else might laugh.

Like many Maritimers, Joe traveled over to Maine and New Hampshire to work in the woods. Alec Underhill remembered their first trip:

> Me and Joe went down to New Hampshire one summer, and the first thing we got was a job haying in a place named Jackson. When we got our pay we went to town, and right away Joe got drunk. I saw he was going to get in trouble, so I stole his wallet and his watch, a big gold pocket watch. Next morning, Joe was feeling pretty bad. "I want to go home, Alec," he said. "Do you want me to buy your ticket, or do you want to go get it yourself?" I said. Joe said he guessed he'd get it himself, so I handed him his wallet. "You had this all along, didn't you?" he said. "Yes," I said, "and this too," and I gave him back his watch.
>
> But I should have bought that ticket, because Joe got in with a crowd and got drinking again, and then he didn't want to go home at all, but I went home anyway without him. Some time later, he came back. He held out fifteen cents to me. "There," he said, "that's what I've got to show for my trip to New Hampshire. I guess I should have gone back with you."

So far there is nothing about Joe's experience in the States that could not have been duplicated by any of a thousand other husky and high-spirited young men from the Miramichi, but I have been told that it was while he was in the States that he began his career as a thief. Grant Forsyth told the story this way:

> When he was still pretty young Joe went over to Maine to work in the woods, but while he was there he fell in with two older men who were already thieves, and he traveled with them for some time. The three of them robbed a jewelry store, Joe said, and they got caught. The older men were given time to do, but the judge told Joe, "You're only a young boy," he said, "and I'm sure you wouldn't have done such a thing if you hadn't been put up to it. I'll give you until tomorrow morning to get clear of this place." Joe came back to Miramichi, and that's where all his stealing started.

Alec Underhill told another story:

> Another time we went to New Hampshire together, up around Berlin somewhere, but it wasn't long before I saw Joe was going to

get in trouble no matter what I said or did, so after a while I came home again. It was some time after that I was down at the crossing one day when who walked down the track but Joe, and he had this story to tell: He'd been in a bar, and there was a drunk sleeping it off on a bench, and Joe saw the man had quite a roll of bills. "The proprietor had his eye on it," Joe said, "and was planning to take it for himself, so I just took it first." Then he said he went out back and put the money on the ground and shit on it to cover it up. But they caught him and threw him in jail for it.

Wherever or however he began it, Joe's thievery was a well-known aspect of his character. "I've seen him go into a store to buy a hat," Silas Curtis told me, "and walk out with two, one under the other. He'd buy one pair of braces and walk out with a bundle of half a dozen. He never made any bones about his habit either. 'I just can't help it,' he said to me once, 'I think my mother was a thief or something.'" Alec Underhill had a like story to tell:

> I went into a store with Joe one day, and I watched him like a hawk. Never saw him take a thing. Then on the way home he took off his big black stetson and underneath it was a gray cap he'd picked up. "Joe," I said, "I never saw you take that. How'd you do it?" Joe just laughed and held the cap out to me. "Here," he said, "I'll give it to you." That's the kind of man he was.

There are plenty of stories of Joe's antic larcenies, and what they reveal is not the desperate thief who steals to keep alive but the rogue outlaw who steals for the sheer hell of it. "It was more like hallowe'en pranks," said Silas Curtis, and Arthur Carr agreed. "It was all for excitement and jokes that he stole," he said. "With his friends Joe was just as honest as a man could be." At one point, Joe got in with a gang known as "The Bouliar Crew,"[16] whose members spent much of their time stealing sheep and chickens and such, and when they had stolen enough for a good feed they would head for one of their several hideouts back in the woods and keep out of sight for a while. In the following song, Joe tells of one of their raids:

THE BOULIAR CREW[17]

1. Come all you people of Renous
   And listen to me a while,
   While I sing you a bit of song,
   Which may cause you for to smile.

2. It was early Monday morning
   I bid the camp adieu
   With my bundle filled with mitts and socks
   From each one of the crew.

3. When I arrived at the settlement,
   About the hour of nine,

> The farmers they all gazed on me,
>   They knew me by a sign.

4. The people they all asked me
       What brought me down to town;
   The answer that I made them,
       For chickens I was bound.

5. As we sat jolly smoking
       Down by the King's Highway,
   My chum being in a sleepy mood,
       And this to him did say;

6. "It's me and you, two of the crew,
       What say we make a plot?
   We'll go down to Donovan's,
       And there we'll steal a pot.

7. "We will act as cute as foxes,
       Some chickens we will steal;
   We will go back of Morgan Hayeses,
       And there we will have a meal."

8. When we arrived at the hen house,
       And boldly stepped in,
   It being a fine large building,
       It was nearly eight by ten.

9. The hens spoke to each other
       In a voice they seemed to say,
   "I think it is the Roving Joe,
       For I seen him around today."

10. We felt the flock all over
        We found them fat and lean,
    And half a dozen shanghais
        Set on a collar beam.

11. We purchased two out of the flock,
        I thought that they would do,
    And the old cock in the upper loft,
        Cried, "Cock-a-doodle-doo."

12. 'Twas early the next morning,
        The news it went around
    Mrs. Donovan she had lost her pot,
        And nowhere could be found.

13. But if she only knew the truth,
        Her pot was quite secure;
    It was left on Baldwin's bankin'
        Just beside the kitchen door.

Michael Sullivan had his orchard robbed by Smith and his gang one night, and Joe had the gall to make a song about it. One verse was recited for me by Grant Forsyth:

One morning as Michael he left his abode
And haughty young Nancy he met on the road;
"Oh Nancy, oh Nancy, don't hold me no spite,
For the boys from the village they robbed me last night."

Obviously not everyone—his victims especially—saw Joe's stealing as pranks. Grant Forsyth's next story makes that very clear:

Welches didn't like Joe and figured he'd been stealing from their well-house, where they kept all kinds of things—milk, cream, butter, eggs, and pies—to keep cool. So one day Welch put a poisoned pie out there. Joe told me he found it all right, but suspected it was too good to be true, so he tossed it over the fence into Welches' pig pen. Next morning Welch went out to find he'd lost his best boar.

At one point, things are supposed to have gotten bad enough so that a detective by the name of Ring was brought upriver to try to deal with Joe. He had never seen his man, until he met him one day right in the middle of the Quarryville bridge. Ring took one look at Joe, and kept right on walking. "I asked Joe what he'd have done if Ring had laid hold of him," said Grant Forsyth, "and he said 'Grant, there's forty feet from that bridge to the river, and I was going over and I was going to take him with me!' And Joe'd have done it too, I know." Forsyth told another little cante-fable about this confrontation:

Another time he was on the south side of the river at Polly Underhill's little tavern, and Ring walked in, and Joe took one look at him and said,

"Detective Ring, you're on my trail,
I guess, my boys, I'd better sail."

And then he went out and jumped right into the river—at spring height, with ice and all!—and he swam clear across to the other side. When he came up on the far bank, he just shook himself like a dog and went right off into the woods. Ring never did get him, of course.

Two more cante-fables are rather widely told about Joe. The first is the most popular and here it is as it was told me by Al Keating:

*Joe one time he went to sleep in a barn way up in Renous someplace, and there was a rooster way up on the collar beam. He dirtied down on Joe's face, see, in the night . . . so in the morning [when] daylight come he says,

"Little bird of little wit,
Who taught you on my head to shit?
But since you've been so jeezly mean,
I'm going to sweep you from the collar beam."

And he killed the rooster.

Everett Price was probably the first to tell me the next one, but I
have heard it several times along the Miramichi. Andy Connors, by
way, ran a little saloon, or at least sold whiskey, at his place in
Renous:

> *[There was] an election down here. This old fellow he was going
> to feed the voters . . . and he told Joe for to—that he'd pay him well
> if he'd get him a sheep. See, he was going to feed them on sheep for
> meat. And Joe he started and he went up in the pasture . . . and he
> caught this fellow's big wether—his own sheep—and killed it and
> sold it to him. That was funny about that—"Two dollars apiece
> without the fleece"—(the way he put it, you know):
>
> "Two dollars apiece without the fleece,
> When money is so shy;
> Tomorrow we'll get rotten drunk
> On Connors' rotten rye."

Many of these stories have the sound of self-told tales; that is they
are not so much eye-witness accounts of Joe's actions as they are
stories that Joe told on himself.[18] There is nothing surprising about
that; "The Roving Joe" was jealous of his reputation. His favorite
story on himself, according to Grant Forsyth, was the following, and
it speaks for itself:

> One time Joe came home after having been away for a while, and
> he asked his wife if there was anything new. No, she said, there
> wasn't. "Well, is the salmon running yet?" he asked. "Yes," his wife
> said, "they are." So Joe went down to Whalen's Pool—that's where
> Renous and Dungarvon join—but when he got nearby he saw two
> guys sweeping the pool with a net. Well, he hid nearby, and when
> they brought out their net they had thirty-two salmon there. "Let's
> try her again," said one, so they threw the salmon they had up the
> bank into the grass. Well, Joe bagged them and took them off. Then
> he came back to see the fun.
>   Well, this second time the two guys got thirteen more, but when
> they went to find their thirty-two other fish of course they weren't
> there. All they could find was the slime in the grass, but the salmon
> weren't there. "Now that just shows you," one of them said. "If Joe
> Smith was in this country now, sure as hell he'd get blamed for this!"

What are we to make of all this? I say it is all one piece. On a
child of questionable birth the world had taken its pious and customary revenge, farming him out and insisting he be grateful for
whatever crust it gave him to eat and corner it gave him to sleep in.
The child grew up and found he could strike back at that world by
making it appear ridiculous through playing jokes on it. What seems
to have saved him from becoming a pure rogue that smashed and
killed was (and I recognize that I am shuffling some rather base

psychological coin around here) some sense of perspective that let him see that that way lay self-destruction. Call it a sense of humor. Joe Smith had been hurt, and I think that hurt and resentment come out rather clearly in a little anecdote Alec Underhill told me:

> Joe and I used to argue a lot about his stealing and all, and one night I told him, "Joe," I said, "if you'd give that up you'd be thought of more than any man on the Miramichi."
>
> "You know better than that, Alec," Joe said. "Nobody cares a damn about me. I'm just a bastard."
>
> "No, Joe," I told him, "you're wrong about that. I'm telling you the truth. But so long as you keep on with this stealing, people will hold it against you."
>
> But he wouldn't listen. A couple of times I almost thought I had him off it, but then he'd go right back to it just as bad as before.

Fortunately, though, the anger bred by that resentment came out as laughter. He would not try to destroy the world; he was content to make it look absurd.

One day Joe came to Alec for some advice. He'd been thinking of getting married, he said, and what did Alec think about it? "Do you think I'd be any better for it?" he said. Alec recommended it, and sure enough, on June 20, 1900, Joe married Florence O'Brien, daughter of Micky "Spoony" O'Brien, and evidently it worked out very well. Joe did not change his ways completely or anything of the sort, but he and his wife took a place up the Dungarvon several miles above Pineville, and started raising a family—two girls and two boys.[19] Joe had always loved children—several people remarked that. "Joe may have been a hell of a scrapper," said Mr. Tucker, for example, "but he was always awful good to kids—kids and old men. And he had plenty of time for both, always." Now he had kids of his own, and he thoroughly enjoyed them.

Joe's end came hard. In November of 1912, he was working in the woods for a Mr. Pratt, and having completed a job repairing the telephone line into Holmes' Lake, he had permission to take a couple of days off to go hunting before the season closed. He and Tom Howe, an older man, were at Holmes' Lake and had just gone around a large cove to reach a log dam where they had seen some caribou. After being there about an hour with no luck, they decided to head back, and while Howe returned along the shore the way they had come, Joe took a short cut across the ice which had recently formed in the cove. He got about a dozen rods out when he broke through. His obituary tells the rest of it:

> [Howe] saw Smith fighting for his life but was powerless to help and, after struggling for nearly an hour, the unfortunate man sank. Mr. Howe gave the alarm and word was sent to a nearby camp,

where two young men, Anthony Gillis and Grant Forsyth were, and they started out to recover his body, but did not succeed in finding it until Sunday night, when it was found in eleven feet of water. Deceased was well known as Big Joe Smith, and a native of Dungarvon, where he leaves a wife and five children to mourn.[20]

"He must have broke thirty feet of ice before he finally went down," Alec Underhill said, "and when they found his body they saw he'd torn off all his fingernails breaking it."

Evidently Mrs. Smith had a hard time of it after Joe's death. Alec Underhill had a remarkable story to tell here:

> I've told you how Joe loved kids. Well, he told me one time, "Alec, after I'm dead if anyone ever uses my kids the way I was used, I swear to you I'll come back!" Up there in Dungarvon after he died there was this big white dog used to come and play with the kids, jumping and running in the fields with them just the way Joe used to do. No-one knows where it came from or where it went to, but there it was. Do you believe that?
>
> And there was one time a man tried to get a piece of land away from Mrs. Smith. He even went up and started to cut some trees there, but every time he'd start to cut, out would jump this big white dog and scare him off. Do you believe that?
>
> Then one time Mrs. Smith went down to the settlement for some supplies, and she had to leave the kids at home alone. When she came back, the place was all picked up, and the kids were all clean and brushed and neat. "Who did all this?" she asked them. "Oh, Daddy was back," they told her.

Once again Alec asked me, "Do you believe that?" I told him I didn't know. "I do," he said. "I believe it. Jesus can do anything!"

It wasn't long before she had to give the children up, though. A family by the name of Dunphy took them in, but when Mrs. Smith remarried in 1914, she soon took them back. Her new husband, I was told, used neither her nor the children well, and, according to Alec, the family had to move out of the house because Joe haunted it so thoroughly. The new husband did not live long, however, and evidently things quieted down.

In writing of Larry Gorman, I said that to think of him "as anything but a poet . . . is to miss the whole point of his character, for that is not only the way his contemporaries saw him, it is the way he saw himself."[21] Nothing was as important to him as his songs; they were at the center of his life. The same cannot be said about Joe Smith. He wrote the same kind of songs Gorman did for most of the same reasons, but while for Larry songs were all he had with which to do battle with the world, for Joe they were only one weapon in a rather formidable arsenal. Both men moved and worked within the same culture, but Larry Gorman was the Loner, always on the edge of things, watching, and his songs were usually responses to specific attacks — real or imagined. Call him a poet on the defensive. Joe Smith, on the other hand, was not only where the action was, often enough he *was* the action, and his songs were simply one strategy in a lifetime of obstreperous and often hilarious attack. Call him a poet on the offensive. I am wary of battle metaphors, but for Larry Gorman and Joe Smith, they are on target.

A few more comments, by way of a coda. Almost all my field work on Smith was done in the early 1960s, at which time I was most interested in talking to people who were old enough to have known Joe and even to have worked with him. Nearly twenty years later (although I knew one could almost always gather new material by returning to the field) I decided that the data I had was both thick enough and consistent enough to allow me to go ahead with a rather complete draft of this essay. Then, in September of 1982, I made a very brief return to Miramichi to conduct three more interviews and examine the records of St. Bridget's R.C. Church in Renous, which had not been open to me before.[22] Nothing I discovered in this three-day foray contradicted or gainsaid anything I had found twenty years before. No-one remembered more than a line or two of his songs, but he himself was still remembered vividly and warmly. His granddaughter recalled that her daughter had recently gone to an Old Home Week celebration up in either Renous or Blackville:

> *There must have been a community hall or something there, and she went in and walked around, and of course there were a lot of elderly people there, and she finally approached someone and asked if they knew Joe Smith. And of course they had known him, and she said, "Well, I'm his great-granddaughter." And she said they were just thrilled to think that there were relatives of Joe Smith, and they made a big time over her. And of course they all had their different stories they wanted to tell her, and oh she had a wonderful time.

To be sure, like the great-granddaughter, I too was still talking to the older people, but they were somewhat younger older people than I had talked to before, and I can safely say that Joe's legend is alive and well in their hands. His larcenies are still recalled, but they are extenuated. *"He just done it to be devilish," said Edith Whalen. "He really didn't mean harm out of it, but he just done it to torment anyone." His granddaughter, Mrs. John Hawthorne, though she could cite no specific instances, said that she had heard stories that showed him as a local Robin Hood. *"There were families who were starving," she said, "and there was someone else who had more than they needed. He wasn't above going and helping himself to what they had to distribute among these poor families." The story of his death, usually including the image of his breaking ice until he tore off his fingernails, occurs over and over again, and while no-one ever put a marker on his grave, evidently someone marked the place of his death: *"We went up one time," said Edith Whalen, "out to Holmes' Lake, and they had a big thing up where Joe was drowned —a sign. Had his name on it and where he was drowned. . . . That would have been about forty years ago," she added, which would place it about 1940, almost thirty years after Joe went down for the last time.

As a songmaker, there is little more to say about Joe Smith. As a local hero, the work has just begun. For the legend—and for the folklorist—in Joe's end is a new beginning.

NOTES

¹For examples of recent satire, and for some fine discussion of the whole subject, see Henry Glassie, "'Take That Night Train to Selma': An Excursion to the Outskirts of Scholarship," and John F. Szwed, "Paul E. Hall: A Newfoundland Song-Maker and His Community of Song," in Henry Glassie, Edward D. Ives, and John F. Szwed, *Folksongs and Their Makers* (Bowling Green, Ohio: Bowling Green University Press, 1970), pp. 3-68 and 149-69.

²For the results of my research, see Edward D. Ives, *Larry Gorman: The Man Who Made the Songs* (Bloomington, Ind.: Indiana University Press, 1964; reprinted New York: Arno Press, 1977); Ives, *Lawrence Doyle: The Farmer-Poet of Prince Edward Island* (Orono, Me.: The University Press, 1971); and Ives, *Joe Scott: The Woodsman Songmaker* (Champaign, Ill.: University of Illinois Press, 1978). As for my parenthetical "never women," I should add that women played an important part as songmakers in Acadian tradition. See the excellent work of Georges Arsenault: *Complaintes acadienne de l'Île-du-Prince-Edouard* (Quebec: LEMEAC, 1980), especially pp. 41-69.

³Throughout this paper, all quotations preceded by an asterisk are taken verbatim from tape recordings on file in the Northeast Archives of Folklore and Oral History, South Stevens Hall, University of Maine, Orono, Maine. All omissions are indicated by standard ellipsis marks. Words or phrases that are not clear on the tape are given in brackets, while words I have added to make the sense of a passage more clear are bracketed and in italics. All other quotations are taken from field notes, and while they are as close as I can possibly get to what was said, I cannot guarantee verbatim accuracy. All Northeast Archives accessions are listed as "NA" followed by the accession number.

⁴For more on the Miramichi Folksong Festivals and Louise Manny's radio programs, see Ives, *Larry Gorman*, p. 171, 211 (and note 21).

⁵See Ives, *Larry Gorman*, pp. 54-56.

⁶For another singing of this song, see Louise Manny and James Reginald Wilson, *Songs of Miramichi* (Fredericton, N.B.: Brunswick Press, 1968), pp. 187-90.

⁷Repeat second half of tune to fill out this stanza.

⁸See Grant Reference Plan No. 77, Department of National Resources, Fredericton, N.B., revised 1977.

⁹For an earlier transcription of this song, see Ives, *Larry Gorman*, pp. 175-76.

[10]For a tune analogue, see Phillips Barry, *The Maine Woods Songster* (Cambridge, Mass.: The Powell Printing Co., 1939), p. 57.

[11]Repeat second half of tune to fill out this stanza.

[12]See Ives, *Larry Gorman*, p. 112, for a reference to the same characteristic. See also Ives, *Lawrence Doyle*, pp. 10-11.

[13]See Ives, *Larry Gorman*, pp. 185-86.

[14]See Ives, *Larry Gorman*, pp. 142-48.

[15]I am grateful to Father Vincent Donovan, Parish Priest of St. Bridget's R.C. Church, Renous, N.B., for making these records available to me.

[16]Probably from the Acadian word *bouilliot* or *bouilliotte*, meaning a thick stew in which leftovers and whatever else is available—pork, beef, chicken, game—are cooked with potatoes and a variety of vegetables until all the meat falls off the bones. I have heard the term used by both French and English-speaking woodsmen.

[17]From Dr. Louise Manny's files. Sent to her by Mrs. Thomas Hallihan, Pineville, N.B.

[18]For a parallel, see Ives, *Larry Gorman*, p. 147.

[19]Elizabeth Christina, b. March 9, 1902; Lucy Dorothea, b. May 29, 1905; James Raymond, b. Dec. 15, 1908; Thomas Luke, b. Feb. 11, 1911. Another child, Mary, b. March 30, 1904, died when one week old. (Parish Records, St. Bridget's Church, Renous, N.B.)

[20]*North Shore Leader* (Newcastle, N.B.), Friday, Nov. 29, 1912, p. 1.

[21]Ives, *Larry Gorman*, p. 187.

[22]I would like to take this opportunity to thank Alec Underhill's granddaughter, Norma (Mrs. Ralph) Mountain of Grey Rapids, N.B., for reawakening my interest in Joe Smith by writing me and mentioning several people she knew who remembered him.

Appendix

List of Informants

Note: Age is given as of date of interview. All tapes referred to are in the Northeast Archives of Folklore and Oral History, South Stevens Hall, University of Maine, Orono, Maine.

Carr, Arthur. Boiestown, N.B. Aet. ca. 85. Interviewed July 19, 1961. Not recorded.

Curtis, Silas. Grey Rapids, N.B. Interviewed July 14, 1961. Not recorded.

Forsyth, Grant. Whitneyville, N.B. Aet. ca. 70. Interviewed July 15, 1961. Not recorded.

Hambrook, Mark. Renous, N.B. Aet. 85. Interviewed July 11, 1961. See NA Ives 1.101-103.

Hawthorne, Mrs. John. St. Stephen, N.B. Interviewed Sept. 17, 1982. See NA 1591 (she is Joe Smith's granddaughter).

Keating, Al. Strathadam, N.B. Aet. ca. 75. Interviewed July 9, 1961. See NA Ives 1.98-101.

McEvoy, Mr. and Mrs. Daniel. Pineville, N.B. Interviewed July 14, 1961. Not recorded.

McEvoy, Vada. Renous, N.B. Aet. 84. Interviewed Sept. 18, 1982. See NA 1588.

Mountain, Eldon. Grey Rapids, N.B. Aet. 94. Interviewed Sept. 17, 1982. See NA 1589.

Price, Everett. Blackville, N.B. Aet. ca. 70. Interviewed July 11, 1961. See NA Ives 1.102.

Tucker, John. Pineville, N.B. Interviewed July 14, 1961. Not recorded.

Underhill, Alec. Barnettville, N.B. Aet. ca. 90. Interviewed July 27, 1961, and again in 1962. Not recorded.

Underhill, Nicholas. Northwest Bridge, N.B. Aet. ca. 60. Interviewed July 8, 1961, July 22, 1961, and at various other times. See NA Ives 1.93-95 and 1.96-98. The songs are located as follows: "A Winter on Renous," 1.93; "Charming Laura Brown," 1.94; "The Belles of Renous," 1.93.

Whalen, Edith. Renous, N.B. Aet. 91. Interviewed Sept. 18, 1982. See NA 1588.

Part 5:
Problems of Oral Re-Creation

Ballad Tradition and Hugh Spencer

David Buchan

The name Bronson, like that of Child, has already achieved the peculiar kind of scholarly distinction that follows the production of a definitive work of its time, when in speech the name itself denotes the work, without the redundancy of title. The editor of *The Traditional Tunes of the Child Ballads,* however, has written widely and well on a plenitude of subjects related directly or at distance to the music. One such subject is the artistically creative capacities of individual singers. This topic, in "Habits of the Ballad as Song," he discusses within the framework of his argument on the "two impulses, of conservation and of re-creation" that operate within tradition. I shall give the passage in full because it constitutes a major statement on the folklorist's perennial and daunting concern, the relationship of stability to change, of constants to variables:

> Now, these two impulses, of conservation and of re-creation, are perhaps not so mutually antagonistic as at first they appear. No doubt the proportions of each vary enormously in different individuals and at different times, or we should not have the unevenness of growth and change that we have been remarking. But it is important to realize that they can exist and interact simultaneously in the same individual. We have parallel evidence on the verbal side in the performance of Mrs. Brown, the Scottish singer of the late eighteenth century, who contributed notably to the traditional stores of Jamieson and Walter Scott. At different times, Mrs. Brown gave widely different texts of some of her ballads to these collectors, and did so apparently with no sense of inconsistency or alteration. She was, incidentally, possessed of some education; but for her songs she was undoubtedly drawing entirely on early memories. Her case is exactly analogous to Larcombe's, and to be explained in the same way. These were singers steeped in the traditional idiom, and whatever they sang, judged traditionally, would sound authentic. They were not automatic transmitters, as we ourselves should be, of a standard, received

text and tune: they were themselves the living authority, personified embodiments of traditional re-creation. What they carried in their memories was not a fixed, memorized series of words and notes, but the fluid idea of a song which so far as they were concerned had never had any other existence than in the fresh evocations it received from singers like themselves. There was no "authoritative" text or tune to which they might refer for the "correct" reading; but instead, only a narrative idea, a melodic idea, floating in their minds in solution, as it were, until it was crystallized by an act of will. This is tradition at its vital best: a marriage of opposites, an example in miniature of the practice of the ancient rhapsode, half recollection, half improvisation.

The point to be emphasized is that the idea which such singers retained in their minds—whether narrative, melodic, or both—was clear and definite enough to be a positive, controlling, but not constricting force. Within limits they were free: they used the words and notes that occurred to them at the moment, like good raconteurs who re-create their stories at each fresh telling. This kind of invention is too rapid and spontaneous to allow of deliberation. But beyond the traditional boundaries they would not stray. To do so would be a betrayal of their trusteeship, a kind of disloyalty almost unthinkable in the faithful transmitters of these venerable songs.

The nature, the laws, and the operation of this loose kind of restraint—or this restrictive liberty—*laxis immissus habenis*—can of course be studied only in its tangible products, either in the particular successive performances of individual singers, when we are so fortunate as to possess this rarest kind of evidence, or in the commoner yet sadly deficient record, scattered through time and space, to which multitudes have contributed in their turn.[1]

Here Bertrand Bronson provides an authoritative exposition of a crucial and complex topic—the tension between the forces of conservation and of re-creation in ballad tradition—that has all too frequently attracted simplistic reactions such as the facile cry of "contradiction" when an attempt is made to consider the two elements in balanced conjunction. He stresses the importance of re-creation, and stress is needed because all too often in ballad criticism this element has been ignored. Modern scholarship in folk narrative and folksong at large, on the other hand, has placed considerable emphasis on the creative and re-creative abilities of performers: here, as elsewhere, a peculiar timelag seems to exist between other folkloristic research and much ballad research. It would, *a priori*, be rather strange if balladry were the only genre in folk literature where traditional creativity is not to be imputed to the performer, as if storytellers were allowed to be creative but ballad-singers not. One can speculate that the inability to conceive of traditional re-creativity may derive from a mental adherence to high literature and a consequent difficulty in adjusting more than minimally to the contexts and canons of folk literature. Whatever its origins, though, the inability to conceive of traditional re-creativity generally leads to an embracing of some version of the memorial theory of ballad transmission. According to this theory ballads, irrespective of temporal or cultural contexts, are assumed to have been transmitted by memorization, not by creative reproduction; it is stated at its baldest by A. B. Friedman: "memorization . . . is the basic vehicle of oral tradition."[2] This theory has, however, to take account of the sometimes extensive differences between versions of the same story type, and it does so normally in one or more of three ways: one, variation is attributed to such negative forces as forgetting, mishearing, omission; two, literate poets are held to have entered tradition and injected some creativity from high culture (an interesting offshoot of *gesunkenes Kulturgut* notions); three, the facts are conflated with process, and "variation" is conceived of as some mysteriously mystical operation that occurs superorganically, without account of the artistic functioning of the performer. Ballad transmission, then, is seen by memorialists as essentially a business of conservation, where the conserving is not very efficient.

For proper perspective, ballad research needs to devote some attention, in the light of modern folkloristic scholarship rather than misapplied assumptions from a high-literature context, to the other element in the balance: re-creation. Bronson's exposition of the balance grows out of an understanding that the singers discussed, Anna Brown and Henry Larcombe, were not "automatic transmitters," that is, they did not work by rote memorization, but were "personified embodiments of traditional re-creation." He emphasizes, however, that the two forces of conservation and re-creation operate together in tradition, and it is important to bear this in mind, especially when scholars concentrate on one or other in their writings, for the methods of traditional re-creation employed by Anna Brown and Henry Larcombe subsume the conserving impulse. An awareness of the precise relationship between the two forces can best be approached through linking the singers, named or nameless, to their contexts and analyzing in their songs the relation of constants to variables.

The relationship of constants to variables in tradition constitutes one of the main concerns—if not *the* primary concern— of the modern structuralist approach to folklore. Vladimir Propp, for example, in his explorations of how texts stand to tale-concepts in the wonder tale has demonstrated how a method of structural analysis based on an awareness of this relationship can lay bare the essential movements and meanings of a story.[3] A structuralist method need not be applied without reference to context, as sometimes happens, for the perceptions of the structuralist approach can, when texts are set in contexts—however minimal certain historical contexts may be compared with today's field-recorded performance contexts—illuminate essential features of compositional and transmissive processes.

In a book which dealt with the changing contexts, functions, transmission methods, and aesthetics in one regional ballad tradition through a concentration on three tradition-bearers, and which illustrated how that tradition moved from a vitally recreative stage to a memorial stage, I attempted to analyse the repertoire of one of the "personified embodiments of traditional re-creation," Anna Brown, paying particular attention to what was revealed from the structuring of her texts.[4] The investigation of Anna Brown's repertoire was an endeavour to study "the nature, the laws, and the operation of this loose kind of restraint—or this restrictive liberty" that animates a vital tradition through examination of its "tangible products" "in the particular successive performances" of an individual singer. In this essay I propose to examine rather the tangible products "in the commoner yet sadly deficient record, scattered through time and space, to which multitudes have contributed in their turn," by considering "Hugh Spencer's Feats in France" (Child 158) in terms of structure, function, and context and whatever light they may shed on processes of traditional re-creation.

"Hugh Spencer" suggests itself initially because it provides in one of its versions a text from approximately the same period as Anna Brown's repertoire but from a different culture area, a combination of factors which should furnish the grounds for instructive comparison and contrast. The story appears in four texts, three published and one unpublished. Child's A version is from the Percy MS., his B from the Percy Papers, "communicated by the Duchess Dowager of Portland," and his C from Dr. Joseph Robertson's *Journal of Excursions,* recorded in the Leochel parish of Aberdeenshire in 1829.[5] The unpublished version ("D") comes from the Glenbuchat Ballad MSS., compiled in the Aberdeenshire parish of Glenbuchat before 1818. There are, then, two English texts, one from the seventeenth and one from the eighteenth century, and two Scottish texts, both collected in western Aberdeenshire parishes in the early decades of the nineteenth century. No tunes or North American texts have been recorded. One English text, B, and one Scottish, D, provide the focus for discussion.

The story, briefly expressed, is this: the King sends a young hero to another country (France) to see if they want peace or war and the hero impresses the King of that country with his feats. Only in A does an overt comment on the fulfillment of the mission appear:

> 'Why then, comend [me] to that Englishe kinge,
> And tell him thus now ffrom mee,
> That there shall neuer be open warres kept in my land
> Whilest peace kept that there may bee.' (A36)

In B, C, and D the fulfillment is implicit, when the King's admiration of the prowess shown indicates that the desired end has been achieved. With the fulfillment explicit or implicit, however, the main narrative theme stands out clearly: the hero performs so redoubtably that the French, taking him as epitomizing his country's martial prowess, will not want war.

Examination of the B version should reveal whether the structural characteristics of Anna Brown's repertoire are also to be found in a text of roughly comparable period. In length (thirty-eight stanzas) it corresponds to a number of the substantial Brown texts, though in content it has no obvious parallel, the nearest probably being "Johnie Scot." The version has three Acts, of three, two, and two scenes:

I   i   The King of England sends the Hero and two companions on a mission to see if France wants peace or war.

     ii   The King of France responds courteously but unfavorably: the English broke the last peace.

     iii   The Queen of France insults the Hero and his companions and issues a challenge to a joust; the hero confers with his companions and accepts.

II   i   The first French Knight offers the hero a choice of steeds.

     ii   The second French Knight is engaged in joust by the Hero and defeated.

III   i   The Queen of France declares he must die for that, but the Hero and his companions slay many of the Queen's guards.

     ii   The King of France asks the Hero to stop, and expresses his admiration.

The five scenes of Acts I and II have each a change in cast, with a different character partnering the hero every time, three royal figures, and two knights. The character structure could be expressed in this way:

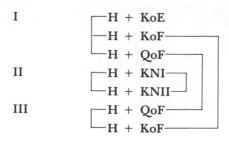

I

II

III

Table 1

Here we have a triad followed by two balances, standard units of arrangement which at first sight do not seem to be bound in an overall symmetry, but there are also annular links between Acts I and III framing the balance of the two Knights in Act II; for full symmetry one would expect a third scene in Act III involving the hero and the King of England. In Anna Brown's repertoire the norm for the ballad cast is three emotionally interacting characters, sometimes accompanied by narrative agents (bonny boys and the like). Clearly here we do not have a simple three-character interaction; what we do have emerges if the basic narrative conflict of the version is borne in mind: the tension between the English and the French. This tension expresses itself in three antithetical pairings: in the apposition of the King of England and the King of France; in the apposition of the generous Knight I who aids the hero and the nasty Queen of France who opposes the hero; and climactically in the direct combat between the hero, the representative of England, and Knight II, the representative of France. The first apposition shows in the characters introduced in the initial two scenes, the second apposition in the next two scenes, and the third apposition in the central fifth scene. In short, there are two sets of three characters, in apposition. While the norm itself, a triad of interacting characters, does not obtain, a standard variation of the norm, a pair of balancing triads, does. In addition to the major six characters, this version contains two shadows of the hero, the companions, who appear frequently in folktales but seldom in ballads.

The major pattern of the narrative structure is embodied in the three narrative concepts of mission, obstacle, and tests. In Act I the King of England gives the hero a mission, the King of France by his unfavorable response raises an obstacle to the success of the mission, and the Queen of France sets a test by which the success or failure of the mission will be judged. In Act II the hero prepares for the test and then in the test gains the victory. In Act III the Queen sets another test which the hero again comes through victoriously, and the King of France in his favorable response alters his attitude, thereby removing the obstacle and implicitly indicating the success of the mission. The main pattern can be expressed schematically in this way:

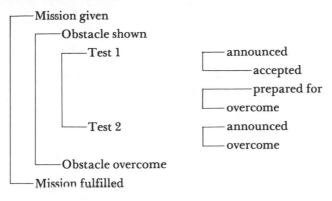

Table 2

Present here are the customary balancing and annular relationships. Also present and pervasive in the central parts of this version is a triadic pattern on and just below the surface which contributes, though in minor fashion, to the structuring organization. In stanza 13 the Queen says:

> I have a steed in my stable
>   that thou canst not ride;
> I have a spear in my keeping
>   that thou canst not guide;
> And I have a knight in my realm
>   that thou darest not abide.   (B13)

These three linked narrative ideas—steed to ride, spear to guide, knight to abide—are used to bind together the test scenes of the version. Stanzas 17 to 23 are concerned with the choice of steed, and then follow stanzas 24 to 26:

> When that *horse* was saddled,
>   and Spencer got on,
> With his *spear* at his foot,
>   O he was portly man!

> "Now I am on that *steede*-back
>   that I could not ride,
> That *spear* in my keeping
>   that I could not guide,
> Come shew me that French *knight*
>   that I dare not abide."

> "It is a sign by thy sharp shin,
>   ay, and thy cropped knee,
> That you are no fit match
>   to justle with me:"
> "Why it makes no matter," says Spencer,
>   "you hear no brags of me."   (B24-26)

The underlined words show how the tripartite idea governs the middle stanza 25 (which echoes 13) and how the first two elements inform stanza 24; the third element turns up in stanza 26 where the knight has his solitary speech. In these stanzas, then, the tripartite idea occurs twice, in one triad embedded within another. After the preparations for the joust the stanzas dramatizing the joust itself, 27 to 31, continue the pattern within the triadic sequence of the courses run; the focus on the spear in the second encounter is framed by the hero's doing more than merely abiding the knight in the first and third encounters:

> The first time they rode together,
>   now Sir Hugh and he,
> He turned him in his saddle
>   like an apple on a tree.
>
> The next time they rode together,
>   now Sir hugh and he,
> He lit upon his breast-plate,
>   and he broke his spear in three.
>
> "A spear now," says Spencer,
>   "a spear now get me:"
> "Thou shalt have one," says Willoughby,
>   "if in France one there be."
>
> "O tye two together
>   and the stronger they'l be,
> For the French is the better,
>   and the better shall be:"
> "Why it makes no matter,' says Spencer,
>   'you hear no brags of me."
>
> The next time they rode together,
>   now Sir Hugh and he,
> He threw him fifteen foot from his saddle,
>   and he broke his back in three:
> "Now I have slain thy justler,
>   Queen Maude, I tell thee."   (B27-31)

The patterning of this tripartite idea, which is employed in both compressed and expanded form, may be given diagrammatic shape thus:

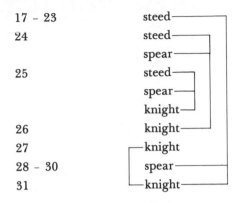

17 – 23	steed
24	steed
	spear
25	steed
	spear
	knight
26	knight
27	knight
28 – 30	spear
31	knight

Table 3

In the narrative as in the character structuring, then, one finds the organization achieved by the balancing, annular, and triadic patterns that also characterize Anna Brown's ballads.

The same statement can be made about the stanzaic structure: Act I, scenes i and ii have each a pair of balances, scene iii a triad of balances, the third framed in *Achtergewicht;* Act II, scene i has a triad and an extended triad, scene ii a triad and a framed triad; and Act III has a framed balance for scene i and a triad for scene ii. The overall architectonic organization of this ballad version can now be portrayed in diagram:

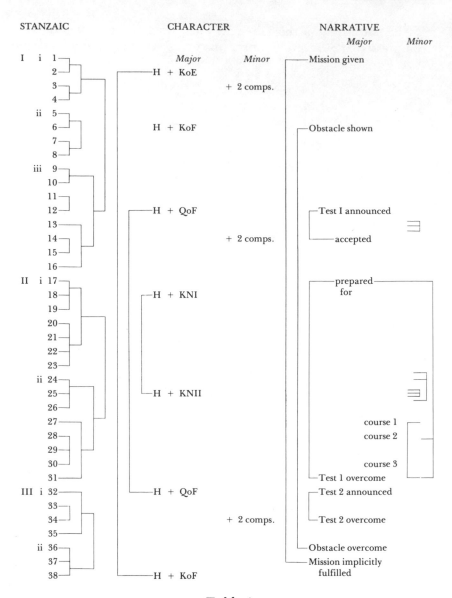

Table 4

The text, then, can be seen to be organized by oral traditional patternings. The ending, while satisfactory, appears to be somewhat contracted, and one's first impression that the success of the mission could well be made more explicit is reinforced by the potential inherent in the patterns for greater symmetry. A fuller symmetry would indicate (and this may have achieved realization at some point in tradition) a third scene in Act III in annular balance with the first scene in Act I, a scene between the hero and the King of

England where the success of the mission and the part played by the two companions are acknowledged. The relationship of Acts I and III would stand in this manner:

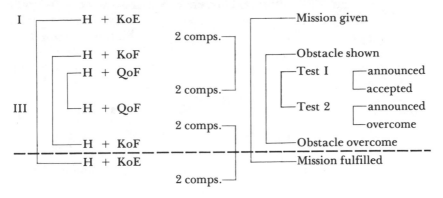

Table 5

That the success of the mission is not elaborated upon (either here or in the other versions) would suggest that its function as framework has been served and that the ballad's main emotional effect has been achieved, a point to be returned to. Another topic raised by the scheme which will receive later consideration is the role of the companions.

In this eighteenth century English version of "Hugh Spencer's Feats in France" the same principles of organization inform the ballad as inform Anna Brown's repertoire. Despite the difference in language, English as opposed to Scots, the essential components of 158B exhibit a remarkable correspondence to those of the Brown ballads. The one noteworthy divergence might appear to lie in the varying of the dramatis personae from the norm of three to include two sets of three, but one finds the same variation in Anna Brown's "Fause Foodrage" and "Rose the Red and White Lily," both of which have two sets of three characters. The same principles of organization exist here as in Anna Brown's ballads, and, it is logical to suggest, for the same reasons: the textual patternings are manifestations of re-creative compositional processes that derive from the exigencies of nonliteracy. It is the textual results of these re-creative compositional processes that give the ballad those hallmarks which demarcate this genre from written literature. This English ballad version also shows that any argument that would dismiss the idea of re-creative oral composition in British balladry through dismissing the possible validity of Anna Brown as a source (the *argumentum ad mulierem* approach?) would have to be rethought. One swallow makes neither a summer nor a drunkard, but the evidences of this text cannot be ignored.

The hitherto unpublished text of "Hugh Spencer's Feats"—D—comes from the Glenbuchat Ballads, collected by the minister of the parish, Rev. Robert Scott, in the first two decades of the nineteenth century. The collection contains representatives of fifty-eight ballad-stories in Child, a remarkable trawl from a small parish which by the 1811 census had only 443 souls. The four-volume MSS were deposited in King's College Library at the University of Aberdeen midway through this century and are being edited for publication.

SIR HUGH

1   It fell about the Martinmas
      The wind blew loud an cauld
   An a the lads in fair Scotlan
      Have drawn them to some haul   house-shelter

2   Except it was him young Sir Hugh
      An he maun sail the sea
   An ay betwixt the kings twa
      Wi leisome letters three   lawful

3   O Monday, Monday he took gate   started out
      An o Tuesday shippit he
   An lang or Friday's afternoon
      In fair France landed he

4   O when he cam before the king
      He fell upon his knee
   Stand up, stand up now young Sir Hugh
      What is your will wi me

5   I am come to your Grace he says
      Wi leisome letters three
   To see if ye'll lay down your wars
      Or leave or let us be

6   Ye know I am an aged man
      An the truth ye do well see
   But I will not lay down my wars
      Nor leave nor let them be

7   O then out spake the Queen hersel
      As in her bower stood she
   I know well by thy lang lang shanks
      An that knap on thy knee   lump

8   That I have a shepherd's son in France
      Will joust an hour with thee
   O by my sooth said young Sir Hugh
      That sight fain would I see

9   But yet I tale my word again
      I'm new come from the sea
   My blood lance knives an harnassed steed
      I left them behind me

10   O then out spak an eldron knight   elderly
          A Scots born man was he
      I have three steeds in my stable
          As good as runs on ground

11   The worstan steed in my stable
          He cost me fifty pounds
      An you shall have the best of them
          To joust an hour wi him

12   I have three brands into my hall
          That cost me lands three
      An you shall have the best o them
          To joust an hour him wi

13   The first an steed that they drew out
          An he was penny grey
      He wouda run oer moss or mold   boggy ground;
          The lang, lang, simmer's day   earth

14   The next an steed that they drew out
          An he was berry brown
      He wouda run oer hill or mold
          Until the day gaed down

15   The next an steed that they drew out
          An he was jet jet black
      His een were rolling in his head
          Like wild fire in a slack   hill-pass
      A boy, a boy said young Sir Hugh
          Put on the saddle on that

16   The first an course of their meeting
          Between Sir Hugh an he
      The brands they brak, an the wight steeds lap   stout
          But still sat he an he

17   A brand, a brand said young Sir Hugh
          A brand for charity
      Cheer up thy heart said the Scottish knight
          A brand soon shalt thou see

18   The next an course of their meeting
          Between Sir Hugh an he
      The bridles brak, an the wight steeds lap
          But still sat he and he

19   A bridle, a bridle said young Sir Hugh
          A bridle for charity
      Cheer up thy heart said the Scottish knight
          A bridle soon shalt thou see

20   The third an course of their meeting
          Between Sir Hugh and he
      He struck that good lord to the heart
          An oer the steed fell he

21 O have ye any more whelps to kill
        Or any more shepherds to die
    Or have ye any more scuddler boys   scullions
        Go bring them here to me

22 Light down light down now young Sir Hugh
        O ill mat be thy chance
    For thou hast slain to me this day
        A shield but an a lance
    The Duke of Darbois ae dear son
        An the best jouster in France

23 I woud I had gien the lands an rents
        An ha's an towers so high
    That thou had jousted wi him an hour
        An left an let him be

24 O never scorn a Scottish knight
        Tho' new come frae the sea
    For if he hae a drap o Scots blood
        He'll no be scorned wi thee[6]

The structuring of this version, rendered in diagrammatic form, is as follows:

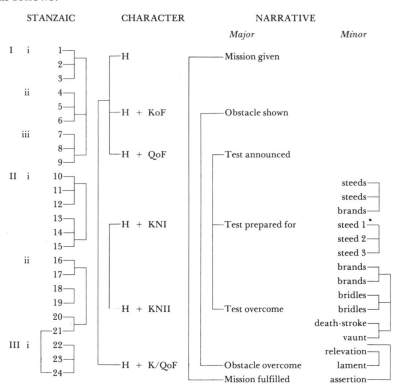

Table 6

The B and D versions exhibit differences. Clearly, there is a wide divergence in the words used to tell the story; adherents of the memorial transmission theory would have a hard task trying to account for this splendid verbal fecundity. The social and cultural contexts of the versions have influenced not only the languages, English and Scots, but also the dramatis personae, for in D the hero is Scottish, as is Knight I, facts to be taken up again. In addition, the two companions do not occur and the King of Scotland, his part in the mission just referred to in passing, makes no actual appearance on stage. In the narrative structure no second test exists and the main one is presented in triadic organization. The D version shows even further compression of the ending, with just one short scene, between the hero and an unnamed interlocutor, either the King or Queen of France. Despite the differences, however, the essential components remain constant, as one can see clearly from the schemas. The constants, in short, are the essentials of the story while the variables are the means, often culturally conditioned, to achieve certain specific ends in the telling of the story. Tristram Coffin's argument that ballads in transmission tend to reduce to a lyric "emotional core"[7] may hold good for a tradition in its declining stages when transmission by rote memorization becomes standard; but when a tradition still thrives, when transmission involves re-creative composition, then the retained core is the narrative, not lyric, essence of the story. The narrative essence, of course, has a crucial relationship to the emotional attitudes expressed by the ballad, as will be discussed shortly; the point being emphasized for the moment is that while the emotional core of a ballad may find lyric expression in the declining stages of a tradition, in the vital re-creative stages it finds narrative expression.

Analysis of the structures of the B and D versions now opens the way for discussion of the ballad's functions. The pervasive narrative tension, we have seen, concerns the conflict between one national group, the English or the Scots and another, the French. This tension expresses itself in a number of ways but centrally in the story's climactic section, in the defeat of the French representative by the English or Scottish hero; the testing of the hero's abilities in the joust corresponds to the testing of national prowess. The ballad as a whole, then, has the effect of raising pride in "Englishness" or "Scottishness." A number of features conduce to this effect, most obviously the frequency, very marked in B but present also in D, of the adjectives and nouns denoting the countries and the peoples. The role of the companions in B now becomes clearer. After the Queen of France has insulted the hero and his companions by calling them "English shepherds" (before the days of the nation of shopkeepers, presumably) and then proposed the joust, he confers with them:

> O then spoke Hugh Willoughby
>   and John of Atherly:
> If you won't take it [in] hand,
>   why turn it unto we.
>
> "It shall neer be said in England,"
>   says Hugh Spencer, he,
> "That I refused a good justling
>   And turned it to ye."   (B15–16)

After the hero has completed the first test, the Queen declares he
by law must die:

> "It shall neer be said in England,"
>   says Hugh Spencer, he;
> "It shall neer be said in England,"
>   says Hugh Willoughby;
>
> "It shall neer be said in England,"
>   says John of Atherly,
> "That a queen of another nation
>   eer had her will of we."
>
> They laid their heads together,
>   and their backs to the wall;
> There were four score of the Queen's guards,
>   and they slew them all.   (B33–35)

The companions are there not only to reflect the hero's prowess but
also to underscore by words and deeds the virtues of Englishmen.

Where in B the Queen insults the three by calling them English
shepherds, in D she insults the Scottish hero by unflattering comments on his physique and then by proposing a joust with not a
noble but a French shepherd's son. (The appearance of the notion
of shepherd in both at this point could hardly be construed as coin-
cidental; it illustrates how an idea or word may be conserved and
put, re-creatively, to different uses.) After the hero has demonstrated
his, and by extension the Scots', capacities, it is dramatically revealed that his knightly opponent was "the best jouster in France,"
which sets the seal on the glorious performance and leads naturally
to the climactic assertion of Scottish worth:

> O never scorn a Scottish knight
>   Tho' new come frae the sea
> For if he hae a drap of Scots blood
>   He'll no be scorned wi thee   (D24)

The reason for the compression of the ending remarked upon earlier
becomes evident: with the victory in the joust and the triumphant
emphasis on Scottish worth the main emotional purpose of the
ballad has been served. The "mission" simply provides the frame-

work for the exploits and once the exploits have been performed and emotional satisfactions gained, its success can be left implicit. On the score of national feeling the B and D versions stand at variance in one interesting regard: where the Scottish version has a single-stranded advocacy of Scottishness, the French being presented in consistently unlikable terms, the English version has a more sophisticated balance between Englishness and Frenchness which accords a civil amount of decent qualities to the adversary. The King of France, it is stressed, speaks "courteously" and reacts to the hero's asking of "peace or war" with the reasonable argument that the English broke the peace last time (B7, 8). Most strikingly, where the generous Knight who supplies the hero with the equipment for combat in IIi is Scottish in the D version, in the English version he is French. In its expression of a sense of national identity, then, the English version is less strident than the Scottish; this difference could lead to interesting cultural speculations, but that hare will not be pursued.

The B and D versions share the same function-on-the-general-level, the reinforcing of group solidarity, but differ in the function-on-the-concrete-level: the one reinforces a sense of Englishness, the other of Scottishness. (Here, as so often in folkloristics, there is a need for terms, corresponding in kind to type and version or motifeme and allomotif, to distinguish between the different levels.) Whereas the folkloristic truism of "stable function, variable agent" holds good for the first level, on the second, if agent is in this case equated with story, it would reverse to "stable agent, variable function." In this ballad the constants are the essential story and the general function, the variables are the means of realizing the story and the concrete function. In the B and D texts the concrete function varies because the versions were intended by singers in different cultural contexts for different audiences, and in like manner the means of realization are fashioned by the singers in accordance with local cultural as well as social and environmental conditions. Here we arrive at a significant element in ballad re-creation: intentional adaptation by the singer so that the story fulfills its function in its performance context. The alteration of function according to performance context demonstrates the importance of the re-creative and the adaptive in the oral traditional processes, not simply in terms of compositional method but also in terms of cultural conditions. It also shows the inutility of assuming that change in a vital ballad tradition happens just negatively (that, in line with the devolutionary premise, there is a deterioration from a mythically "good" text), or superorganically, that is, without the conscious artistic participation of actual people. Ballad versions have always been sung by specific performers in specific cultural settings, and from those texts from the vital stage of tradition one can learn the nature of the interaction. Among the singers of a flourishing tradition there thrives, as an essential element of their art, conscious re-creation, which can operate both in compositional response to the exigencies of nonliteracy or in functional response to the emotional needs of a culture.

"Hugh Spencer" has a certain relevance for the question of the relationship to history of the historical ballads. The standard non-folkloristic approach concerns itself with the literal truth or otherwise of the texts; normally, the ballads are found wanting in the literal truths that can be corroborated from documents. It was an intrinsic part of Child's meticulous nineteenth-century philological approach to sift the details of historical ballad texts and study them against documentary information. In his head-notes to this ballad-story, for example, he discusses two English fourteenth-century Hugh Spensers and declares that none of the four wives of Charles IV and Charles VI was called Maude. What study of tradition reveals, however, is that details, and especially names, are among the most mutable variables in a re-creative tradition; while details may on occasion provide valuable clues and insights, they do not afford a ubiquitously reliable foundation for generalizations about the literal truth of ballad-stories. Whether ballads are literally true or not, however, is not the prime question (though it can be an interesting topic in several instances), the prime question is how they function in their contexts, and the answers to that can illuminate the study of the past. They are rarely documents of literal fact, but they can, as "Hugh Spencer" shows, be invaluable revelations of the emotional forces and social attitudes that operated within a culture and were given expressive form within sections of society which, historically, are otherwise mute.

Re-creation, both compositional and functional, permeates the processes of a vital ballad tradition. The ballad performer re-creates his versions, both artistically and culturally, in accordance with the conditions of his context and his individual flair. Many contemporary ballad scholars (D. K. Wilgus, James Porter, Iørn Piø, for example) have stressed the necessity for paying profound attention to living singers in living contexts, as a corrective to the literary superorganic treatment of balladry that held sway for so long. The main concerns of this kind of synchronic study—concerns with functions, contexts (social, cultural, and performance), essential structures, and the individual creative singer—can fruitfully inform diachronic study of the ballad genre as well. "Hugh Spencer" demonstrates how an exploration of the eighteenth and nineteenth century versions of a ballad-type which relates the versions functionally to their contexts and the nameless performers to their audiences, and which examines the constants and the variables through the essential structures, can illuminate the re-creative element within tradition and contribute to an increased understanding of the two forces, of conservation and of re-creation, to which Bertrand Bronson, with the grace, perception, and human sympathy that have characterized his writings for four decades, has directed the ballad scholar's attention.

NOTES

[1]Bertrand Harris Bronson, "Habits of the Ballad As Song," in *The Ballad As Song* (Berkeley and Los Angeles: University of California Press, 1969), pp. 105-107; first published in *Five Gayley Lectures, 1947-1954* (University of California Publications: English Studies, no. 10. [1954]).

[2]"The Formulaic Improvisation Theory of Ballad Tradition—A Counterstatement," *Journal of American Folklore*, 74 (1961), 114.

[3]Vladimir Propp, *Morphology of the Folktale*, 2d. edition, ed. Louis A. Wagner (Austin: University of Texas Press, 1968); "Transformations in Fairy Tales," in *Mythology: Selected Readings*, comp. Pierre Maranda (Harmondsworth; Baltimore: Penguin Books, 1972).

[4]*The Ballad and the Folk* (London and Boston: Routledge and Kegan Paul, 1972).

[5]Francis J. Child, *The English and Scottish Popular Ballads* (Boston: Houghton, Mifflin and Co., 1882-1898), vol. 3, pp. 275-82.

[6]In the transcription of the text, capitalization has been regularized and "&" silently expanded. Line 8[1] of the manuscript has "'s son" scored out and "swain" inserted above. Since the alteration probably resulted from an editorial fear of an indelicate misinterpretation, the original has been restored. That such an interpretation was current is clear from Joseph Robertson's recorded "comment of the reciter" of the C version: "The shepherd's son was the Queen's own son" (Child, vol. 3, p. 282).

[7]"'Mary Hamilton' and the Anglo-American Ballad as an Art Form," *Journal of American Folklore*, 70 (1957), 208-14; reprinted in *The Critics and the Ballad*, eds. MacEdward Leach and Tristram P. Coffin (Carbondale, Ill.: Southern Illinois University Press, 1961), pp. 245-56.

Impossibles in Ballad Style

Hugh Shields

The rhetoric of oral literature is a neglected subject, except for that quantifiable class which can be used to show just how oral a particular branch of oral literature may be. Within that class, the more easily quantifiable matter gets the greater attention; thus computers work overtime on formulaic style so that authors may prove this or that work or genre orally composed, improvised or re-created. In this endeavor, ballads have not been left untouched, though it remains to prove—or to abandon—the hypothesis of an exclusively oral-formulaic mode of composition in them.[1] It is becoming clearer that the demarcation of oral and literate modes of composition is not easy to draw nor probably very precise. Features apparently characteristic of oral expression occur as well in written literature which, after all, is written by people accustomed also to speak. Terms to describe such features exist already, having long since been invented for application to written texts. So it is with the device called *adynaton* in Greek, "impossible,"[2] which the second part of this article will examine in the ballads of English. But the *adynaton* is not unique of its kind nor is it an isolated feature of oral expression. The first part therefore, by way of introduction, will sketch a context for this device, ranging as convenient over languages and beyond the ballad genre, so that the rhetorical impossible may be seen as one of a variety of means of literary emphasis in oral style extending from simple hyperbole to actual negation of reality.

1

Such features are not of course excluded from the literature which is a function of writing and reading; but it may well be that they flourish in direct proportion to the oral scope of literature. The rational, objectivizing processes of writing and reading seem to curb in the writer a natural inclination to enhance by exaggeration, to which on the other hand oral media give free play. Simple hyperbole is an excellent illustration. Its use is most intense in the genre which was first and has been foremost in providing matter for research in formulaic composition: the epic. The Old French *chansons de geste* offer many illustrations, the most startling of which for a modern reader is no doubt the motif of vertical cleavage of an enemy, saddle, horse and all, so that the sword may even remain embedded in the earth.[3] Christians put to flight Moslem forces who implausibly outnumber them, as it happens with William of Orange when

> Pur un sul home en fuïrent vint mil.[4]
> *Before a single man twenty thousand fled.*

The arbitrary choice of some large number is not confined to epic; in a ballad a man may bet as much as 10,000 to 1 that a girl will not preserve her virtue with him "in yonder shady trees," so that the subject of "The Broomfield Wager" appears as a quasi-impossible (43.16).[5] Quasi-impossibles have many functions in folksong; a string of them affirms that "love will find out the way" on a sheet of the Euing Collection thus subtitled,[6] while others are the object of tasks or riddles, perhaps better called pseudo-impossibles in such a ballad as "Captain Wedderburn" (46). Such elements of contest lead normally to a solution or fulfillment; otherwise they must be considered impossibles, though not necessarily following the rhetorical pattern with which we shall be principally concerned in due course. When a girl orders a suitor, "Apportez-moi la lune, le soleil à la main," it is foolish of him in one version to try, for we already knew that "La chos' fut impossible, la bell' le savait bien" without the addition of so explicit an authorial comment.[7] Its curious rationality, which is that of the *adynaton,* may seem to set it off from the non-rational impulse towards hyperbole which we have noticed in the *chansons de geste.* Yet it would be wrong to dissociate positive and negative expressions of the impossible or near impossible, since they share the common intention of stimulating reflection on the notion expressed, whether its actuality is denied, envisaged or narrated.

Here we might notice that type of hyperbole which seeks embellishment of ordinary things. Much of the mobile text in ballads enshrines pictures of a gilded reality, like that of the ship manned by girls in "Le Merveilleux Navire," of modern tradition, or of a fifteenth-century precursor:

>   . . . veez cy mes amours venir,
> En ung beau basteau sur Seine   qui est couvert de sappin;
> Les cordons en sont de saye,   la voille en est de satin;
> Le grant mast en est d'iviere,   l'estournay en est d'or fin;
> Les mariniers qui le meynent   ne sont pas de ce païs.
> L'ung est filz du roy de France,   il porte la fleur de lis,
> L'aultre est filz . . .   cestuy la est mon amy.[8]

. . . here is my love coming   In a fine ship on the Seine   all covered in firwood;   Her sheets are of silk,   her sail of satin, Her mainmast of ivory,   her helm of pure gold;   The sailors who sail her   are not of this country.   One is the king of France's son,   he wears the lily flower,   The other is son. . . ,   he is the one who is my lover.

A well-known sixteenth-century text of a Spanish ballad offers similar motifs:

. . . vio venir una galera	que a tierra quiere llegar.
Las velas traía de seda,	la ejercia de un cendal;
marinero que la manda	diciendo viene un cantar
que la mar hacía en calma,	los vientos hace amainar,
los peces que andan al hondo	arriba los hace andar,
las aves que andan volando	en el mástil las hace posar . . .[9]

He saw a galley coming,   making for land.   She has sails of silk and tackle of fine silk;   The sailor who commands her   is singing a song   Which calms the sea   and abates the winds,   The fish that swim at the bottom   to the surface it attracts,   The fowl that fly,   it makes them light upon the mast . . .

But pictorial description here gives way quickly to the enchantment of a song sung by the sailor which compels all nature to listen along with Count Arnaldos. Hyperbole thus can permit an easy passage from experienced reality to a degree of the supernatural. Discontinuity between the two is still less evident in an Occitanian ballad narrating the apocryphal attendance of Mary Magdalen at Mass to hear and see a handsome preacher (who is Christ); description of her dazzlingly beautiful toilet is followed by details, both extravagant and unnatural, of its effect in church:

Mas sa maire la n'a cueifada	em' un penchon d'argentol;
Mas la rauba que la li dona	lo solelh li es pertot,
Lo davantal que la li dona	la luna li es pertot,
Dins lo colet que la li dona	las estialas son pertot.
Quand ela entret dins la gleisa	los benitiers fasián lo torn,
Quand fuguet al mieg dins la gleisa	los altars trambleron tots.
[Los prestres quitan la messa	e los clerjons las leissons . . .][10]

Her mother had dressed her hair   with a comb of silver;   The dress she gives her,   the sun is all over it,   The apron she gives her,   the moon is all over it,   On the collar she gives her   the stars are everywhere.   When she went into the church   the vessels of holy water overturned,   When she came to the middle of the church   all the altars trembled.   The priests leave the Mass,   the clerks leave the lessons . . .

During and after the Middle Ages, it sometimes happened that an extravagant nobility strove to make their ships, costumes, etc., as beautiful in actuality as in these pictures.[11] But they did not thereby invalidate hyperbole in poetry; they introduced it into another branch of art. To realize the "impossible" was in no sense to disqualify it from use as such in literary convention.

Ballads in English also use hyperbolic embellishment in motifs of limited scope. As well, they seem inclined, more than those of France or Spain, to make supernatural motifs the essential motivation of action. For our present purpose, such motifs as shapechanging can be defined as the effecting of the impossible. Just as in oral poetry there is no clear dividing line between the hyperbolic and the impossible, neither is there one between the supernatural and the impossible. "The Two Magicians" — and to take an example from modern oral tradition, "Tam Lin" — show serial shape-changing as actually happening:

> He grew into her arms two
> Like to a savage wild (. . . adder, snake etc.)   (39D)

In French tradition, on the other hand, "Les Transformations" only verbalizes about envisaged shape-changing:

> Oh si tu te mets biche   dans un beau champ
> Je me mettrai chasseure   pour te chasser . . .[12]
>
> *Oh if you make yourself a doe   in a fair field   I shall make myself*
> *a huntsman   to hunt you . . .*

To this may be compared the English song "Hares on the Mountains," in which shape-changing is not actual; either the provoking young women run *like* hares on the mountains etc., or else the hypothesis is made, "*If* all the young women were hares . . ." (44.2-12). In a well-known Anglo-Irish broadside ballad, "Molly Bawn," metamorphosis is not even envisaged; the huntsman simply mistakes his sweetheart for a swan/fawn/heron.[13] All these songs have been commonly considered, not textually, but thematically related. And it would be easy to multiply examples showing that between the extraordinary, the impossible and the unnatural happening there may be poetic equivalence in folksong.

Among the varied means by which "non-transformations" may be expressed, hypothesis is the most interesting since it is very prevalent in the folksong of many languages. Often it expresses a wish which cannot be fulfilled, no wish more common in lyric than to be able to fly like a bird. The motif occurs in the ballad genre:

> If I was as swift as any swallow (I would cry vengeance).
>   (196B, cf. C, 2)[14]

Alongside this kind of desired but unreal hypothesis we might range such optative expressions of strong emotion (curses) as

May the very grass he treads upon the ground refuse to grow
(now that he has been unfaithful).[15]

But another hardly less common form of hypothesis regards in at
least ostensibly more detached fashion the realization of what we
might call an impossible "of quantity": one having to do with
magnitude either temporal or spatial. The pains of Hell, laments
Dives, will not end

> . . . had I as many years to abide
> As there are blades of grass.   (56)

Dives certainly draws the literary form of his thought from medieval
homiletic writing; compare the comment on the pains of Hell—
similarly conceived—in the *Vision of St. Paul:*

> Postea interrogavit Paulus angelum, "Quot sunt pene inferni?" Et
> dixit ei angelus, "Pene inferni sunt centum quadraginta quatuor
> milia; et si essent centum viri loquentes ab inicio mundi, et unusquis-
> que habuisset quatuor linguas ferreas, non possent dinumerare ceteras
> penas (*var.* unam penam de penis) inferni."[16]

> *Then Paul asked the angel, 'What is the extent of the torments of
> Hell?' And the angel said to him, 'The torments of Hell number one
> hundred and forty-four thousand; and if a hundred men had been
> talking since the beginning of the world and each one had four
> tongues of iron, they could not have enumerated the other torments
> (*var. one of the torments) of Hell.*

Secular songs also use hypothetical "impossibles of quantity." One
which has been well documented in its extension and age ends up
distorted in the nursery rhyme "If All the World Were Paper": an
eminently translatable commonplace, as this parallel between Irish
and English texts will illustrate:

> If Killyboyne (?) it was mine in chorus (*recte* inkhorn/inkhorns)
> And the green fields they were mine in white
> And if my pen it was made of the temperéd steel
> Sure my true love's praises I could never write.[17]

Dá mbudh dubhach uilig an fháirrge 's a' talamh bheith 'na pháipéar
          bhán,
Cleití fada geala 's na h-ealuigheacha ba chiún a' snámh,
Cléirigh Eireanna & Alabainn, Sasanaigh a bheith do'n Fhrainnc
          's do'n Spáinn,
Geanúileacht mo chailín-sa níor bhféidir damh fhagháil scríobhtha
          i mbán.[18]

If the sea was all ink and the land white paper,   [*If I had*] *long,
white quills of the swans most gently swimming,   The clerks of Ireland and Scotland, Englishmen (foreigners?) from France and Spain,*

The comeliness of my sweetheart, I could not get it written down in white.

Returning to "reality," but to that of the future, we may notice prophecies. The Christian supernatural is not to be strictly cut off from the pre-Christian magic which nourishes many English, Scandinavian and other ballads; of this fact the Otherworld of "Draumkvedet" is probably the best illustration. On the other hand, the two are not to be simply confused. Often ballad narratives are too explicitly Christian in character. The miracle of the bending fruit tree retains its significance in the grand design of Christian history at the same time as it operates on an interpersonal level. Signs in Nature prophesied by the infant Christ at the end of the English version belong to the grand design:

> 'O I shall be as dead, mother,
>   As the stones in the wall;
> O the stones in the streets, mother,
>   Shall mourn for me all.
>
> Upon Easter-day, mother,
>   My uprising shall be;
> O the sun and the moon, mother,
>   Shall both rise with me.'   (54A)

In French folksong, such prophetic motifs acquired penitential value. "La Passion de Jésus-Christ,"[19] in ballad form, became a Holy Week begging song; the same function belongs to a recently recorded millennial text in Occitanian:

> Quand lo jorn del Jutjament vendrá
> Lo cial, la terra tramblará;
> Lo cial será coma un quiejor
> E la terra coma un blandor.
> Las estialas qu'al cel serán
> Totas en terra descendrán
> E descendrán de jorn en jorn
> Coma las fuelhas e las flors.
> Tots los enfants nascuts serán ⎤
> Davant lhors maires creiarán ⎥ *repeated*
> E cridarán grands e petits,
> "Senhor, donatz nos lo paradís . . ."[20]

*When the day of Judgment comes   Heaven and earth will tremble; Heaven shall be mute (?)   And earth shall be softened (?)   The stars in the sky   All shall descend to earth   And they shall descend day after day   Like the leaves and the flowers.   All the children [who] are born (*recte* unborn?)   Before (*recte* Inside?) their mothers shall cry out   And great and small shall cry "Lord, give us paradise . . ."*

Though textually corrupt, this passage gives a clue to an important medieval influence on religious folksong. The "Fifteen Signs of the Day of Judgment" was a medieval commonplace which lingered on in chapbook literature; a popular early medieval French poem on the subject uses terms similar to those of the Occitanian song in describing the descent of the stars and—more noteworthy—predicting that unborn children will cry out to God to let them not be born (evidently the folksong has lost a negative in line 9 above)[21] [figs. 1, 2]. Thus we may once again invoke, for our denials of reality in modern oral literature, a medieval written source with a significant oral function. To actual narration and to hypothesis of unnatural or extraordinary phenomena (statements in the past or the conditional) Christian prophecy adds their prediction (statements in the future). And the affinity of such predictions with the rhetorical impossible is evident in the Danish "Sven i Rosengård" with its concluding chain of *adynata* the last of which is

> Naar ser vi Havet braende?
> Naar vi ser Verdens Ende.[22]

When will the seas burn?   At the world's end.

So far we have been concerned with serious if not sacred texts. But we have also to notice the comic potential of the impossible or near impossible. The range of resources is hardly less. Hyperbole, in both epic and ballad, serves notably to describe ugliness or strangeness ("Kempy Kay," 33; cf. 34, 36, 99L etc., 129, 156). In "The Boy and the Mantle" (29), it neatly characterizes Queen Guinevere's jealousy of a virtuous rival, "I have seene tane out of her bedd Of men fiveteene." Quasi-impossibles figure again in riddles ("King John and the Bishop," 45) and in wagers (the Anglo-Irish "Seducer Outwitted")[23] etc. A quality of self-parody is often to be surmised, and to state that a narrative is conceived as either mainly comic or mainly serious is often impossible; what Child apparently called the "diverting absurdity" of "The Bold Lieutenant" must have diverted more than professors of folklore (lady rewards suitor for outdoing his brother by retrieving the fan she has dropped into a den of lions).[24] Absurdity for its own sake is the simple basis of a great deal of popular comic literature; medieval *facetiae,* fools' plays, etc. are often nothing else than a string of nonsensical statements, and to that tradition we may certainly attach oral songs of lies and boasting. The "Land of Cokayne" left its legacy to folk tradition. And the "world turned upside down" became so great a commonplace of chapbooks that it could provoke double meaning in a French song in which a boy promises to show a girl "le monde à l'envers" and takes her to the wood to do so [figs. 3, 4].[25]

e second jour la mer descendra en bas en tant que apame la po
rt on veoir. Car de quāt cōme elle se sera esleuee plus hault q̄
les montaignes vers le ciel dune part. & tant se esleuent dail trepet
en hault uers le ciel qui est dessoubz terre. Et pō ce a pame la poinra
on veoir. Et de ce peut estre entendu ce que dit lapōm lipse caplo xxi.
Et mare iam non est. id est non apparet more solito.

FIGS. 1 and 2. The Fifteen Signs of the Day of Judgment, *from the "Desrain Livre de la Vigne Nostre Seigneur," MS Douce 134 (fifteenth century): f. 42ʳ, the* sea disappears *(second sign), and f. 42ᵛ,* sea monsters appear and cry out unin- telligibly *(third sign). By permission of the Bodleian Library, Oxford University.*

Le tiers jour les monstres de mer apparerõt. et donerõt
luoix et gemissemens que nul nentendra sinon dieu. Ces
monstres de mer sont les balaines et les serraines et aultres
mueilleux poissons qui seront assemblez par lieux sur la mer.
ainsi que dit le prophete. Osee iij. Sed et pisces maris congregabut.
Et elleront et plaindront icellon sappete. qui sera vne mer
ueillense chose a ouyr.

FIGS. 3 and 4. The World Upside Down, *from an eighteenth-century London chapbook in the Houghton Library, Harvard University.* Catalogue of English and American chapbooks and broadside ballads in Harvard College Library. *Cambridge, Mass., 1905, no. 1870 (58[ii]. 25), last two of twelve woodcuts: 11,* fishes fly and fish for men, *and 12,* earth and heavenly bodies are transposed. *By permission of the Houghton Library, Harvard University.*

Thus intellectual verbal play, in negating or otherwise modifying reality by various quite simple means, reinforces elements of narration or discourse which seem to deserve prominence. Whereas the means employed are relatively few—hyperbole, enigma and solution, hypothesis, absurd or predictive statement etc.—they have at their disposal a range of subject-matter embracing whatever is admitted as imaginable (possible through human effort, magic, miracles etc.) by the conventions of belief proper to a particular society cultivating oral traditions. We are not concerned here with the deployment of subject-matter in ballad narratives as a whole, but with detailed means of embellishing the action that throw highlights on motivation: means which, since they have to do with affective or non-rational elements, tend to seek striking and memorable presentation and so to be formulated with a high degree of conventionality. This is the character of the *adynaton,* to which we now turn our attention.

2

From the evidence of Child and Bronson, only a small number of ballads utilize the rhetorical *adynaton.* In most cases, moreover, the form of the device may be defined quite narrowly: a comparative proposition with two elements—one a subordinate temporal clause—emphasizing affective content in the narrative by means of a periphrasis signifying "never" through some natural or other impossibility. The periphrasis may occupy the main clause:

> The sun and the moon shall dance on the green
>> That night when I come hame.
>>> (51A)

More usually, however, it occupies the subordinate clause, while the main clause, a statement in the future, can be implied in a preceding question rather than actually expressed (and the periphrasis can moreover be followed by what may seem an unnecessary elucidation):

> "Whan will ye come hame again, Willie,
>> Now, Willie, tell to me?"
> "Whan the sun and the moon dances on the green,
>> And that will never be."
>>> (49D)

An appendix lists all obvious or potential *adynata* I have found in the two collections. Perusal of it will reveal two kinds of problem which our definition raises: that of aberrant forms and that of motifs which are not certain to have been intended as absurd. As we consider each of these categories in turn, the more normal ballad *adynaton* just defined will be by contrast brought better into focus.

Formally aberrant are the unaccomplished tasks proposed by a dead lover in some versions of "The Unquiet Grave": "Go fetch me a nut from a dungcon deep, etc." (78E) — a verse of three motifs is usual. No reward is held out, and the implication seems to be that none is possible: "I shall return when you fetch . . ." = "I shall not return." A rejoinder of the living lover expressed in a few cases — by putting the imperative in question form ("How can I fetch . . .") — confirms this interpretation.[26] If it is right to think that the "quasi-impossible" riddling form is here converted to an actual *adynaton,* then we have a rare case of this device in versions of a revenant ballad (for which also see below).

Less noteworthy probably than a deliberately incomplete riddle is a hypothesis left hanging in 114B:

> [For if?] a bird in a' the wood
>   Could sing as I could say,
> It would go in to my mother's bower,
>   And bid her kiss me, and take me away.

In other versions, Johnny Cock's wish that a bird/boy might carry the news of his wounding to his mother is fulfilled. In Child B however this verse is final, leaving doubt whether a wish or an impossible is intended, since either the text may be fragmentary or a bird's ability to act in this manner, even in ballads, may be doubted. It remains difficult, in the latter case, to frame the thought in *adynaton* form without departing considerably from its verbal formulation in the text.

On the other hand, we may with little doubt discern an *adynaton* in a single, albeit textually shaky, version of "The Fire of Frendraught" (196A), though in a form in which the logicality of a comparison is more implied than verbally articulate:

> The fish shall never swim in the flood,
>   Nor corn grow through the clay,
> Nor the fiercest fire that ever was kindled
>   Twin me and Rothiemay.

which seems to say, "Fish shall cease to swim . . . and corn to grow . . . before I part from Rothiemay," passing over the third, simply hyperbolic, line referring to the fire which threatens both their lives. But the third line is of special interest, for it shows the combining of *adynaton* motifs with a more straightforward form of emphasis, hyperbole, and that at the expense of syntax since the sentence is an anacoluthon.

Another form of emphasis in ballads appears actually to complement the *adynaton:* one in which, instead of an absurd motif, the
syntax of a temporal clause expresses a perfectly acceptable notion.
At least twice in Child we find such expression. "Young Peggy"
counters her mother's hostility to a match by declaring that she
will sleep in her lover's arms "When his grave's growing green" and
again "When your een winna see" (298). The king makes the outlaw
Murray sheriff of Ettrick forest "Surely while upwards grows the
trie" (305A, v. 68; cf. B, v. 55). Both ballads are exclusively Scottish,
both seem extinct, neither has survived in many texts, and the
motifs do not recur in other ballads. Probably then this device is an
artistic adaptation of the conventional impossible which replaces
"never" by "always"[27] but which did not find enough favor in sung
poetry to become conventional itself.

The association of impossibles with other forms of emphatic
proposition is apparent not only in examples drawing attention to
variation in form but also in others illustrating a certain fixity of
content. Our ballad impossibles use images or motifs which recur
in applications other than the *adynaton.* Fidelity is represented
metaphorically by images of rock not only in the impossible "rocks
will melt" but in the strict simile "as true . . . As the stones that lie
under yon ground."[28] Sun and moon are invoked in oaths,[29] assever-
ations and prophecies (54AB, 110E, 156F, 200BE, 209I etc.) as
readily as in imagined phenomena against nature. Wine, which by
not dripping "red frae ilka tree" confirms that Jamie Douglas and
his wife will never be reconciled (204L), does "drop" from trees in
what passes for a real description of the "Lowlands of Holland"
(92.5-6). Here if need be is evidence that the impossible of the
ballad *adynaton* is primarily that which is deemed by convention
to be so rather than a rational impossible. We shall not overlook
this distinction in now considering those motifs which are included
in our list of *adynata* thought not certain to have been intended
as absurd.

A few "non-impossibles" may be despatched before the rest: cases
in which uncertainty arises from the fact that something which
reason regards as genuinely impossible, or at least highly implausible, is subsequently put into effect. The roasted cock which crows
(22, 55) is primarily a miraculous motif. But a prior statement of
its impossibility, by Herod the unbeliever, differs formally so little
from the regular ballad *adynaton* that it may easily be reconstructed
on normal lines:

> þat is al so soþ, Stevyn, al so soþ, iwys,
> As þis capoun crowe xal þat lyþ here in myn dysh.
>
> (22)

= "That will take place when this cock . . .". Once more the *adynaton* shows its affinity with other forms of emphasis (the miracle) by association with one of them. The two remaining cases of "fulfilled impossibles" need scarcely detain us for their eccentric motifs may be at least in part due to the editing of Peter Buchan's texts. A lady gives her lord the task of drowning an unwanted child, apparently not his, which, she says, need not return "Till white *fish* he bring hame" (264). Because the lord is kind-hearted the child does return, though without the white fish which would have reduced an apparent impossible to the stranger-than-fiction kind of truth. Another woman seeks revenge for her husband's death by shutting up his blameless soldiers in a cellar "Till my gude *lord* return to me" (265). His appearance as a revenant induces, and enables, her to free them (he is carrying the cellar keys which she had thrown into the sea). In each of these two cases action is dominated by feeble play on the *adynaton* convention, whereas King Herod's "impossible" is a use of convention to enhance action of broader scope.

Next we may notice some motifs the impossibility of which seems to require a special view of reality as apprehended by the singer. "When the *sun* sets in yanders hill/sycamore tree" must have originated as a locally apt expression of "When the sun sets in the East" (cf. Appendix, other images of *sun, sun and moon*). Where topographical confirmation of such impossibles eludes us, we can generally take them as confirmed by their formal character and by the context of their use, including sometimes their association with other obvious impossibles. Surprise that heather cannot grow "on yonder knowes" is dispelled when we notice that this motif belongs to a ballad in which enumeration of impossibles extends at times over two, three or even four verses, "Trooper and Maid" (299). More difficult in the same ballad is to know whether another motif is an ironic impossible or represents a re-interpretation of the narrative conclusion: the soldier lover will return "When peace and truth come to this land." In one American text (299.8) the motif stands alone, permitting interpretation at face value: = I will come back when the war is over. But a Scots text (299.25) links it with one of the most conventional of *adynata,* "When cockle-shells grow silvery bells" and so suggests that peace and truth are in the indefinite future (a satiric use of the impossible more to be expected in written literature).[30]

Having as best we could traced the limits of the ballad *adynaton* in English through a miscellany of more or less eccentric cases, we can now go on to refine our definition by considering its scope and purpose in more normal usage.

The material of our repertory of motifs, the antiquity or sources of which it is beyond our scope here to examine, provides a modest range of images drawn almost entirely from nature inanimate or generalized. A few of these are concerned with apparent trivia: cockle-shells, mussels, heather etc. But major cosmic categories are preferred: sun, moon, water, birds, fish, trees, grass etc.[31] In both cases, the impossible phenomena consist in a change of nature, which, if the produce of nature is in question, may introduce a quantitative aspect: wine drips from or gold grows on trees. We notice only one impossible exclusively of quantity—a conventional though not a rational impossible—heather is burnt and grows again nine times (218).[32]

The number of ballads using *adynata* is also small—our list mentions twenty-four—and smaller still if we exclude the eccentric cases already discussed. Of the remainder, some ballads have impossibles only in one or two versions of recent date or limited extension. A general scrutiny of usage shows that impossibles figure mainly in interpersonal action and predominantly in tragic love ballads.[33] Other kinds of narrative may call for strong negative emphasis without receiving it through the *adynaton:* for example, the conclusion of "Sir Patrick Spens" (58). The device has no place in combat situations; Robin Hood ballads lack it as do for the most part border ballads. Yet many interpersonal narratives and even tragic love ballads also make no use of the *adynaton:* "Sweet William's Ghost" (77), "Geordie" (209).

The distribution of impossibles within the ballad genre may have a historical explanation. Such explanation might seek to show, among other things, the especial fitness of certain motifs to figure in certain narratives. Yet we must start by noticing that several motifs furnish *adynata* in more than one ballad, and at times in ballads quite diverse in tone:

> *Appendix:* seashells cannot become silver bells (204, 299)
>   fish cannot fly (204, 248, 299); (cannot cease to swim, 196)
>   frost cannot warm (204, 299)
>   rocks cannot melt (76, 248, 293)
>   sea cannot run dry (76, 248, 267, 204?); cannot burn
>   (76, 243, 293)
>   sun's course cannot change (4, 13, 68, 243)
>   sun's and moon's courses cannot change (13, 49, 51, 299)
>   cf. corn cannot grow on trees/cease to grow and fire
>   cannot cool/freeze (196, 299)

Thirteen ballads are represented here; but if we put aside those to which the use of the *adynaton* seems incidental—occurring in one or two texts only—together with "The Heir of Linne" (267), for which see below, only six remain in which the device seems to some degree characteristic. Noticing distribution of motifs in these, we find we can make a rough grouping: 13, 49, 51, images of sun or sun and moon; 204, 248, 299, diverse images mostly excluding sun and moon. The impossible motifs of "Lizie Wan" (51), narrating murder of a sister after incest, are regularly of sun *and* moon. The same is true of "The Two Brothers" (49); is the image then proper to fratricide/sororicide rather than incest? But "Edward" (13), also dealing with fratricide, prefers on a numerical count of versions "sun" to "sun and moon." It is not clear if any conclusions may be drawn from these details, or whether they can be viewed profitably in conjunction with Taylor's study of "Edward" and its Scandinavian counterpart. But these three ballads give the only weighty evidence I can report in confirmation of a view that Taylor took for granted, namely that we can indeed expect to find specific meaning in at least part of the repertory of *adynaton* motifs.[34] As for the group using diverse motifs, it is surprising how many of these are shared by "Jamie Douglas" (204) and "Trooper and Maid" (299), which deal respectively with serious marital estrangement and, exceptionally among our ballads of *adynata*, with comic infidelity.

The passe-partout character of many motifs underlines the formulaic aspect of the impossible, involving not only meter and rhyme, but linked motifs, and situation in context. Before we try to draw some conclusions, the context of our impossibles deserves some comment here.

Because of their emphatic character these occupy a strong position in the narrative, usually in its final phase. They are rarely tossed off casually, as in some versions of "The Heir of Linne" (267): disinherited Willie receives alms out of charity and not in expectation that his property will be restored, "ye'll pay me when the *seas* gang dry For ye'll ne'er be heir o Linne" (B). But this ballad breaks a rule of the normal ballad *adynaton* which seems the very reason for its use, being itself the motive of emphatic expression: the narrative "never" is always true and no reversal follows it (Willie on the other hand does regain Linne and boasts "Seas ebb and flow [as] they wont to do," the literal "never" is untrue; again in 22, 55, 264, 265, discussed above, both literal and metaphoric "never" are untrue). The normal *adynaton* then has a static, not dynamic, narrative function in that no important narrative development flows from it. "Jamie Douglas" is the most notable case of a non-final *adynaton,* and it admits, after the impossible has been expressed, only action in confirmation of it and verses of lyric lamentation.

The lyric conclusion of "Jamie Douglas" is somewhat unusual in the ballad genre. As a rule the *adynaton* serves to distinguish the ballad from non-narrative lyric. In ballads it is almost always reserved to dialogue and usually moreover to the answering of a question. We may try to characterize the ballad *adynaton* by its emotive content; fidelity and infidelity are the commonest emotive themes, the rest is less straightforward. But it is easier to find an organizing principle in terms of objective narrative: most ballads using *adynata* share the common narrative theme of irreversible separation.

In conclusion, then, we may state that ballad impossibles normally figure in an action between partners which culminates in dissolution of the partnership. An additional characteristic seems to be that action is conceived in wholly human terms (no magic, no supernatural). Provided these traits can be established as conventional, then *adynata* which lack them, as well as those which are aberrant in respect of form, content or context, may be scrutinized for their value as proper currency. This is not to suggest a naive search for "authenticity" in texts, but rather to facilitate study in diachronic perspective and study of genre and sub-genre.

So for example the unique impossible of quantity already noted in "The False Lover Won Back" (218) is reversed in what follows and thus untypical in function and context since it opens a narrative of the reconciliation of partners. Untypical in context also is the motif "*salt and oatmeal* grow both of a tree," found in a solitary version of "The Two Sisters" (10A), where it emphasizes, but in a non-final phase, the jealous woman's resolve to let her sister drown. We may guess that this seventeenth-century version has probably undergone revision for the popular press. In two versions of "The Famous Flower of Serving-Men" (106) the lady turned serving-man refuses to marry the king, affirming her refusal in an *adynaton* which functions normally in respect of narrative but not of matter since it is uncharacteristic of ballads though recurring in non-narrative lyric. These versions have evidently introduced a new conclusion.[35] Untypical narrative function elsewhere suggests that *adynata* have been borrowed from outside the repertory, where they express a vow about to be broken, "May the *sun* turn to blood," or a confession of credulity with consequences to be narrated, "the *sun* rose in the West." Finally, impossibles confirm separation after death in some versions of "The Grey Cock" (248), in a partnership, that is, already dissolved. But *adynata* are never linked with revenants in other ballads, unless we count the unfulfilled riddles of some versions of "The Unquiet Grave" (78, discussed above), these perhaps also an elaboration.[36]

With "The Grey Cock," which for me initiated this inquiry, it is appropriate to end our detailed discussion. But I expect the subject to prompt many detailed questions which for want of time, space or ability I have left untouched. A few may be suggested. Do singers hold in the memory the notion of a rhetorical impossible more than the detailed motif or motifs? Is the impossible readily borrowed, and does it thus provide a focus of thematic change? Are some individuals more attached to this device than others? Can we know more about the distribution of motifs, according to specific meaning, across the ballad genre? To what extent do the same motifs recur in non-narrative songs? Are the textual miscellanies which Child and Bronson offer here used too indiscriminately? Is, finally, the *adynaton* of ballads in English paralleled, with its characteristics, in other languages? There is much uncharted territory in the study of oral literary composition: less perhaps than might be written of *si totum mundum esset pergamenum*, yet quite enough to keep the clerks of Ireland, Britain, France and Spain — and places East and West — busy for some time to come.

NOTES

References to Child's *The English and Scottish Popular Ballads* use the number of the ballad followed if necessary by a letter indicating one of Child's versions: 10A. References to Bronson's *The Traditional Tunes of the Child Ballads* use the Child number followed by the numbers of versions in Bronson: 43.16 = Child 43, Bronson's 16th version.

[1] References to the attempted proofs, refutations and other contributions to the debate offered from 1961 onwards may be found in a recent article described by its authors as "entirely negative": F. G. Andersen and T. Pettitt, "Mrs. Brown of Falkland: A Singer of Tales?", *Journal of American Folklore*, 92(1979), 1-24.

[2] See H. V. Canter, "The Figure ἀδύνατον in Greek and Latin Poetry," *American Journal of Philology*, 51(1930), 32-41, esp. 32. I use the Greek term for the comparative rhetorical device discussed below, though it is sometimes applied more generally to the impossible motifs themselves, as by E. R. Curtius, *European Literature and the Latin Middle Ages* (New York: Harper, 1953), pp. 94-98. For Classical literature see also E. Dutoit, *Le Thème de l'adynaton dans la poésie antique* (Paris: Société d'Edition "Les Belles Lettres," 1936).

[3] *Chanson de Roland*, ll. 1324-34; *Voyage de Charlemagne*, ll. 454-64. Cf. Child 18D.

[4] *Chanson de Guillaume*, ed. D. McMillan (Paris: Société des Anciens Textes Français, 1949-50), l. 1859.

[5] In "Judas" (Child, vol. 5, p. 288) St. Peter declares he would fight for Christ though Pilate should come "wid ten hundred cnistes."

[6] *Euing Collection of English Broadside Ballads*, ed. J. Holloway (Glasgow: University of Glasgow Publications, 1971), p. 594.

[7] J. Tiersot, *Chansons populaires recueillies dans les Alpes françaises* (Grenoble & Moutiers: H. Falque et F. Perrin, 1903), p. 225.

[8]G. Paris & A. Gevaert, *Chansons du quinzième siècle* (Paris: Société des Anciens Textes Français, 1875), p. 96. For the modern song: G. Doncieux, *Romancéro populaire de la France* (Paris: E. Bouillon, 1904), pp. 417–21.

[9]C. C. Smith ed., *Spanish Ballads* (Oxford: Pergamon Press, 1964), pp. 208–9.

[10]Sung by Raymond Buche, rec. H. Shields (7204), Brive, Corrèze, 1972 (text in brackets sung by Jean Mouzat, of Corrèze, 1970, tape 7007); cf. Doncieux, *Romancéro populaire*, pp. 166–73.

[11]Child, vol. 5, p. 285.

[12]Rec. National Museum of Man, Ottawa (JO 29–450) at Saint-Louis, Saskatchewan, 1957.

[13]Laws O 36; H. Shields in *Ulster Folklife*, 17 (1971), 8, 21; 18 (1972), 36–37.

[14]Cf. 99A, 4.105, 107, 138. More gloomily, "Fair Annie" (62) wishes she were a cat (hound, etc.) and her sons rats (hares, etc.) so that she might worry them, the impulse to repudiate being sometimes replaced by passive grief through a reversal of the hypothetical roles (G, 3, 4).

[15]F. Kidson, *Traditional Tunes* (Oxford: C. Taphouse and Son, 1891; repr. ed. 1970), p. 114.

[16]T. Silverstein, *Visio Sancti Pauli* (Studies and Documents 4) (London: Christophers, 1935), p. 202, cf. pp. 213, 155, and for a source in Virgil, pp. 65–66.

[17]*Adam in Paradise*, EP disc and pamphlet, Ulster Folk Museum (1969); from Co. Derry, Ulster. For this commonplace see *Journal of the English Folk Dance and Song Society*, 1 (1932), 69–70, (1933), 111; 3 (1937), 155, (1938), 201.

[18]"Ag éirigh amach mé damh," from a MS lent me by Liam MacMenamin, Falcarragh, Co. Donegal, who noted it in Donegal in 1935/6.

[19]*French Folk Songs from Corrèze*, ed. H. Shields, Topic LP 12T 246 (London, 1974); cf. Doncieux, *Romancéro populaire*, pp. 61–70.

[20]Sung by Raymond Buche, rec. H. Shields (7301), Lafage, Corrèze, 1973.

[21]*Les Quinze Signes du Jugement dernier*, ed. E. von Kraemer (Helsinki: Societas Scientiarum Fennica, 1966), pp. 66–68, ll. 77–101. Cf. Jacqueline Simpson, "The World Upside Down Shall Be: A Note on the Folklore of Doomsday," *Journal of American Folklore*, 91 (1978), 559–67.

[22]A. Taylor, *"Edward" and "Sven i Rosengård"* (Chicago: University of Chicago Press, 1931), p. 67.

[23]Sung by Charlie Somers, Co. Derry 1969, rec. H. Shields (6921, "It's of a Young Gentleman"). See H. Shields ed., *Shamrock Rose and Thistle. Folk Singing in North Derry* (Belfast: Blackstaff Press, 1981), pp. 100–101.

[24]Laws O 25; for the reference to Child see *Modern Language Notes*, 26 (1911), 167.

[25]Noted from an unrecorded rendition, Corrèze 1973, by H. Shields. For recent studies of this commonplace see Ian Donaldson, *The World Upside Down* (Oxford: Clarendon Press, 1970), esp. pp. 14–23 (on the commonplace as a source of comic drama); D. Hook and J. R. Williamson, " 'Pensastes el mundo por vos trastornar': The World Upside Down in the *Dança general de la muerte*," *Medium Aevum*, 48 (1979), 90–101; Simpson, "The World Upside Down," (see n. 21).

[26]In 78.3, from Baring-Gould's papers, an extra verse relates how the tasks are actually accomplished; but this is evidently editorial: it is not in Child's text from the same source (Hb, vol. 4, p. 475).

[27]It is common in Classical literature; see Dutoit, *Le Thème de l'adynaton*, in n. 2 above, pp. 36–44, 50, 160 and passim; Dutoit calls it "le thème complémentaire de l'adynaton" (p. 50).

[28]In a version of "The Grey Cock" (248) sung by Joe Holmes, Co. Antrim, Ulster, 1975, rec. H. Shields (7503), and on the disc *Chaste Muses, Bards and Sages*, Free Reed LP FRR 007 (Derby, 1976).

[29]L. C. Wimberly, *Folklore in the English and Scottish Ballads* (Chicago: University of Chicago Press, 1928; reprint ed. New York, 1965), p. 362.

[30]In Child, the *peace and truth* verse is an addendum to his version D: a full text with *cockle-shells*, text and addendum both from relatives of Macmath; it is not clear whether the two motifs figured in one version. The case of the more recent Scottish text which contains them both (299.25) is also problematic; it is somewhat confused, and the two motifs could possibly be taken to signify successive states of mind in a wavering lover.

[31]For general use of such images in ballads see Wimberly, *Folklore in the English and Scottish Ballads,* passim.

[32]Cf. also Appendix, *moon* "seventh m. is done and passed . . ." (but versions of the ballad in question [248] not in Child or Bronson indicate an unnatural rather than a quantitative impossible, "seven moons shine brightly o'er yon lea" — version cited in n. 27), *grass, stars* (these two motifs comprise in 243.25 no more than a banal comment on womankind).

[33]Cf. Chaucer's use of impossibles: C. Brookhouse in *Medium Aevum,* 34 (1965), 40-42. The vogue for *adynata* in literary poetry of unrequited love (often in the form of antithesis) seems to go back to Petrarch; see J. G. Fucilla in *Zeitschrift für romanische Philologie,* 56 (1936), 671-81.

[34]Taylor, *"Edward,"* in n. 22, pp. 43-51, esp. p. 44.

[35]Appendix, *"apple* grows on an orange tree," and Department of Irish Folklore, University College, Dublin, MS 736, pp. 298-301 (Co. Cork, 1940: ". . . ivy tree"). The motif is apt to the situation of a woman of low standing (albeit a former noblewoman) wooed by a king. But it does not recur in Child or Bronson except once in reverse: see *orange.*

[36]For impossibles in 248, see H. Shields, "The *Grey Cock:* Dawn Song or Revenant Ballad?" in *Ballad Studies,* ed. E. B. Lyle (Cambridge: D. S. Brewer, 1976), pp. 70-71, 90-91, 188, 196-97.

[37]For a miscellany of continental *adynata* see Child, vol. 1, p. 437.

Appendix

Adynata *motifs in Child and Bronson*

All potential, as well as ascertained, *adynata* are listed. Motifs are arranged alphabetically by their principal noun, usually the first. Before each quoted passage, "when" is to be understood as omitted, unless a different syntax is shown in brackets. Text is quoted from the first version listed after it, and only materially significant variants are noted.

apple   (whilst) an — grows on an orange tree 106.3.3., cf. *orange*
apple trees grow in the seas 299A
blood   (fetch me) — from out of the stone 78.10
(cock)   (al so soþ . . . As) þis capoun crowe xal þat lyþ here in myn dysh 22,55A,2,3

cockle/conk shells turn/grow silver bells 204A–D, F–M, 1 (cf. Child vol. 4, p. 93), 8, 299A–C, D = 3, 10, 12, 25–7

corn shall never . . . (= cease to?) grow through the clay (Nor 196A; grows on a white-oak tree 299.9

fire the — its breeze shall blow no more (if) 76.12; the — shall freeze to ice (if) 293.3.

fish the — shall never (= cease to?) swim the flood (Nor) 196A; -es fly 299A, 248.3–5, 11, 13, 16; -es flee frae tree to tree 204D; (till) white — he bring hame 264

frost and snaw turn fiery baas/beams/bombs/brands 204B–D, F–H, JK; turns fire to burn 204A; will warm us a' 204LM, 1 (cf. Child vol. 4, p. 93), 299A

gold it grows on every tree 204J; grows o'er yon lily lea 204H

grass grows over the highest tree 204G; Oh had I as many years to abide As there are blades of — 56A, 1, 3, 6; (she'll tell you) more lies than . . . the — that grows in the ground 243.25

heather growes on yonder k'nowes 299.17, 20–1, 24; knowes growe owsen-bows 299.19; knaps grow siller taps 299A; cows grow/turn owsen bows 299AC; hills are nine times brunt And a' grown green again 218B = 1,218.2, 4

letter (fetch me) a — from the deserts so deep 78.10

light (fetch me) a — from a dungeon deep 78H = 3

lord (till) my gude — return to me 265

milk (fetch me) white — from a maiden's breast. . . . 78F = 41, 78H = 3, 78.10, 12, 14

moon may . . . the — shade the earth (if) 243.18; the seventh — is done and passed And shines on yonder lea 248.6–7; (made me believe) the — in the South 68.23; see also *sun*

mussels they bud on a tree/grow/hing on every t. 204A–C, FIKM, 1 (cf. Child vol. 4, p. 93)

note (fetch me) a — from the dungeon dark 78E

nut (fetch me) a — from a dungeon deep 78F = 41, 78.12

oatmeal see *salt*

orange an — grows on an apple tree 299.5, cf. *apple*

peace and truth come to this land 299D addendum; is made an' the soldiers are at home 299.8; the queen cries —, the war will cease 299.25

quills gray goose — turn to silver pins 299.16

rocks the hard — will melt with the sun 248.3–5, 11, 13, 16; the — will/must melt in the sun (if) 76.12, 293.3; (till) the — lay in the sun 76.18

roses blow in wintry snow 204.8

(rushes) rashin rinds grow gay gowd rings 299A

salt and oatmeal (till) — grow both of a tree 10A

sand   see *sea*

sea   -s gang dry 299A, 248.3–5, 11, 13, 16, 267B, 4; the -s will be dry (ere) 267.1, 2; (till) the -s run dry 76.18; the saut — shall be frozen (before) 92.6, 14; the ragin' — shall burn (if) 76.12, 293.3; may . . . the raging billows burn (if) 243.18

sea and sand   turns foreign land 204I

snow   see *frost*

stars   (she'll tell you) more lies than the — in the skies 243.24

sun   the — shall set in yonders East 13.17; the — rises in the West and sets in the East 13.15; the — goes East and West 13.21; the — rises never to set 13.6b; the — sets into yanders sycamore tree 13.1, 2, 5; the — sets on yonders green hill 13.4; the — sets on yonder hill forever 13.3; (made me believe) the — it rose in the West 4.119, 68.23, 243.89; may the — turn to blood (if) 243.18

sun and (the) moon   the — shall set in yonders East 13.12; the — sets in yonders (green) hill 13.14, 19, 22, 51.2, 4, 6; the — rises over yonder hill 51.3; the — meet on yon hill/ yonders green hills 51B, 5b; the — meets in yon glen 13.3.1, 3.2; the — leap on yon hill 49E; the — shines both at once 49I; the — passes over the broom 49H; gae three times round 49F; the — dances on the green 49D, 10.1, 299C; the — shall dance on the green (when) 51A; sunlight and moonbeams meet on the green 49.41

water   (fetch me) — from a stone 783, 12, 78F = 41, 78H = 3; (fetch me) — from a dungeon stone 78.14; (to seik) het — beneth cauld yce 169C

wine   drieps red frae ilka tree 204L

Ballads listed

("etc." indicates inclusion of derivative songs from Bronson)

4. "Lady Isabel and the Elf Knight," see: sun. 10. "The Two Sisters": salt and oatmeal. 13. "Edward": sun, sun and moon. 22. "St. Stephen and Herod": cock. 49. "The Two Brothers": sun and moon. 51. "Lizie Wan": sun and moon. 55. "The Carnal and the Crane": cock. 56. "Dives and Lazarus": grass. 68. "Young Hunting" etc.: moon, sun. 76. "The Lass of Roch Royal" etc.: fire, rocks, sea. 78. "The Unquiet Grave": blood, letter, light, milk, note, nut, water. 92. "Bonny Bee Hom" etc.: sea. 106. "The Famous Flower of Serving-Men": apple. 169. "Johnny Armstrong": water. 196.

"The Fire of Frendraught": corn, fish. 204. "Jamie Douglas" etc.: cockle/conk shells, fish, frost and snaw, gold, mussels, roses, sea and sand, wine. 218. "The False Lover Won Back": heather. 243. "James Harris": grass, moon, sea, stars, sun. 248. "The Grey Cock" etc.: fish, moon, rocks, sea. 264. "The White Fisher": fish. 265. "The Knight's Ghost": lord. 267. "The Heir of Linne": sea. 293. "John of Hazelgreen": fire, rocks, sea. 299. "Trooper and Maid" etc.: apple trees, cockle/conk shells, corn, fish, frost and snaw, heather, orange, peace, quills, rushes, sea, sun and moon.

The Oral-Formulaic Theory of Balladry
— a Re-rebuttal

Albert B. Friedman

Perhaps no book in the last fifty years has so fluttered the dove-cotes of philology as *The Singer of Tales*, Albert B. Lord's study of how Serbocroatian singers recompose their folk epics at each per-formance with the help of a system of isochronous formulas and of themes, the latter an organizing principle variously understood as a cluster of motifs, "type-scene" in the folkloric sense, archetypical narrative pattern or, most recently, myth.[1] Shortly after putting the book down, Marshall McLuhan lit the fuses to his pyrotechnic displays on media and culture, while less sensational scholars began busily tabulating the density of formulas in every likely text from Hittite epics to chivalric romances by way of establishing their aboriginal orality. Seven years earlier F. P. Magoun, Jr., had stolen a march on his colleagues by applying the theories of Milman Parry, Lord's mentor, as well as Lord's own researches to *Beowulf* and other Old English narrative poems. But philology, as George Steiner has said, brings out the worst in men. No sooner had the oral formu-laic theory begun to carry all before it, when pockets of resistance developed, reactionaries mounted needling attacks, and to such telling effect that the advocates of the Parry-Lord thesis since about 1970 have spent much of their effort qualifying their rash early statements and working out compromises with the proofs mustered against them.[2]

In most formulaic studies a written text, like the *Iliad, Beowulf,* the *Heliand* or the *Nibelungenlied,* is analyzed to prove that it derived from an oral past which conditioned its style. About the orality of the ballad there has of course never been any question, but there is a question as to whether the specific operations described by the oral-formulaic theorists apply to the Child corpus of English and Scottish popular ballads. The first attempt to make such an application was by James H. Jones in an article that represented itself as overwhelming all the current theories of how ballads were composed and transmitted.[3] Jones divided the ballads into the couplet variety and the quatrain: the couplet belongs to an archaic fashion of dramatic improvisation; the quatrain ballads are governed by the oral formulaic theory. For, according to Jones, the commonplaces, so badly misunderstood by previous ballad scholars, are actually the balladic equivalent of the oral formula (defined by Parry as "a group of words which is regularly employed under the same metrical conditions to express a given essential idea"[4]). Thanks to the formulaic technique, the ballad singer is freed from "the restrictions of memorization" and enabled "to compose rather than merely transmit. . . . The commonplaces belong not to the ballad but to the singers. . . . Like the epic formulas they enabled the singer to improve a song by filling in a story outline."[5] Jones is not speaking of some distant past. The singers of the English and Scottish popular ballads, "at least until the middle of the nineteenth century — Child's ballads were mostly collected by that time — transmitted their ballads in the same way" as the "Yugoslavic epic singers," who composed a new ballad to the same story at each separate performance.[6]

To the oral-formulaic theory Jones opposes the theory of "communal re-creation" sponsored by Cecil Sharp and G. H. Gerould (and he might have added Phillips Barry), which holds that though folksongs once had a beginning in the work of an individual poet, in the course of transmission they are varied and reshaped, producing new varieties and new species.[7] Since Gerould speaks of singers forgetting musical and verbal phrases and filling them in as best they can, he clearly believes that the singer learns his ballads by memorizing them. The communal re-creation theory, then, considers that ballad versions are variant readings of a specific *text*.[8] Perhaps hundreds of years before the Child ballads were collected, Jones goes on, oral tradition began as memorization of specific texts, "but little of this has been true with regard to the variants in the Child collection."[9] Gerould and Sharp based their theory on a "dying tradition" — twentieth-century balladry — "a tradition in which memorization plays a role far different from that which it plays in a thriving tradition" i.e., the "flourishing" tradition of eighteenth- and nineteenth-century England and Scotland, whose products are preserved in Child.[10] "Tradition and composition must have been identical (as Lord demonstrated with regard to the oral epic) when the ballad tradition was thriving."[11] "The singers," says Jones in his emphatic core statement, "were not simply transmitting memorized ballads but were consciously composing their own versions, and . . . they could have done so *even if they had never heard the ballad sung before:* all they needed to know was the story outline. . . ."[12]

Before publishing Jones's article, the editor of the *Journal of American Folklore* at the time, Richard Dorson, allowed me to write a brief undocumented counterstatement by way of *caveat lector*.[13] Much as I admired the daring of the piece, the theoretical passages struck me as a blind, doctrinaire imposition of Parry-Lord on recalcitrant materials. Jones's summary statement quoted just above seemed to me so preposterous as to wipe out whatever impression his conjectural passages on dramatic improvisation, incremental repetition and commonplaces had made. It seemed sufficient to point out that the Serbocroatian epics recorded by Parry and Lord ran from 600 to 13,000 lines; that the shortest were longer than the longest ballads; and that one such improvised epic required 199 twelve-inch discs in the recording. "Every improvised epic is unique: none resembles another in the way a given ballad is a version or variant of another."[14] My capping point was to ask the reader to open Child to the display of versions he offers for a widely-diffused ballad. "The similarities among the versions, to say nothing of the variants, make it inconceivable that these texts were recorded from improvisations—were improvised, that is, by singers who knew only the story outline of the ballad and had never heard it rendered before."[15] Jones had analyzed "Johnie Scot" (Child 99) as an example of a ballad composed almost entirely of commonplaces. But how could he explain the stanza about the Italian (Taliant) champion with its locutions peculiar to this ballad, or the amazing stability and identity of phrasing in the strophe in which Johnie rejects a proffered dowry, a strophe found in twelve of the fourteen complete versions of "Johnie Scot"? Can anything but memory account for the "four Maries" stanza, almost all identically worded, in fourteen of the twenty-one full versions of "Mary Hamilton" (173) printed by Child? Indeed, any Child ballad with multiple versions would clinch the point. Ruth Finnegan, in her recent wide-ranging book on oral poetry, adopts the same strategy for showing memorial transmission in balladry. She prints in parallel columns the version of "Barbara Allen" (no. 84B) from Percy's *Reliques* against one recorded by Sharp in the Appalachians 150 years later, pointing up the striking verbal resemblances.[16]

Jones ruled out appeals to the tunes for evidence. If he had not, the readers would have been invited not only to open Child but to open the first volume of Bronson's great thesaurus of ballad music (the only one published at that time) for corroborating evidence in the traditional tunes. Bronson's practice throughout is to sort the melodic sets by groups on the basis of family resemblances, and though he is alert to the enhancing variations of gifted singers and the crossings and garblings of forgetful or uncreative ones, clearly no radical improvising of tunes was taking place during performances to complement the total improvisation by formula and theme that is alleged by the oral-formula school to be going on during the verbal dimension of the ballad performance. The ninety-nine tunes for "The Two Sisters" (10), for example, fall into only four groups, one of which (B) alone furnishes fifty-five tunes, although the variations in the group make six subheads prudent. The tune family of group A of no. 10 embraces a text from Scotland published in 1824 (but doubtless older since it belongs to the Binnorie group of refrains, the verbal counterpart of one member of which was published by Scott in 1802) as well as a tune discovered in Southern Michigan over a hundred years later.[17] If anything, the stability of the melodies over time and terrain is much greater than that of the verses since music observes a more strictly binding logic of progression and arrangement, holding the tunes in tidier shape. The distinct and stable configurations of the tunes show them to be even more decisively than the verbal texts the products of memorial transmission. And easier than the verses for the singer to remember: the tune, being repeated for every strophe, gets more deeply incised in the memory than the narrative, which must necessarily change in the course of unfolding.[18]

In stressing emphatically that "the basic vehicle of ballad transmission is memorization"[19] I did not wish to deny or disparage the crucial factor of variation. But ballad variation is a far less radical operation than the recomposition from scratch, from a story outline, from a tradition of unexpressed prose synopses of ballads, which in the oral-formulaic hypothesis mystically parallels ballad tradition itself. The communal re-creation doctrine I was defending and expanding makes variation vital to the health of the genre. But variation, as we have seen, may be enhancing or diminishing, depending on the singer's skill, the taste of the audience to which he appeals, and whether the tradition out of which he comes is thriving or moribund. Indeed, one can go so far as to say that most of our extant ballads were probably made (and some unmade) by variation. Once the ballad style had crystallized in the late Middle Ages, it was the cumulative variations over decades and centuries that remade all manner of diverse poetry—carols, episodes from romances, debates, coronachs, and the multifarious poetry of the minstrel repertory—into ballads. Since the sixteenth century many of our ballads have been set afloat in tradition from broadsides (themselves the urban sport of the ballad habit) which fluttered from the press in such numbers that they strained the power of ballad tradition to digest them—an incapacity which may explain why in recent tradition broadside styles have come to exist side by side with the "classic" folk ballad styles.

"Communal recreation" suggests the communalists' bankrupt notion of composition by committee or dancing throngs, but "communal" in the Sharp-Gerould-Barry doctrine is to be understood

in a diachronic sense: the line of singers who, over time, have altered
the song toward the ballad form. Under this dispensation each
proto-ballad and ballad version had an individual author. But until
the ballad had undergone a tour in tradition and been accepted
by the ballad audience, it was not theoretically a true ballad. If
the initial maker was someone who was grounded in balladry and
who in the act of composition felt himself not an exalted creator
but the humble deputy of the public voice, the re-creating tour
might be very short because acceptance would be bound to come
early.

In two particular cases, often overlooked, words and tunes had
definitely to be created and mated at one time. As the distribution
studies of the Finnish school have shown, there was an international
traffic in balladry no less than other folk genres. For a ballad to
cross from one language to another, not only did the story have to
be translated but also, since the ballad meter, style and format vary
in the different geographical areas, the ballad, tune and words, had
also to be entirely recast. This activity doubtless took place, as
Nygard has suggested, in the overlapping bilingual fringes of con-
tiguous language areas,[20] the work probably of bilingual minstrels
or travelling folk. The second case: a radical mutation must have
occurred in the tradition of a given ballad, Bronson argues, when
there was a shift in the type of refrain or when there was, for whatever reason, "a conscious shift from one tune to another."[21]

Foreign balladries have also inevitably been subjected to tests
for oral formulaic composition with inconclusive or downright negative results. James Ross, in testing Gaelic oral literature for signs
of oral composition, found himself making the same fudging shifts
as Magoun had resorted to when adapting Parry's formula to fit
"the more restrictive nature" of Old English poetic narrative.[22]
Indeed, Ross's own adaptations lead him to question "the metrical
utility criterion for determining what a formula is."[23] In certain
instances Ross seems to be taking any stylized poetic diction for
evidence of formulas, a practice which could be extended to the
absurdity of making Pope and Dryden "singers of tales." Moving
from poetry to the complex rhythmical prose of Gaelic storytellers,
Ross finds that extemporizing seemed to play "no certain role,"
and that in the Highlands "a good tradition-bearer is one who does
not reformulate or alter what he has heard."[24]

Since the Spanish ballads are longer than other European ballads
and uniquely stichic, resembling thus the *laisses* of traditional
French and Spanish epics, Bruce A. Beatie thought them promising
for consideration as oral formulaic compositions.[25] Menéndez
Pidal's dominant communal recreation theory, which like that of
Sharp and Gerould recognizes the importance of recomposition
through variation ("la reelaboración de la poesía por medio de las

variantes") similarly emphasizes memorial transmission and "the totally *collective* nature of the ballad tradition."[26] Assuming the validity of previous formula studies, Beatie proceeds to dissect evidence of oral composition from the very *romancero* texts on which Menéndez Pidal based his theories. The contradiction between Parry-Lord and Menéndez Pidal is adroitly reduced to the gulf between epic and ballad in order that a reconciliation can be patched up. Certain *romances* belong to an "intermediary type between the two genres," the contradictory theories of composition "represent two separate ways of looking at essentially similar material."[27]

Both W. Edson Richmond and Otto Holzapfel have tested the oral-formulaic theory of Scandinavian ballads, and in Holzapfel's writings, on German ballads as well. Richmond's remarks at a recent international conference[28] are bafflingly equivocal. In one paragraph he finds the applications of the Parry-Lord theory to balladry just another ballad fad ("ballad scholarship . . . has been haunted by faddism"); in the next paragraph he asserts that "the oral formulaic theory of ballad creation has become as important for ballad scholarship as the concept of survival of the fittest for the biological sciences." A few sentences along we learn "there is evidence which gives [the hypothesis] strong support," but "there is also a considerable body of evidence to suggest that it is at best but a partial answer to the questions surrounding ballad composition and transmission."[29]

In another article, Richmond feels he clearly demonstrated "that a considerable number of ballad singers have at their command a body of formulaic phrases and commonplace stanzas which they may employ to reconstruct a ballad text for which they remember primarily only the basic narrative."[30] Here he is countering, Klaus Roth remarks, the notion that "die Theorie der mündlichen Komposition impliziere eine Tradition von Prosaresumées."[31] "The singer," Richmond says, "need merely have heard a song, remembered only its basic narrative content, and delved into his own genius and the accepted patterns of his own tradition to reconstitute his own version of the song."[32] And after this position, with civilized evenhandedness comes the expected antistrophe: "But it is also true that memorization played a significant role in Norwegian ballad transmission and that the peculiarities of human memory brought about some major changes both in the ballad corpus in general and in the nature of particular ballad types. . . ."[33] Richmond discusses one of Moltke Moe's most forthcoming informants, whose habits were directly contrary to an ideal Parry-Lord singer of tales. For one thing, she "could not sing, but *recited* her ballads."[34] She also wanted to do no more than reproduce the ballads from memory, but in actuality they were different from their sources: they were shorter — "so, in a sense, she does re-create ballads, but her re-creation is the result of omissions, not of imaginative additions."[35]

Holzapfel speaks much of formulas, but neither of the two varieties he is at pains to distinguish in Danish and German ballads would pass muster with the oral-formulaic school. One variety is the ornamental formula (stereotype, commonplace), which mainly pads "empty lines"; the other is an element which furthers the plot: the structural formula. The latter he sometimes calls "epic formulas," an unfortunate term since it has been preempted by the Parry-Lord advocates in America for their special use, but Holzapfel means his epic formulas to further memorial transmission both in their mnemonic value and as a stylized norm toward which the singer varies memorized lines extemporaneously in performance.[36] "These epic formulas do not indicate ornamental improvisation or oral re-creation. Instead, they are on the one hand the result of stylistic concentration during transmission over the centuries, and on the other hand the result of a more or less fixed verbal tradition."[37]

Neither in these articles nor in the magisterial surveys of Michael Curschmann and Klaus Roth on how literary scholarship has reacted to the oral-formulaic theory has the theory emerged as a lively option for explaining ballad transmission even in those adaptations which almost sacrifice its identity for the sake of compromise. And with the two book-length monographs on the ballads' relation to the oral-formulaic theory it is much the same story.

The later of the two, Wolfhart H. Anders's book[38] may be dismissed as an unedifying curiosity. Even when Anders is speaking about ballads in twentieth-century American and British collections, he ignores the evidence of tapes, discs and what the singers themselves say, holding slavishly to the impossible position that the ballads were freshly improvised at each performance from "narratal skeletons." Jones's thesis on commonplaces he confirms with irrelevant statistics, embellishing his pages with pointless lists and charts to shore up a dogmatic argument which can be faulted as to logic — and has been — at every crucial juncture.[39]

Called "the most significant study of the ballad in recent years"[40] and "die bisher beste Studie zu diesem Thema"[41] by scholars who were at that very moment sharpening their pencils to refute crucial passages in the book, David Buchan's *The Ballad and the Folk* is a splendid network of error, and all the more mischievous for its splendor.[42] The sophisticated surface with its trendy terminology belies the gullibility which has drawn him into building on assumptions that are provably erroneous and undermine the whole structure of his argument. Even his engagingly detailed ethnological chapters on the conditions in the Northeast of Scotland that once made it particularly fertile soil for balladry run afoul of critics like

Jack Goody and Ian Watts who challenge H. M. Chadwick's "heroic age" and the whole notion that poetry is the reflection and consequence of social forms.[43]

Our concern is with the body of the book, the introduction and the eight chapters wholly or mainly about Mrs. Brown of Falkland as the composer of ballads in the way described by Albert Lord. Although Buchan is never explicit about it, he appears to concede that since the 1830s or so in the Northeast of Scotland, and even sooner in those parts of the British Isles where literacy had established itself earlier, the ballads have indeed been transmitted by memory with a narrow margin for variation. Such transmission he calls "verbal" as opposed to the "oral" way of Lord's Yugoslav singers and Mrs. Brown, who dictated her songs in 1783–1805. In Northeast Scotland from about 1350 until the early 1800s, the true "oral" ballad tradition prevailed; singers composed their songs anew during each performance, having only a vague outline of the story in mind but equipped with training in how to manipulate a repertory of formulas and further endowed with a set of deep generative structures, a poetic grammar which facilitated the unfolding of the narrative:

> In the Scottish Northeast, and presumably elsewhere, ballads were once composed in traditional fashion by local singers of tales who had mastered the patterns and systems of their poetic language. The strongest evidence of this lies in the texts of the ballads of Mrs. Anna Brown.[44]

In point of fact, as we shall come to see, the texts of Mrs. Brown are strong evidence exactly to the contrary.

Buchan accepts the commonplaces as "formulas intrinsic to the oral mode of composition,"[45] though he has surprisingly little to say about them. Lord's "theme," the other arm of the oral singer's technique, however, cannot be carried over in any form that resembles Lord's description. Yugoslav tradition may mold the story "in shaping dies, verbal and architectonic," along the same principles as Scottish tradition, but "because one is creating epic song in thousands of unrhymed decasyllables" and the end product of the other is "the tight ballad-drama whose main unit is the rhyming stanza . . . the tactics, the particular acts of composition and the particular textual results" would have to be different.[46] This need to supply correlative "tactics" to replace Lord's themes leads Buchan into long chapters analyzing Mrs. Brown's genuine examples of the "old oral mode" of composition, exposing in them the latent patterns, "the stanzaic, character, and narrative structures" (later "tonal, atmospheric structure" is inserted) which "together make up the ballad architectonic." Axel Olrik's laws of oral poetry are recast

as binary (balanced), triadal and annular (framing) patterns; pre-
sumptive analogies with Lévi-Straussian interpretation of myths,
structural linguistics and transformational grammar are lightly
exploited; Cedric H. Whitman's revelation of geometric structuring
in Homer is clearly an inspiration; the chapters on narrative patterns
derive from Propp, though the Proppian units in Buchan do not
follow out a linear group of consequences but are made to fall
rather into binary and triadal sets within annular frames.[47]

After these elaborate analyses, meant to show that Mrs. Brown's
texts reveal the essential operations of the oral ballad tradition, the
"structural and formulaic patternings" by means of which the
ballad maker actually "re-creates" the ballad stories every time he
performs, Buchan in his summing-up begins subverting his own
thesis:

> Because re-composing marks the essential difference between oral
> and written poetry, it is natural to emphasize the re-creative element
> in oral composition, but it is perhaps more necessary, as a corrective,
> to emphasize that the re-creative method produces story-texts remark-
> able for stability rather than innovation.[48]

Apparently in his analyses of the Brown corpus it at last dawned
on him that though this "maker" had "the means to re-create a story
afresh each time," she passed up the option most of the time and
did not make "wholesale alterations" in the texts:

> In fact, it is rather paradoxical that a re-creative technique should
> produce the degree of narrative conservatism it does. Variation, of
> course, exists but it is often made up of verbal minutiae and is
> frequently unimportant. Stability comes about, first, because the
> maker normally tries to tell the right and true story, the one he
> heard, and, second, because each story in a regional tradition carries
> with it its own inherited patterns — the structural, aural, and other
> formulaic patterns.[49]

The last sentence implies that the story and its expression in a given
region are mated despite the freedom of patterned improvisation
available to the singer. Memory then could have played a larger
part in preserving Mrs. Brown's ballads than Buchan had been
willing to grant.

When Bronson wrote his elegant article on Mrs. Brown of Falkland's way with ballads in 1945[50] the oral-formulaic theory was
restricted to Homeric scholarship and was a minor issue even there.
To emphasize dramatically that singers could vary or improve their
texts in a creative fashion he wrote — rather too raptly, it turned
out — of the changes between the texts Child's most important
ballad source Mrs. Brown had dictated on separate occasions

between 1783 and 1805. Bronson was particularly eloquent in stressing the wide divergence between her two versions of "The Lass of
Roch Royal" (Child 76D and 76E), which he took to be persuasive
evidence of imaginative re-creation — re-creation to be sure, in the
Sharp-Gerould sense.[51] Once the oral-formulaic theory appeared
on the scene, these few sentences, charged as they were with Bronson's authority, produced unintended repercussions. They launched
Buchan's book, and even so tough-minded a student of oral poetry
as Ruth Finnegan fell in with Buchan's erroneous thesis that in Mrs.
Brown we have a Scottish singer of tales on the Yugoslav model.[52]

Erroneous because, as Holger Nygard has meticulously demonstrated, Mrs. Brown was no singer of tales.[53] Her ballads came from
probing her memory. She was a cultured woman, wrote conventional poetry; collected differing versions of ballads, comparing her
own with those printed by Herd and Percy. Her textual variations
have been "overstated," deriving less from her desire to improve
or imaginatively vary her text or to give scope to the Scottish side
of her "bicameral mind"[54] than to the carelessness and inexperience
of the kinsman to whom she dictated. Child had been right: she
knew two discrete versions of "The Lass of Roch Royal," each from
independent strands of tradition, neither of her personal making.
Her two versions are not examples of oral-formulaic recomposition.
Nygard's conclusions about Mrs. Brown have been repeated inde-
pendently, with particular reference to Buchan's elaboration, by
two scholars in Denmark, Andersen and Pettitt, who did not know
they had been anticipated.[55] They likewise show that "the process
involved in her transmission is overwhelmingly the memorization
of a fixed text."[56] Reviewing Buchan's work as a whole, they
conclude that "the oral-formulaic theory has . . . almost by definition little relevance for English balladry"[57] — a point I had made in
the same journal eighteen years before.

Though Buchan laments Jones's "literate conceptions,"[58] he has
much the same views on the ballad commonplaces ("clichés, stereotyped phrases, frequently recurring lines, stanzas, clusters of stanzas") as Jones: "These recurrent lines and part-lines . . . can now,
in the light of Lord, be seen as the formulas intrinsic to the oral
mode of composition."[59] The formulas grow out of the "oral poet's
need to fit his narrative ideas to metre while he is re-creating a story
rapidly in performance"; they "belong to tradition"; "they are
assimilated by young singers . . . and used by these singers, when
mature, in their re-creation of the stories . . . the only way possible
in nonliterate communities"; Buchan, however, finds it "unwise
to abstract the formulas from their context, for the ballad language
to which they belong is really completely formulaic."[60] In his book,
as we have already noted, Buchan employs a special elaboration of

Lord's concept of "theme" to illustrate that ballads were once (1350–1750) and lingeringly in the period of Mrs. Brown (1750–1830) as much oral compositions as the Serbocroatian epics.

The inadequacy of Buchan's structural analyses has already been discussed. It remains only to point out the peculiar way Buchan manages to bolster his argument by appealing to authorities whose remarks only serve his purpose if they are arbitrarily pruned, misinterpreted and cut off before they go on to say something embarrassingly contradictory. The words "oral," "formula," "form," "re-creation," etc., have been used in ballad scholarship since the eighteenth century; only in the last twenty years have they become colored with the stipulative meanings of the oral-formulaic theory. In the same way, scholars who cannot subscribe to the theory, indeed combat it, have long been saying that it is pointless to look for the original of a ballad, that all versions are of equal authenticity, that ballads are not composed like literary poetry and tethered to a canonical, unchangeable text, but are creatively remade by the selective or unconscious variation of the singers. Bronson's paean on Mrs. Brown's creativity, like Sharp's on blind Henry Larcombe's "inspired invention," belongs to this dispensation, and it was a result of Buchan's reading of Bronson "in the light of Lord" that got him entangled in the network of contradictions, labelled as paradoxes, in his summation. At several points in his book, Buchan gives Lord's special meanings to conventional ballad terminology and by semantic juggling makes prophets of some of the old worthies of ballad scholarship, representing them as scholars who "probed near or into the [oral-formulaic] method of composition through considering the significance of ballad style or form."[61]

Jones felt it necessary to contest Motherwell's making the commonplace a part of the mechanism of the ballad instead of the method of the singer. Buchan, on the other hand, found Motherwell supplied "the most enlightening insight into the relationship between ballad style and the oral process. . . ." According to Motherwell, the "general structure" of the ballad and "those commonplaces and curious burdens . . . [constitute] the bounding line which exists between what is the Oral and what is the Written poetry of a people."[62] W. P. Ker did indeed declare "the ballad is *form*," meaning the genre's "power of taking up new subjects, and treating them according to the laws of the Ballad"; but when Entwistle says "the course of the tale must have the prescribed order and formulas,"[63] he is not anticipating oral-formulaic composition; he is speaking rather of the peculiarly distinct stylization of the ballad and the ability of ballad tradition to remake an episode of a romance like "Hind Horn" into a ballad. Similarly, Entwistle may say "ballad language is formula," but in elaborating on this pronouncement he comes out in the course of a single page with statements absolutely heretical to the oral-formulaic school, such as "The accuracy of the reciter's memory and his private interests will affect the recitation" or "A long memory is a pearl of price. If the singer forgets, there may be those in the audience who can correct him"—assistance a singer could hardly get if he were genuinely recomposing a ballad afresh.[64] When Buchan has Motherwell, after quoting Jamieson, write,

> To these peculiarities [the ballad's formulaic characteristics], in what may be styled the mechanism of the ancient ballad . . . may be attributed the purity and integrity with which a great body of it has been transmitted to the present day.[65]

the square brackets are deceptive. Jamieson spoke of "the recurrence of certain terms, epithets, metaphors and phrases" and of "hackneyed" lines and stanzas.[66] He does not use the word formula and certainly does not see his itemized commonplaces as structural formulas in the Parry-Lord sense.

2

Buchan locates the "oral composition" phase of the ballad between 1350 to 1750, followed by an adaptive phase 1750–1830 or so; then ensued a phase of aural memorization lasting to the present.[67] Jones, on the other hand, starts with a period when ballads were memorized, modulates into an oral improvisatory phase extending from 1450 to 1900, the years arching Child's corpus, then returns to memorization as the "modality" for the post-Child dying tradition. "Perhaps hundreds of years before Child ballads were collected," Jones conjectures, "oral tradition began as memorization of specific texts, and . . . variations resulted from lapses of memory—but little of this has been true with regard to the variants in the Child collection."[68] The return to memorial composition and transmission after four hundred years of Parry-Lord-type oral composition is a most unlikely development. Ironically it is to avoid a yet more damaging inconsistency in his argument that Jones commits himself to this implausible sequence.

According to Jones, the ballads were originally couplets of four-stress lines with intercalated refrains.[69] In this he is following Child, who, acting on the advice of Grundtvig, took the couplet ballads to be the oldest, and indeed several of the most venerable specimens have this metrical shape, though they are not always the normal four-stress line. From this couplet ballad—actually a strophe of four lines with the second and fourth refrains—developed the quatrain ballad through what Gummere misleadingly called "an epic process."[70] Gradually, J. H. Boynton theorizes,[71] the refrain lines began to succumb to the narrative; there was an intermediate stage of variable refrains that complemented the story line; finally there emerged a ballad, without refrain, of stresses heard 4/3/4/3, rhymed *abab* or *xaxa*. But the three-stress lines, the former refrain lines, tended to be less essential to the narrative than the first and third lines, the original substantial story lines, and it is these inessential lines which came to be the favored habitat of the commonplaces. It is, thus, only the quatrain ballads that are rich in commonplaces. Now commonplaces mean oral-formulaic composition in Jones's thesis, the couplet ballads, being spare in commonplaces, cannot be the products of oral formulaic composition even though they are the oldest stratum of ballads. This chain of reasoning lies behind Jones's conjecture that "oral tradition began as memorization of specific texts," that is, begun the same way modern decadent tradition is ending.[72] Evolution came a full circle!

This scheme of the genre's development not only buys consistency at a high price, but leads to two further cloudinesses in Jones's argument. For one thing, the couplet ballads and the quatrain ballads represent for Jones two different ways of telling a story, one by memorial transmission, the other by oral-formulaic composition. Since the couplet ballads are older and not formulaic, on Jones's terms, the unwary reader might infer that the couplet ballad died out with the coming of the later stanza form. But the demoralizing truth is that couplet ballads, for which Jones's theory cannot account, have persisted side by side with the quatrain ballads throughout the recorded history of the genre.

Secondly, to make the commonplaces the counterpart of the Parry-Lord formulas is difficult when one is maintaining at the same time that the commonplaces normally occur in the lines and passages which least further the narrative. In the Parry-Lord system oral formulas may be ornamental or padding at times, but they are the sole vehicle of the narrative as well. "Remove the cliché," Horace P. Beck remarks of ballad commonplaces, "and one still has a narrative."[73] Buchan illustrates just that point in his analysis of Mrs. Brown's "Sir Hugh." The second line has been dotted out in fourteen of the seventeen stanzas; the fourth line in five stanzas; the story remains intact. Lines one and three, however, are always indispensable. The second and fourth lines, it should be remembered, are the former refrain lines become commonplace spaces. Here they are dispensable — from the textual point of view — despite the fact they are the rhyming lines.[74]

To be fair, Jones admits the commonplaces generally "have no effect upon the story"; to be structurally significant they must group themselves into thematic configurations.[75] The grouping may seem to satisfy Lord's dictum that formulas build lines and themes build songs, but the dictum has a different meaning in stichic poetry, where the line is the narrative unit, than in strophic poetry, and the difference cannot be planed away simply by making theme the plural of the formula-commonplace. Gradually in the course of his argument, therefore, Jones swells the commonplace unit from a single line to one of seven stresses, to a whole stanza, to a set of stanzas, and finally in his analysis of "Johnie Scot" he is found claiming that "the ballad is composed almost entirely of . . . commonplaces."[76] In a Yugoslav epic that blanket statement is always theoretically true. But how is one to deal with those ballads which are not the nearly complete tissue of commonplaces that "Johnie Scot" is alleged to be? Jones does so in a manner which undermines the exclusive sufficiency of the oral method of composition. "In the older British tradition," he says, meaning the oral-formulaic phase, "memory filled gaps for which the singer had no commonplace."[77]

Let us grant "Johnie Scot" (Child 99) is unusually rich in commonplaces. Does that automatically mean, as Jones would have it — and must have it, for this is the capstone to his edifice — that the versions of the ballad are the products of oral composition? The mere fact that the organization of the ballad in almost all versions is so similar argues against uniquely-improvised performances of the Parry-Lord type. Version A, one of the two texts Jones especially singles out for analysis, is one of Mrs. Brown's texts, and she, we now know, recited from memory and was not a singer of tales. And, as I asked rhetorically before, how is Jones to explain the resemblances in the stanza about the Italian (Taliant) champion, with its locutions peculiar to this ballad, or how explain the amazing stability and identity of diction and phrasing in the strophe in which Johnie rejects a proffered dowry, a strophe found in twelve of the fourteen complete versions of "Johnie Scot"? One must assume a mystic communion and "conspiracy of co-inspiration" among the Scottish oral singers to explain how fourteen versions of the ballad recorded from several parts of Scotland over a period of one hundred years could read so much alike.

"An integrant portion of the original mechanism of all our ancient ballads" and "landmarks, and helps to the memory of the reciter," Motherwell had called the commonplaces.[78] Jones, we saw, must necessarily contradict him: "The aesthetic significance of the commonplace," quite on the contrary, is that "they freed the singer from memorization. Variation in the use of commonplace rarely affects the story. . . ."[79] And again, "the commonplace may be used in a variety of situations" and "has no necessary effect upon the story. . . . The wide variation in the handling of themes as in the handling of commonplaces implies the singer's selectiveness rather than his memorization."[80] These cryptic remarks do not follow easily from Jones's position but, as the mention of themes hints, are Jones's attempts to get into line with Lord's emphasis on the discreteness between the formulas employed by the singer and the formulas common to the tradition. Jones's allegiance leads him to a peculiar conclusion: "That commonplaces belonged not to the ballads but to the singers is suggested by the fact that they are not always used in all versions of the same ballad or in similar situations in other ballads."[81] But surely the fact that a commonplace is not in the repertory of a hypothetical singer or does not "always" appear in "all" versions of a given ballad does not mean it is not a commonplace within the total corpus of a regional balladry.

3

It is not hard to understand what has started and sustained this controversy. The oral-formulaic theory, for good or ill, legitimately or otherwise, has energized several fields of philology from the poetries of African and Polynesian tribes to Homeric and biblical form criticism. Its adherents have involved the theory in each brand of modern linguistics as that brand has circulated to the peak of the wheel of fashion; many voguish if ephemeral trends in the social sciences have exploited the theory; and almost from the beginning the writings of Parry, Lord and company were brought into play in media and communication theory. Naturally ballad scholars would like to participate in this lively circus. But as we have seen, and as it is coming more and more generally to be seen, the ballads are not and have never been oral-formulaic in composition or transmission. And this is nothing to be sad about. The ballads are the more distinct, the more aesthetically pleasing, the more culturally and philologically interesting precisely because they cannot be accommodated to the oral-formulaic theory.

To fit the ballad into the spectrum of European narrative poetry requires a wrenching of criteria. The other genres, the chivalric romances say, come down to us in written form; their oral qualities have been largely submerged in literary conventions. The *Nibelungenlied*, for instance, may be the written canonical collation of several oral versions of the story, and these and other oral strands may have persisted alongside the manuscript tradition of the romance and influenced it during the tradition's incipient stages. Very early, however, these oral versions fell away and their very existence can now only be conjectured.[82] Of all the medieval narrative genres, the ballad is the one which is actually, overtly oral; we may know it mainly from records—very sparse ones in the early centuries, admittedly. Such are the chances of oral poetry—but there are records, more or less accurate, of later oral performances which link up with the performances heard by eighteenth-century collectors and audiences since. Because of its continuous orality, its non-literary method of transmission and its comparative isolation from the currents of literary practice and fashion, and, most important, because of its uniquely composite nature as song, ballad narration is too highly special, too idiosyncratic to be comfortably fitted into the narrative line-up.

This composite nature, the tense balance of narration, song, drama, dance and (if one must be fancy) ritual, is a leading reason for the ballad's distinctive style. Individual ballads evolved from the stylization into ballad form of a situation, a story, an episode borrowed from another genre, or a topical event recast to accord with archetypal expectations. Among the many reasons for rejecting the oral-formulaic theory of balladry, the argument from style may well be the most convincing. For if one accepts that the ballads are transmitted by memory, most elements of ballad style can be interpreted as devices that came into habitual use to facilitate memorial transmission—many of them elements about which the oral-formulaic theory has very little to say. "To facilitate memorial transmission," to be sure, is looking at the ballads from the singers' point of view. Many typical ballad devices, rhetorical patterns, turns of phrase, syntactical habits, etc., are there principally to accommodate the hearer of oral poetry. The ubiquity and variety of repetition is obviously of this sort. When instructions are carried out in a stanza fully as circumstantial and word-for-word the same, except for the tense and agent, as the one in which the instructions were given, the critical action is subtly reinforced, as is also, incidentally, the emotional impact. Key facts are everywhere incised by repetition in case the first utterance may have slipped by in a moment of inattention. But no hard and fast line has to be drawn between the memorizable and the memorable—the needs of the singer and those of the hearer. They are both reciprocally active in the performance whether vocal audience participation occurs or not.

If the complex of idiosyncrasies which make up the ballad style is a reflection of memorial transmission, it follows that the genre from its inception was transmitted by memory. Those adherents of oral-formulaic composition who say that only since 1830 or since 1900 has this decadent mode of transmission prevailed are thus ruled out of court. But, to be just, one must concede that relating style to function, the function in this case being the technique of oral transmission, is a tricky business. By analyzing the style and narrative organization of Mrs. Brown's corpus of ballads Buchan thought to demonstrate they had been composed during performance according to his fabricated set of oral techniques. Buchan was unfortunate: both external and internal evidence dug up by other researchers proved her ballads to be unquestionably the products of memorial transmission. But Buchan's unsuccess does not make otiose the theoretical possibility that a stylistic feature that once had a specific function may in the course of time persist as a mere habit or an empty rhetorical flourish.

The notion of feature as equivalent to function has perpetrated bold errors even in the best of hands. Kittredge was operating on this principle when he argued that incremental repetition over a succession of stanzas was the residuum of, and therefore another proof of the ballad's origin in communal dramatic improvisation. The argument was plausible in the abstract and remained plausible when applied to a particular text of "The Hangman's Tree" (Child 95):

> So inevitable is the course of the narrative, so conventionally fixed the turn of the phraseology, that [the audience] could almost finish the piece by themselves if the author remained silent.[83]

In a brilliant paragraph, however, Bronson has dismantled Kitt tredge's elaborate example, demonstrating that the great man failed to look at the music closely, for its intricacy and the variation within the symmetrical stanzas show that the tune does not develop with the inevitability the verbal text implies. The tune could not have been made up by the audience improvising along with the "author"; the well-formed tune was already completely worked out in the singer's head before he uttered the first word/note.[84] From Kittredge's "muddle" we can see that the function of a stylistic technique is by no means obvious, necessary or constant. Perhaps the greatest fallacy in oral-formulaic scholarship generally also grows out of the failure to recognize how hard it is to establish a necessary relationship among style, technique and function. Since formulas are the technique of oral composition-transmission, pro-ponents of oral formulas assume that any written text dense in formulaic phrasing must automatically be the dictation of an oral performance. But when a densely formulaic poem which is a close translation into English of a learned Latin treatise comes along, it is obviously a case of a literate tradition's taking over the conventions of its oral-formulaic predecessors.[85]

4

"Memorial transmission" has a dull ring to it, and not solely because of the morbid connotations of the adjective. It implies constrained, unimaginative reproduction of an earlier text, a singer who represses his personal expressiveness and submits to the tyranny of tradition. Ballad transmission is by no means so static a process. The ballad, to reiterate, is created in the first place through adapta-tion and variation, and it recreates and renews itself by a variety of substitutional devices which are lively and flexible at a time and in a region where ballad tradition is healthy. Ballads are thus marked by a mutually sustaining tension between conserving and innovating. The vital stylization of the ballad form would have crumbled long ago if the conservative impulse relaxed. And if there were no margin for change, for the ballads to adapt to new material conditions, language, customs and tastes, the genre would just as surely have died of inanition. Admittedly the traditional process is full of contradictions. On the one hand, variation progressively renews the ballad, bringing the stories and manners up to date, localizing incidents, and in other ways preserving the relevance and immediacy of what is being sung; on the other hand, singers will cling to "old-timey" expressions, symbols from dead mythological systems and archaisms whose meaning neither they nor their audience understand.

Unique as ballad tradition is, it is not unique in being basically an art of memory. One of the more troubling dogmas of the oral-formulaic theory is its idea that "oral narrative is not, *cannot* be memorized." Oral presentation is irrelevant; "oral" means "composition during oral performance."[86] Parry and Lord, overreacting to the widespread naive notion that rote memory was all there was to tradition, spoke so strongly against memorial transmission, however qualified, that field workers slighted the role of memory in oral poetry when it showed up in their ethnological data. Ruth Finnegan confesses to having been herself among the "misled."[87] In actual fact, memory plays a significant role in oral poetry.

Strict memorization to be sure may be dubious despite all the claims of legends being handed down from time immemorial. Yet word-for-word transmission of poems, usually sacred, occurs exceptionally. The classic instance of course is the *Rigveda,* a three-thousand-year-old collection of more than a thousand hymns, whose canonical fixity is such that supposedly the whole could be recreated from the memories of the holy men if all written texts were lost. Among African peoples panegyrics, legends and genealogies, not to mention the much shorter lyrics and riddles, have sometimes been handed down for generations with demonstrably amazing stability. As to contemporary oral poetry, tribes differ as to the scope they allow to improvising during the performance of what is essentially a memorized "standard, neutral version." Just as the Chadwicks found that the Turkoman Tatars insisted on "exact verbal memorization" from their minstrels while the nearby related Kara Kirghiz Tatars, if one may trust Radlov's description, encouraged "extempore composition"[88] — probably of a more controlled type than pre-Parry-Lord investigators realized — so Africanists contrast Zulu, Ruanda and Yoruba strictness with regard to reproducing songs with Xhosa and Hausa permissiveness.[89] The "essential qualification" of a Zulu praise-singer is "an excellent memory," says Trevor Cope, for much of the material he will have to rattle off about the ancestors of the chief he is eulogizing "is often meaningless to him."[90] The Mandinka griot, according to Gordon Innes, performs a version of a legend reshaped from the songs of other griots encountered in his travels. "With repetition this version will become more or less fixed . . . but even this version will vary from performance to performance," altered to introduce praises of the "reputed ancester" of someone in the audience from whom a reward is expected.[91] The Norse skaldic poets and the "tame bards" of medieval regal and baronial courts were no less venal. When the Nyanga bard sings and narrates in tandem the Congolese Mwindo epic, he is assisted by apprentice bards who "know large fragments of the epic, and, whenever necessary, help the bard to remember and to find the thread of his story. . . ."[92] If oral poetry is always made only during performance, what is to be done with the Eskimo, Gilbert Island and Dinka poets who, like the medieval Gaelic *filid*, composed their songs with great deliberation privately and performed them from memory publicly? Or, similarly, how is one to deal with the Benin bardic guilds of Nigeria described by Ben-Amos or with the self-censoring Hawaiian singing groups, both of which put together compositions in committee to be memorized and exactly reproduced at popular assemblies?

When one reads of Somali poetry and how the composing bard held a sort of copyright on his work and made the passive talents who recited them from memory acknowledge his authorship at each recital,[93] one is reminded of the troubadours, many of whom hired jongleurs to disseminate their compositions, but who were nonetheless jealous of their authorship. Of the three thousand troubadour songs which survive, many made their way into the hundred or so extant *chansonniers* several generations after their original composition. How the songs were transmitted during the interval is currently a lively question among scholars of Provençal culture. Most of the *chansonniers* were compiled from loose parchment sheets, earlier patron manuscripts or from jongleur promptbooks, but the variation in those songs that exist in multiple copies suggest some degree of memorial transmission, with alterations hewing to the original authors' intentions. Moshe Lazar believes the troubadours purposely complicated their texts in order to inhibit performers from altering them out of shape (the ingenious and seemingly gratuitous complexity of skaldic verse may perhaps be explained in the same way). The music seems to have done little to preserve the integrity of troubadour poems, at least as regards the arrangement of stanzas. This varies widely among the exemplars of the same song because, most of the songs being lyrics, there is no narrative progression to keep the sequence orderly[94] — a point which brings us to the role of music in abetting the basically memorial transmission of ballads.

Significantly, in every attempt to foist the oral-formulaic theory upon balladry, ballad music has been ignored. Jones and Anders simply choose not to deal with it; Buchan excuses himself after a paragraph on the grounds that the subject demands a book of its own.[95] The avoidance of music is good strategy: in no other area does the Yugoslav analogy break down so badly.

The *gusle,* the instrument of Lord's singers, has an ambitus of only five notes, the open string and four finger positions. The singing that accompanies the instrument may have subtle changes in rhythm and pitch, but the short melodies (one third the length of a ballad set) have little variety and color, and since they are repeated for every ten-syllable line of an epic of many thousands of lines, a certain monotony is assured. It is no wonder that Lord occasionally falls into speaking of the songs being "chanted."[96] As contrasted with the improvising Kirghiz minstrels, who were said to have only one or two tunes to service their entire repertories of heroic songs[97] (Lord implies the melodic repertories of their Yugoslav counterparts are also limited), the British singers are remarkably unthrifty. According to K. A. Thigpen's analysis of Bronson's data, they employ a ballad tune for only one or two texts.[98] Clearly the musical dimension is much less important in the oral-formulaic performance than it is to the ballad performance; composing the story apparently exhausts the creative energy of the *guslar.* The tunes he learned in his apprenticeship stay with him throughout his career. Yet the oral formula school would have the ballad singer composing ballad texts and tunes *de novo* simultaneously! Buchan takes advantage of an ambiguously formulated statement of Samuel P. Bayard, in which he happens to use "formulae" to suggest that ballad music may have gone through a stage of "disciplined re-creation," too, and that the ballad singer's attitude "may have been, or in certain areas may still be, akin to the oral maker's attitude to his texts."[99] But later on the same page, Bayard says, in a passage not quoted by Buchan:

> The fact is worth emphasizing that most of our folk tunes cannot be regarded primarily as bundles of formulae combined momentarily or on occasion in a semi-extemporaneous way. The presence of numerous cognate tune-versions in our tradition closes the door on that possibility.[100]

Earlier we observed that the stability of ballad tunes is much greater than the verses and that the distinct and stable configurations of the tunes show them, even more decisively than the verbal texts, to be the products of memorial transmission. Here one should extend the point by quoting Bronson's remarks on the tune as a powerful aid to the memory. With its "inner unity that makes it shapely to the ear and mind . . . individual, recognizable, and welcome on repetition," and repeated indeed "as a near-constant throughout the ballad," words positively "cling" to the notes of the tune. So much so that were it not for the tune, he asserts, many a fragmentary or disordered ballad would have been entirely lost.[101] But the mutual and synergistic mnemonic reinforcement which tune and text lend each other need hardly be detailed. Too many collectors have shared Sharp's experience of singers who find it impossible to go on with the story when the tune fails them or to separate words from tunes when they were used to singing them together.[102]

To exploit Bronson's words and arguments further, it is "the tune, not the text, [that] has given its formal structure to the ballad."[103] The oral formula school, in trying to find an equivalent for the additive style of the epic singers and the infrequency of run-on lines, mistakenly take the ballad strophe as the sole structural unit. "Since the epic is unrhymed, the epic singer can develop his theme by adding line to line. . . , but the ballad singer can only add strophe after strophe."[104] Ballad verse too has a paratactic style — a result, I would emphasize, of the lyrical dimension's influence on the narrative. But the break between stanzas is not the crucial juncture; that will be found rather in the discreteness of lines within the strophe. In stanzas with interspersed refrains, the lyrical interruption "has . . . compelled a syntax in lines one and three such as would sustain these lines as separable units of thought."[105] And even the narrative of refrainless quatrain ballads, since the stanzas are musically parsed into four phrases, must submit to the musical division and complete themselves in some degree within the line, no matter what the loss in dramatic or narrative momentum.

> Since the thought is conveyed in a series of musical phrases, it must be understood as they are sung, not wait for clarifying essentials; so the meaning of a line is not in suspense, nor often split between two melodic units. The stanza's length and pattern seldom escape the fixed control of the tune, the cadence-points of which determine rhetorical pauses.[106]

Finally we come full circle to the ballad commonplace, which advocates of oral-formulaic balladry make the primary means of "oral recomposition." Ironically, the early ballad collectors and scholars were apologetic about these "overscutched" phrases, regarding them as inevitable if lamentable traits of "traditionary poetry." Elsewhere I have offered various aesthetic justifications for the ballad commonplaces;[107] here it is relevant only to suggest that the commonplaces arise primarily because the ballad is song, that is, a naturally indivisible combination of words and music — no matter how often, for purposes of discussion, the ballad must be artificially so divided.

Commonplaces, according to the oral formula school's tabulations, are most frequent in the second and fourth lines of quatrain ballads, the lines which correspond to the intercalated refrain of the couplet ballad. A facile explanation for the tendency of the commonplaces to inhabit these lines is that they are filler for the superseded refrain, a refrain lost because the ballad is moving "epicward" (in Gummere's view) and losing its choral and lyrical impulse.[108] Or one could say in contradiction that since these lines end in rhymes, usually the only rhymes in the stanza, the singer is actually slighting the narrative during the course of these lines because his attention is on the duty to rhyme, the easy commonplace allowing him to go on "automatic pilot" so far as the narrative is concerned. But if one looks at the music more closely, one will see that the lyrical obligation, so to speak, is stronger than merely the necessity to manage a rhyme. The chiming of rhyme sounds is the event in the verbal text that most closely approximates the quality of music. With particular suitability, thus, it happens that the ends of the second and fourth lines, the normal rhyme word positions in ballads, coincide with the medial and final cadences of the music, the points of musical variation, determination and resolution. There is indeed an overbalancing of the narrative by the lyrical in these lines, and this action makes the commonplace all the frailer as the basis of the substitutional system required by the oral-formulaic theory of balladry.

There is yet another and more general way in which the commonplace can be seen as the story's concession to the tune which floats it. These conventional ballad locutions, turns of phrase, expected metaphors, stereotyped comparisons, etc., dilute the texture of ballad language and make the syntactically simple and repetitious texts even rarer in semantic density. The very thinness of the language and the semantic valence argue the importance of the ballad music. It is precisely because ballad tunes are sufficiently "thick," sufficiently engaging to the hearers — though perhaps the tunes would not be felt as such if they stood alone — that the verbal component has to space out meaning, avoid complex syntax, incise crucial narrative conditions by repetition, signal junctures in the articulation of the story clearly, and indeed work all its rhetorical effects in a thin linguistic medium. "Hearing verse set to music," said Valéry, "is like looking at a painting through a stained glass window."[109] The ballad form, however, has achieved a happy complementarity of verse and music, as Bronson has taught us to understand, and as the oral-formulaic school, in forcing an analogy with a kind of poetry in which music counts for little, would obscure from us.

NOTES

[1]*The Singer of Tales* (Cambridge, Mass.: Harvard University Press, 1960), pp. 68–98. On theme as myth, see *Oral Literature and the Formula*, eds. B. A. Stolz and R. S. Shannon (Ann Arbor, Mich.: Center for the Coordination of Ancient and Modern Studies, 1976), pp. 1–2.

[2]See the listing, soon to be brought up to date, by E. R. Haymes, *A Bibliography of Studies Relating to Parry's and Lord's Oral Theory* (Cambridge, Mass.: Publ. of the Milman Parry Collection, 1973) and review by S. G. Armistead, *Modern Language Notes*, 90 (1975), 296–99. Lord's "Perspectives on Recent Work in Oral Literature," *Forum for Modern Language Studies*, 10 (1974), 187–210, is mainly a parrying of objection to the oral theory. For the reaction of Homer scholars, see *The Making of Homeric Verse: Collected Papers of Milman Parry*, ed. Adam Parry (Oxford: Clarendon Press, 1971), pp. xlvii–lxii. Michael Curschmann, "Oral Poetry in Mediaeval Literature," *Speculum*, 72 (1967), 35–52, judiciously surveys the earlier years of controversy in one large area. For the oral theory as applied to African poetics, see Ruth Finnegan, *Oral Poetry* (Cambridge: Cambridge University Press, 1977), pp. 97–102.

[3]"Commonplace and Memorization in the Oral Tradition of the English and Scottish Popular Ballads," *Journal of American Folklore*, 74 (1961), 97–112.

[4]Lord, *The Singer of Tales*, p. 30. See Milman Parry, "Studies in the Epic Technique of Oral Verse-Making, 1: Homer and Homeric Style," *Harvard Studies in Classical Philology*, 41 (1930), 80.

[5]Jones, "Commonplace and Memorization," 103, 105–6.

[6]Ibid., 101.

[7]G. H. Gerould, *The Ballad of Tradition* (Oxford: Oxford University Press, 1932), p. 78; see also Cecil J. Sharp, *English Folk-Song: Some Conclusions*, 4th rev. edition, ed. Maud Karpeles (Belmont, Calif.: Wadsworth Publishing Co., Inc., 1965), passim.

[8]Gerould, *The Ballad of Tradition*, pp. 163–88.

[9]Jones, "Commonplace and Memorization," 102.

[10]Ibid., 101–4.

[11]Ibid., 105.

[12]Ibid.

[13]Albert B. Friedman, "The Formulaic Improvisation Theory of Ballad Tradition—A Counterstatement," *JAF*, 74 (1961), 113–15.

[14]Ibid., 114.

[15]Ibid.

[16]Finnegan, *Oral Poetry*, pp. 136–38.

[17]Bertrand Harris Bronson, *The Traditional Tunes of the Child Ballads*, vol. 1 (Princeton, N.J.: Princeton University Press, 1959), pp. 143–84.

[18]Cf. Bertrand Harris Bronson, *The Ballad as Song* (Berkeley and Los Angeles: University of California Press, 1969), pp. 60–63.

[19]Friedman, "The Formulaic Improvisation Theory," 114.

[20]H. O. Nygard, *The Ballad of Heer Halewijn* (Knoxville, Tenn.: University of Tennessee Press, 1958), p. 13.

[21]Bronson, *The Ballad as Song*, p. 44.

[22]James Ross, "Formulaic Composition in Gaelic Oral Literature," *Modern Philology*, 57 (1959), 1–12.

[23]Ibid., 5, n. 19.

[24]Ibid., 12.

[25]Bruce A. Beatie, "Oral-Traditional Composition in the Spanish *Romancero* of the Sixteenth Century." *Journal of the Folklore Institute*, 1 (1964), 92–113.

[26]Ibid., 97.

[27]Ibid., 108.

[28]W. Edson Richmond, "Rhyme, Reason and Re-Creation," in *Ballads and Ballad Research*, ed. Patricia Conroy (Seattle: University of Washington Press, 1978), pp. 58–67.

[29]Ibid., p. 58.

[30]Ibid., pp. 58–59. See W. Edson Richmond, " 'Den utrue egtemann': A Norwegian Ballad and Formulaic Composition," *Norveg*, 10 (1963), 59–88.

[31]Klaus Roth, "Zur mündlichen Komposition von Volksballaden," *Jahrbuch für Volksliedforschung*, 22 (1977), 52.

[32]Richmond, " 'Den utrue egtemann'," 59.

[33]Richmond, "Rhyme, Reason, and Re-Creation," p. 59.

[34]Ibid., p. 63, quoting from *Norsk Folkeminnesamling, MS M. Moe XXV*, p. 42.

[35]Ibid., p. 65.

[36]Otto Holzapfel, "Scandinavian Folk Ballad Symbols, Epic Formulas and Verbal Traditions," in *Ballads and Ballad Research*, ed. Conroy, pp. 113–21; cf. Roth, "Zur mündlichen Komposition," pp. 52–53.

[37]Holzapfel, "Scandinavian Folk Ballad Symbols," p. 120.

[38]Wolfhart H. Anders, *Balladensänger und mündliche Komposition* (Munich: W. Fink Verlag, 1974). According to Roth, "Zur mündlichen Komposition," 53, the book was finished in 1968.

[39]See Flemming G. Andersen and Thomas Pettitt, "Mrs. Brown of Falkland: A Singer of Tales?" *JAF*, 92 (1979), 1–24, esp. 4–6; Roth, "Zur mündlichen Komposition," 53–54.

[40]Andersen and Pettitt, "Mrs. Brown of Falkland," 6.

[41]Roth, "Zur mündlichen Komposition," 54.

[42]David Buchan, *The Ballad and the Folk* (London and Boston: Routledge and Kegan Paul, 1972).

[43]See Jack Goody and Ian Watt, "The Consequences of Literacy," in *Literacy in Traditional Societies*, ed. Jack Goody (Cambridge: Cambridge University Press, 1968), pp. 27–68. Cf. Finnegan, *Oral Poetry*, pp. 244–71. I must confess that I have held a version of this position: see A. B. Friedman, *The Ballad Revival* (Chicago: University of Chicago Press, 1961), pp. 16–34.

[44]Buchan, *The Ballad and the Folk*, p. 61.

[45]Ibid., p. 145.

[46]Ibid., pp. 58–59.

[47]Ibid., pp. 87–144.

[48]Ibid., p. 166. See Axel Olrik, "Epische Gesetze der Volksdichtung," *Zeitschrift für deutsches Altertum*, 1 (1909), 1–12, reprinted as "Epic Laws of Folk Narrative," ed. Alan Dundes, *The Study of Folklore* (Englewood Cliffs, N.J.: Prentice-Hall, 1965), pp. 131–41; Claude Lévi-Strauss, "The Structural Study of Myth," *JAF* 68 (1955), 428–44; Cedric R. Whitman, *Homer and the Heroic Tradition* (Cambridge, Mass.: Cambridge University Press, 1958); Vladimir Propp, *The Morphol-*

ogy of the Folktale, trans. Laurence Scott, ed. Svatava Pirkova-Jakobson (Bloomington, Ind.: Indiana University Press, 1958).

⁴⁹Buchan, *The Ballad and the Folk*, p. 167.

⁵⁰B. H. Bronson, "Mrs. Brown and the Ballad," *California Folklore Quarterly*, 4 (1945), 129-40; reprinted in *The Ballad as Song*, pp. 64-78.

⁵¹Bronson, *The Ballad as Song*, p. 75.

⁵²Finnegan, *Oral Poetry*, p. 56.

⁵³H. O. Nygard, "Mrs. Brown's Recollected Ballads," in *Ballads and Ballad Research*, ed. Conroy, pp. 68-87.

⁵⁴Buchan, *The Ballad as Song*, p. 68.

⁵⁵See above, n. 39.

⁵⁶Andersen and Pettitt, "Mrs. Brown of Falkland," 23; cf. also 12-18.

⁵⁷Ibid., 23.

⁵⁸Buchan, *The Ballad and the Folk*, p. 297.

⁵⁹Ibid., p. 145.

⁶⁰Ibid., p. 146.

⁶¹Ibid., p. 60.

⁶²Ibid.

⁶³Ibid.

⁶⁴Buchan, *The Ballad and the Folk*, p. 274. See W. J. Entwistle, *European Balladry* (Oxford: Clarendon Press, 1939), p. 29.

⁶⁵Buchan, *The Ballad and the Folk*, p. 166.

⁶⁶See William Motherwell, *Minstrelsy Ancient and Modern* (Paisley: Alexander Gardner, 1873, orig. 1827), p. xxiv.

⁶⁷Buchan, *The Ballad and the Folk*, pp. 10, 177, 247, 271.

⁶⁸Jones, "Commonplace and Memorization," 102.

⁶⁹Ibid., 98.

⁷⁰Francis B. Gummere, *The Popular Ballad* (Boston and New York: Houghton, Mifflin and Co., 1907), pp. 77-85.

⁷¹J. H. Boynton, "Studies in the English Ballad Refrain," (Ph.D. dissertation, Harvard University, 1897), p. 58A.

⁷²Jones, "Commonplace and Memorization," 102.

⁷³Quoted by Jones, ibid., 110 from "Ballads," *Midwest Folklore*, 6 (1956), 54.

⁷⁴Buchan, *The Ballad and the Folk*, pp. 148-50.

⁷⁵Jones, "Commonplace and Memorization," 106.

⁷⁶Ibid., 108.

⁷⁷Ibid., 110.

⁷⁸Motherwell, *Minstrelsy*, p. xi.

⁷⁹Jones, "Commonplace and Memorization," 105.

⁸⁰Ibid., 106.

⁸¹Ibid., 105.

⁸²See Michael Curschmann, "The Concept of the Oral Formula as an Impediment to Our Understanding of Medieval Oral Poetry," in *Medievalia et Humanistica*, n.s. 8 (1977), 63-76.

⁸³*The English and Scottish Popular Ballads*, eds. H. C. Sargent and G. L. Kittredge (Boston: Houghton Mifflin Co., 1904), pp. xxiv-xxvi.

⁸⁴Bertrand Harris Bronson, *The Singing Tradition of Child's Popular Ballads* (Princeton, N.J.: Princeton University Press, 1976), pp. xxiii-xxiv.

⁸⁵See Larry D. Benson, "The Literary Character of Anglo-Saxon Formulaic Poetry," *Publications of the Modern Language Association*, 81 (1966), 334-41.

⁸⁶See Lord's article, "Oral Poetry," in *Encyclopaedia of Poetry and Poetics*, ed. Alex Preminger (Princeton, N.J.: Princeton University Press, 1965); *The Singer of Tales*, pp. 5-7. Habit becomes suspiciously like memory in Lord. Note the

remark in *The Singer of Tales*, p. 17: "One of the reasons also why different singings of the same song by the same man vary most in their endings is that the end of a song is sung less often by the singer." It is a general law in Bronson's collection that the tunes most sung are the most stable. On this point see also J. W. Hendren, *A Study of Ballad Rhythm* (Princeton, N.J.: Princeton University Press, 1936), p. 57.

[87]Finnegan, *Oral Poetry*, p. 73. But Finnegan still follows Buchan's interpretation of Bronson as to Mrs. Brown (p. 56), and his and Jones's views on memorization (p. 69). Justifying the need for this present essay, she observes that "in specialist circles analyses in terms of 'memorization' have become unpopular" (p. 53).

[88]H. M. and N. K. Chadwick, *The Growth of Literature*, 3 vols. (Cambridge: Cambridge University Press, 1932–40), vol. 3 (1940), pp. 174–91. Cf. N. K. Chadwick and Victor Zhirmunsky, *Oral Epics of Central Asia* (Cambridge: Cambridge University Press, 1969), pp. 213–33.

[89]The data on the African tribes in this paragraph are from Finnegan, *Oral Poetry*, pp. 73–87 and from her *Oral Literature in Africa* (Nairobi: Oxford University Press, 1977, orig. 1970). The Polynesian and Eskimo examples I also owe to her.

[90]*Izibongo: Zulu Praise Poems*, ed. Trevor Cope (Oxford: Clarendon Press, 1968), pp. 27–29, 35.

[91]Gordon Innes, "Stability and Change in Griots' Narrations," *African Language Studies*, 14 (1973), 118. Cf. S. A. Babalǫla, *The Content and Form of Yoruba Ijala* (Oxford: Clarendon Press, 1966), pp. 40–55.

[92]*The Mwindo Epic*, eds. and trans. Daniel Biebuyck and Kahombo C. Mateene (Berkeley and Los Angeles: University of California Press, 1969), pp. 5–13.

[93]Finnegan, *Oral Poetry*, pp. 73–75.

[94]See Paul Zumthor, *Essai de poétique médiévale* (Paris: Editions du Seuil, 1972), pp. 190–94. The remark by Lazar alluded to in this paragraph occurred during a symposium on the troubadours at the University of California, Los Angeles, March 3, 1979. On the same occasion, Joseph J. Duggan delivered a paper on the strong possibility of oral transmission of troubadour poetry.

[95]Buchan, *The Ballad and the Folk*, p. 274.

[96]Lord, *The Singer of Tales, p. 33.*

[97]Chadwicks, *The Growth of Literature*, vol. 3, p. 181, but note the warning in n. 2 that Radlov may have underestimated the variety of melodies because his ear was unattuned to the Tatar musical tradition.

[98]Kenneth A. Thigpen, "A Reconsideration of the Commonplace Phrase and Commonplace Theme in the Child Ballads," *Southern Folklore Quarterly*, 37 (1973), 387; cf. *The Ballad as Song*, pp. 112–17.

[99]Buchan, *The Ballad and the Folk*, p. 274.

[100]Samuel P. Bayard, "Prolegomena to a Study of the Principal Melodic Families of Folk Song," in *The Critics and the Ballad*, eds. MacEdward Leach and Tristram P. Coffin (Carbondale: Southern Illinois University Press, 1961), p. 110.

[101]Bronson, *The Singing Tradition*, p. xxv.

[102]Sharp, *English Folk-Song*, pp. 25–26.

[103]Bronson, *The Ballad as Song*, p. 264.

[104]Jones, "Commonplace and Memorization," 106.

[105]Bronson, *The Ballad as Song*, p. 265.

[106]Bronson, *The Singing Tradition*, p. xxvii.

[107]A. B. Friedman, ed., *The Viking Book of Folk Ballads* (New York: Viking Press, 1956), p. xv; *The Ballad Revival*, pp. 293–98.

[108]Gummere, *The Popular Ballad*, pp. 79–85.

[109]Quoted by R. W. Ingram, "Words and Music," in *Elizabethan Poetry*, eds. J. R. Brown and Bernard Harris (London: Edward Arnold, 1960), p. 133.

A Tension of Essences in Murdered-Sweetheart Ballads

D. K. Wilgus

By "tension of essences" I refer to the concept set forth by Albert B. Lord — the recognition that certain elements tend to be so inherent in a story pattern that, even when they do not occur explicitly, they can be recognized as underlying and explaining obscure, incongruous, or "irrational" items in a text.[1] For example, Lord has suggested in a public lecture that the apparently inconsequential detail of Odysseus's companion Elpenor's breaking his neck in a fall from Circe's roof occurs at this point in the *Odyssey* because at least this portion of the story parallels the death of Enkidu and the descent of Gilgamesh into the underworld in the Sumerian-Babylonian epic. Thus certain elements in Anglo-American "returned-unrecognized-true lover" ballads occur because the story parallels "return" stories exemplified by the *Odyssey*. The disguise element on the one hand will "retain" the beggar or the mask, or the beggar with a patch on his eye; on the other hand it will be manifested in simple nonrecognition or the use of a surrogate "tester."[2] The years of absence of the lover (varying from three to ten) tend to be seven, perhaps testifying to a "mythological" background.[3] Consider the incident in "Young Beichan" (Child 53) when the Turkish lady, seeking her lover separated from her for seven years, arrives decked in rich array and engages in a none-too-meaningful conversation with the porter of the castle in which her lover is about to marry another girl.[4] First it must be recognized that "Young Beichan" belongs to the so-called "female warrior" type of ballad in which a girl disguises herself (usually as a soldier or sailor) and goes in search of her lover.[5] The "female warrior" element, which occurs in story types other than this, is but an allo-motif of the disguise unit in the story pattern in which two lovers are separated and one journeys to find the other and test her or him, normally with disguise and recognition devices. I shall not speak of a "sex-reversal" pattern,

241

because we do not know the sex of the tester in the origin of the pattern, but the tester may be male or female, whether disguised as a beggar or a soldier, and recognized by a scar, a love token, the exposure of a breast when a button pops off a uniform, etc. Thus the Turkish lady's jewelry, the conversation with the porter, who reports her arrival to his lord, and the rejection of the new love for the old fill the *Disguise, Test,* and *Recognition* slots.

The Anglo-American "murdered sweetheart" pattern should be familiar. A lad who has seduced a lass, who usually becomes pregnant, takes her on a journey on the pretext of marriage. He murders her and is subsequently apprehended and punished (there are of course often variations and omissions — as there are in the "returned-unrecognized-true lover" pattern). Many tensions within this pattern could be discussed, but I shall limit myself to one — which I call for the moment the *Denunciation* element. I shall grant to begin with that a *Denunciation* element — often in guises identical or similar to those to be discussed — occurs in other patterns. And I shall further grant that on the one hand such an element seems "normal" in "true life" situations (on which the ballads are often based) and on the other the element is not always present in ballads in the "murdered sweetheart" pattern. But I wish to consider examples in which it does occur and the manner in which it occurs.

In a study of a group of American "murdered sweetheart" ballads, Anne B. Cohen distinguishes between the "murdered girl" formula and the "criminal-brought-to-justice" formula ("youth, upbringing, or past deeds of criminal; crucial crime and events leading to it; pursuit, capture, and trial; execution"). "Sometimes the murdered-girl formula combines with the second half of the criminal formula to produce ballads in which the capture and punishment of the lover-murderer are reported."[6] Although a number of "murdered sweetheart" ballads contain more than the second half of the "criminal-brought-to-justice" pattern, Cohen may be correct in seeing the "pulls" of the two patterns in traditional texts. However, the relation of *Denunciation* to *Punishment* raises issues larger than I wish to discuss here.

In the ballad earliest known as "The Gosport Tragedy" (Laws P 36A) the murderer buries the girl and attempts to escape to sea. The girl's ghost appears on shipboard, resulting in the confession of the culprit and the subsequent discovery of the body by the girl's parents. In an apparently derived form ("Pretty Polly," Laws P 36B) the ghost tears the villain to pieces. Finally, in blues ballad forms of "Pretty Polly," the ghost has disappeared, but after the villain has buried his victim (in some variants of course) he departs, leaving some beasts, or more usually birds or a bird "for to mourn." This incident occurs in the earliest known text of P 36A:

He covered her body and home he did run
Leaving nothing but birds her death to mourn.[7]

In an Irish murdered-sweetheart ballad, "Young Ellen Maguire," the murderer leaves the girl with the birds mourning.[8] Is the incident a kind of decorative device in the first place and a kind of "survival" in the second? I shall content that a supernatural device is the "essence" of the *Denunciation* element and that the "survival" of the birds is the "tension."

First, one can cite murdered-sweetheart ballads in which the *Denunciation* is provided by an avenging ghost.[9] In the seventeenth-century "Dorsetshire Tragedy," for example, the girl prophesies that *"Conscience shall you molest,"* and "As home his coast he stear'd" he hears a "frightful Voice" and "Sometimes her bleeding Ghost in flames appear'd."[10] In "Pat O'Brien" (Laws P 39) the girl's ghost reports her death to her mother and then appears to the murderer in his cell. "The Sailor's Tragedy" (Laws P 34) differs from the usual pattern in having the pregnant girl commit suicide after being deserted; but her ghost follows her lover to sea and causes his death. The ghost of "Poor Omie" (Laws F 4) follows after him, and in another ballad on the event ("Naomi Wise," Laws F 31) her spirit still "lingers round the place."[11] "John Gorman" married a girl, but three years later "thro' lonesome groves and Vallies he led her astray," murdered her, telling her mother she stayed at a house near Castlereagh. That night the mother heard the daughter's voice telling her of the murder[12] (we have already noticed the voice in conjunction with the ghost; thus we can certainly treat a voice as a synecdoche). The murder of "The Colleen Bawn" was again that of a wife, but of a woman who was an "encumbrance" to her "rakish" husband, John Scanlan. His servant, Stephen Sullivan, was supposedly the actual murderer, and a broadside recounts how he was plagued by visions of the dead girl.[13] Three stanzas of another ballad (or ballads) on the murder recall that "many a burning curse pursued/The heartless villain who betrayed her."[14] What seems a clear sex-reversal occurs in the Irish broadside, "The Lamentation of Thomas Nolan."[15] Nolan courts a girl who murders him with a razor. His ghost appears to his servant and reveals the crime. The girl flees and boards a ship for America. In five days Nolan's ghost appears and casts her into the sea.

Next surrogate forms of the ghost appear. A quite clear substitute occurs in "James MacDonald" (Laws P 38). The girl survives until the next morning and reports the assault before she dies. More prevalent are "tokens" of some sort reflecting the supernatural. After the body of the murdered girl in "The Old Oak Tree" (Laws P 37) is discovered, the corpse bleeds in the presence of the murderer (sometimes he *thinks* he sees her bleeding corpse as well). When Patrick Daly sees the bones of his former sweetheart, whom he has thrown into a lime kiln, he trembles and is arrested.[16] After Henry stabs Mary Benfield, he faints (for no apparent reason) and confesses.[17] Andrew Carr cut off the head of Margret Murphy with an army razor because she "proved inconstant." In a public house he saw blood on his hand and gave himself up to the law.[18] The ghost in "Pat O'Brien" was noted above, but in some versions the corpse also dashes blood in Pat's face. Thus we may see the "tension" in "The Wexford Girl" (Laws P 35). Upon returning home from the murder,the villain explains the blood on his clothes by claiming a nosebleed. We know that bleeding at the nose — like the breaking of rings, the losing of heels, and the stumbling of horses — is an ill omen, so we are not surprised at his arrest and conviction.[19]

A significant example of the function of the "token" occurs in the tradition of "Fair Rosanna,"[20] in which a flower grows out of the girl's hidden grave. Whenever it is cropped, it instantly grows up again. Curious, the murderer crops the rose, which withers instantly, and he confesses. A Nova Scotia singer remembered the tune and sang only two lines of a ballad called "The Magic Flower":

> And wondered how so fair a flower
> Could bloom and flourish there.

The lines do not seem to appear in variants of "Fair Rosanna," but the singer's prose summary of the plucked flower turning to blood in the hands of the murderer[21] agrees with "Fair Rosanna":

> He cried, this is Rosanna's blood
> That did spring from her fair body.

The rather slight "tension" in texts of "The Wexford Girl" has been noted above. However, an Ohio performer told the following story as a "sequel" to the song:

> Not long after the murder, a hunter found the new mound, and on it was growing a wonderful flower. He gathered it for his wife, and was surprised to see another blossom at once to take its place. He pulled it, too, and a third flower at once appeared. When this story became known, people went to the scene. The murderer was asked to go, too, but declined on the ground of illness. His friends insisted, however, and he at length went with them to the grave in the wood. After each had gathered one of the mysterious flowers, the murderer broke one off. At once the plant withered and died.[22]

Whether one wishes to postulate a knowledge of the "Fair Rosanna" ballad or of a prose tradition stemming from or parallel with it, it is difficult to escape the evidence of the "tension" operating.

We have seen how, in the "Dorsetshire Tragedy," "conscience" is added to the overtly supernatural; and in "The Wexford Girl" the troubled sleeper sees the flames of hell all around his bed. But in many of the ballads *Denunciation* is attributed directly to a Supreme Being, as indeed in early forms of "The Wexford Girl": "Heaven had a watchful eye."[23] The murderer of "Polly Williams" (Laws dF 39) cannot escape

> For though he thought his crime was well
> hidden from all eyes,
> There's One who's always watching from His
> palace in the skies.

As for "The Murder of Grace Brown" (Laws F 7),

> . . . nobody knows how it happened
> But Gillette and God knows it all.

The villain cannot escape "the all-seeing eye" ("Pearl Bryan IV" [Laws dF 59]) or the "one seeing eye" ("The Millman Song" [Laws dF 60]), for "the power of Almighty was there for to see."[24] And in the end

> . . . the great Judge of Mercy looked down
> from on high,
> And he said, "Now, Young Millman, for this
> deed you shall die."[25]

For "a witness there who sees a crime with an all-seeing eye," the ballad composer can substitute a mortal witness, sometimes as an addition as in the "Lamentation of William Thompson for the Murder of Betsy Ryan."[26] "Someone" winding hay nearby sees Thompson dash out Betsy's brains and swears against him at the trial; but the murdered girl's ghost appears to Thompson every night in his cell. Usually the mortal witness suffices. Eliza Walker, who runs off with her father's desk and gold, is murdered by her lover. A gentleman passing by recognizes the desk and sees Miss Walker's cloak; he apprehends the culprit.[27] Stephen McKeown, who ambushed and murdered Mary McShane, was captured and convicted on the evidence of a female witness.[28] A witness may, however, be even more helpful, as is Young Forbes in "Bally Mount Forest So Green."[29] Fowling in the forest, Forbes overhears Jamie about to murder his sweetheart. He apprehends Jamie, who is lodged in Monaghan Jail.

The "tensions" noted thus far have been more or less lineal, that is they occur at the place in the story line where *Denunciation* would be expected. There are, however, instances of nonlineal tension in which the supernatural, like the ghost of Naomi Wise, "lingers round the place." One occurs in the tradition of the Irish ballad, "The Hanging of John Roddy."[30] The ballad itself tells of the capture of two men charged with the murder of Mary Maguire, the "Flower of Canaboe." John Roddy is convicted and hanged. The prose comment denies Roddy's guilt and lays the murder on a tinsmith. This is borne out by the curse in the ballad:

> That the porringers and pints may be sawdered
>   round his joints
> And burned day and night in his fire.
> It is then he'll plainly say, My curse
>   light on the day
> That I murdered you sweet Mary Maguire.

There is a further account of a cure: "A rope that was used to hang a man named Roddy in Carrick Jail for a crime for which he was sentenced to death but of which he was innocent, is called Roddy's rope. Portion of the rope is kept in this parish and rubbed on the sick person by a member of the family owning the rope at special times in each month until the patient is cured."

Perhaps a more extreme example of nonlineal tension is that of an Irish ballad, "Bella Brooks."[31] Near Castlefinn, Co. Donegal, a farmer's daughter gives her favor to a neighboring farmer's son. He takes her to his father's house and chloroforms her. Then with the help of a servant he throws her into the waters of the Finn. Her body is discovered and police and coroner are sent for. Apparently because Bella is an orphan she does not get fair play and no one is arrested. But the coroner breaks his neck in a fall from his gig (if it didn't happen, it probably should have).

In the light of the previous discussion, the following text should occasion no surprise:

MURDER OF
MARIA MARTEN,
BY WILLIAM CORDER

E. Hodges, Printer, Wholesale Toy and Marble Warehouse, 26 Grafton Street, Soho Where may be obtained all the old & new Songs of the day, Childrens Books, &c.

COME all you thoughtless young men a warning take by me
And think on my unhappy fate, to be hang'd upon a tree
My name is William Corder to you I do declare
I courted Maria Marten most beautiful and fair.

I promised I would marry her, upon a certain day,
Instead of that I was resolved to take her life away,
I went into her father's house the 18th day of May,
O, come my dear Maria we'll fix the wedding day!

If you'll meet me at the red barn as sure as I have life
I'll take you to Ipswich town, & there make you my wife,
I straight went home & fetch'd my gun, my pickaxe, and my spade,
I went into the red barn and there I dug her grave.

With heart so light she thought no harm to meet him she did go,
He murder'd her all in the barn & laid her body low
The horrid deed that he had done she lay bleeding in her gore,
Her bleeding mangled body he threw under the red barn floor.

Now all things being silent she could not take no rest
She appear'd in her mother's house, who suckled her at her breast;
For many a long month or more her mind being sorely oppress'd,
Neither night nor day she could not take no rest.

Her mother's mind being so disturbed, she dreamed three nights o'er
Her daughter she lay murder'd under the red barn floor
She sent her father to the barn when under the ground he thrust,
And there found his daughter mingling with the dust

My trial I could not stand most woeful was the sight,
When her jaw bone was brought to prove, which pierced my heart
     quite;
His aged mother standing by, likewise his loving wife
And with her grief, her hair she tore, she scarcely could keep life,

Adieu, adieu my loving friends my glass is almost run
On Monday next will be my last when I'm to be hangd
All young men as you pass by with pity look on me,
For the murder of Maria Marten I was hanged upon a tree[32]

While not a perfect example of the murdered-sweetheart plus criminal-brought-to-justice patterns, it is close (it does not turn Maria,
who had given birth to three illegitimate children — one by William
Corder's brother Thomas, one by a Peter Matthews, and one by
William Corder — into an innocent, trusting maiden; however,
writers of popular histories and melodramas did portray Maria as
the "innocent village maiden"[33]). Yet, though it oversimplifies, it
is remarkably close to the reported facts of the 18 May, 1827 murder
of Maria Marten in Suffolk and the 1828 execution of William
Corder outside Bury St. Edmunds Jail. My concern, however, is with
the dream of Maria's mother (actually her stepmother) in which
Maria reveals that she is buried in the red barn.

The dream was no creation of the ballad composer. After Maria
disappeared with Corder on 18 May, and while William was assur-
ing her family that she was alive and well elsewhere, Mrs. Marten
questioned Corder and villagers in Polstead, insisting "something
dreadful must have happened to our Maria." Mrs. Marten testified
that during the winter Maria appeared to her in dreams shouting
for help. Finally, in early April Mrs. Marten told her husband that
she had dreamed Maria had been murdered and "that her corpse

was buried 'underneath the righthand bay of the further side of Corder's Red Barn'." Eventually Thomas Marten obtained permission to examine the barn, and on 19 April Maria's body was discovered where Mrs. Marten had indicated, in a short grave, "legs . . . up and head bent down into the earth."[34]

> Within a few months of Corder's execution few people in the village believed the dream story and Anne Marten was regarded as a somewhat sinister figure who knew more of the events than she would relate. . . . The suspicion that the dream was an invention became a certainty when it was learned that among the books in the Marten cottage was a romance entitled *The Old English Baron.* The story told of a father who, following the directions given him in his wife's dream, found the place where the daughter was buried.[35]

Well, not quite. *The Old English Baron* is a gothic novel by Clara Reeve (1729–1807) of neighboring Ipswich, originally published anonymously in Colchester as *The Champion of Virtue* and revised in 1778 under the new title with the author's name. There are certainly dreams and ghosts in the romance. Lady Lovel says her husband's ghost appears to her and reveals his base murder. Sir Philip Harclay dreams Lord Lovel sends for him and shows him a cave, similar to the location where Lovel's body is later discovered. Edmund (Lovel's lost son) dreams that his father and mother appear in a dream and recognize him. There are indeed interesting "coincidences": a borrowed pickaxe, a drowned woman secretly buried. Lord Lovel's skeleton is found with neck and heels together and forced into a trunk.[36] But it is not a murdered-sweetheart plot. If, as Donald McCormick and others believe,[37] Mrs. Marten was involved in the murder at least to the extent that she had knowledge after the fact, her fabrication of the dream does not seem to have stemmed solely or directly from *The Old English Baron.* It might well have been stimulated by a knowledge of the murdered-sweetheart pattern.

Having considered such an interrelation of fact and fancy, we now observe how *Denunciation* can enter a ballad text in which it was apparently absent. The ballad of "The Jealous Lover" (Laws F 1) is practically archetypal in its adherence to the murdered-sweetheart pattern, with the exception that the motive is jealousy rather than the girl's pregnancy. The lover entices the girl from home into the woods; on her knees she pleads for her life; he stabs her. Seldom is there reference to his punishment. The song has been popular throughout North America and has been adapted to fit known events ("Pearl Bryan II," "Neil Cropsey II," etc.). No clear British antecedent text has been discovered, although Phillips Barry[38] argued that the ballad derived from a nineteenth-century Manchester broadside, "The Murder of Betsy Smith." Laws disputes the claim and, although I cannot completely agree with his reason-ing,[39] he is probably correct. The resemblances cited by Barry tend to be endemic in murdered-sweetheart ballads. But Barry also pointed out the debt many texts of "The Jealous Lover" owe to Thomas Haynes Bayly's "She Never Blamed Him" (1829), a song of an abandoned (not murdered) girl.[40] The lines I am concerned with are:

> The banners waved around her,
> And she heard the bugle sound;
> They pass'd — and strangers found her
> Cold and lifeless on the ground.

Without postulating any direct line of development, I can note interesting variations of the lines as they appear in "The Jealous Lover":

> The banners waved above her,
> Shrill was the bugle sound,
> But strangers came and found her
> Cold lifeless on the ground.[41]

> *   *   *   *   *   *

> The banners waved around her
> And she heard the bugle sound[42]

> *   *   *   *   *   *

> The banner waves above her,
> Shrill was the bugle sound
> The angels found her body,
> Cold, lifeless on the ground.[43]

> *   *   *   *   *   *

> The angels waved above her
> And thrilled the bugle sound[44]

> *   *   *   *   *   *

> The birds sang in the morning,
> But mournful was their song;
> A stranger found her body
> In a cold and lifeless form.[45]

In the process of attempting to make sense of a none-too-relevant stanza, singers seem to have responded to a tension, introducing supernatural elements in differing rationalizations, as in:

> The buzzards hovered o'er her
> And loud did the bugle sound.[46]

The birds in "The Jealous Lover" have brought us full circle as far as vulgar ballads in the murdered-sweetheart pattern are concerned. I can now turn to consideration of three "classic" ballads in the light of the argument I have presented.

The first problem concerns the parrot in variants of "The Outlandish Knight" (Child 4). The girl runs off with a lover who intends to kill her (taking "some of her father's gold" as does Miss Walker). She outwits him and kills him, then returns home and bribes the parrot not to tell on her. It has been suggested that the parrot sequence is borrowed from "Young Hunting" (Child 68), sometimes the reverse;[47] indeed some stanzas are parallel, sometimes including the accusation. But assuming the borrowing, mutual or otherwise, it is the *why* rather than the *what* that is significant. I shall not be concerned at the moment with the sometimes supernatural character of the male in Child 4, which is relatively insignificant in Anglo-American tradition though a supernatural aura may have some relevance to tension in the ballad. On the periphery of the ballad's international tradition are "The Maid Is Killed" forms which, because the girl does not outwit the lover, the plot becomes essentially a murdered-sweetheart ballad (indeed a student of the ballad's international tradition included a text of "The Cruel Ship's Carpenter" as a "literary variant"[48]). However, most texts abort the murdered-sweetheart plot or in effect reverse it. The tension seems to arise because a killing has been committed in a plot similar to that of a murdered-sweetheart ballad, and therefore *Denunciation* is expected. But because the killing seems justified, the denunciation is usually prevented. That the parrot—the "modern" form of the talking bird—is the spirit of the murdered abductor is not maintained, but it stands in that relation, just as does the bird (or birds) in murdered-sweetheart ballads just discussed. A comparison with "Young Hunting," whether or not it is the donor of the parrot sequence, may be revealing.

In this ballad, a lover comes to tell his sweetheart that he is leaving her for another. She kills him and usually has his body thrown into a body of water. She is then accused of the murder by a bird. She attempts to bribe the bird (threatens to kill him in some texts), and in some variants the bird reveals the murder and the girl is executed. This ballad—in terms of its history—is not simply a kind of off-beat sex-reversal type of a murdered-sweetheart ballad. It is a rationalized form of the "fairy lover" type exemplified by "Clerk Colvill" (Child 42), in which a man renounces his supernatural lover for a mortal woman and is consequently killed. "Young Hunting" is in the tradition that lies between the Scandinavian

"Elveskud" (DgF 47[49]) and "Frillens Haevn" (DgF 208).[50] But I am not concerned here with directions of transmission, whether to or from Scandinavia, but with the relationship in story pattern. The knight in "Elveskud," out hunting, visits an elf woman. After he tells her he is forsaking her for a mortal woman, she fatally wounds him. The young man in "Frillens Haevn" rides to his old love's house, where she welcomes him with wine and beer. When he tells her that he is on his way to his bride, she stabs him and he rides home to his death. A recently recorded version of "Young Hunting" in its text and prose gloss makes clear the enticement/seduction elements which tie the ballad to "Frillens Haevn" and to the underlying fairy lover pattern. The singer recalls his aunt's telling of the tale:

> She told a story of a castle a-bein' near a wooded country. The hunters would go in there to hunt. They [the woman's servants] would fill up the pathways with brush, but leave the path open that come through the lands of this castle. And there was a woman lived in that castle who wasn't what you'd call at this day and time, you wouldn't call her a good woman, and not at that time, either, of course. Anyways, she was a-seekin' lovers. I don't think she was so very good looking, what I remember about the tale, so she kindly made some effort to get lovers. So she'd have her servant men to fill up the pathways, the way they went in there, and then make a very good pathway a-leading by her land. And then she'd accuse 'em to get the subject started, she'd accuse them of being on her land—of trespassing. And so she'd try to get 'em to come down and rest up, you know, and she'd killed several that way. And this song of young Henry, the hunter—why he come by. She tried to get him to come down and he wouldn't but she stobbed him anyway—that's according to the song—and hid him away . . .

> > Pitch black was the night, as black as could be,
> > Lost from his hunting was poor Henery.
> > His true love is a-waiting, a-tearing her hair,
> > A-waiting to see her love all so fair. (2)

> > "Who rides on my land at such an hour?
> > Who is it die?" cried she.
> > "Only I ride at such an hour,"
> > So said my love Henery. (2)

> > "Come down, come down, my love Henery,
> > And stay this night with me,
> > My bed is made of soft and warm,
> > And just for you and me." (2)[51]

                    *   *   *   *   *   *

There is certainly a murdered-sweetheart pattern here, and one which emphasizes that we should not think of sex reversal or inversion, but alternate possibilities.

Denunciation is lacking in the international fairy lover tradition, perhaps understandably in that the killer is a supernatural being. Thus it may also be understandable that when the killer becomes mortal the denunciation has a supernatural tension relating to the underlying fairy lover story. The way in which tension—in a larger sense—can operate is revealed in "Sir Hugh" (Child 155). Gavin I. Langmuir has pointed out that

> the events surrounding the death of Hugh of Lincoln in 1255, for which nineteen Jews were executed by King Henry III . . . inspired two quite different literary and popular traditions. In the first place, the alleged ritual murder was described in three contemporary chronicles and an Anglo-Norman ballad, and Hugh's shrine at Lincoln and these writings preserved the memory of his fate for centuries. The event did not seem distant to Chaucer some 135 years later.[52]

Chaucer's prioress recounts the legend of the "singing boy," who after being killed by Jews continues singing until his mother discovers his body in a privy. She concludes her tale with mention of "young Hugh of Lincoln slayn also."

We are concerned with the "second tradition inspired by the events of 1255" which "bears scant resemblance to either the legend of the singing boy or ritual murder."[53] The Anglo-Norman ballad (of ninety-two stanzas) is thoroughly "vulgar" is style, and begins:

> Ore oez bel chancon
> Des Jues de Nicole,
>   qui par tré ison
> Firent la cruel occision
> De un enfant que Huchon
>   out non.[54]

The text sticks close to the "facts" of the case, including the refusal of the boy's body to remain buried or in the privy where it was then thrown—and adds another miracle:

> Une femme vint à cel ur
> Qe aveit perdu avant meint jur
> La we del oil par aventure,
> Cum Deu voleit nostre Seignur.

> La femme mult tost di seit tant:
> "Allas! Huet de juven enfant
> Qe si beals fustes avant,
> Pur quei estes ici gisant?"

> De ces mains ie cors mania,
> Le oil que out perdu après tocha;
> Deu sa grace à lui mustra,
> La we del oil à lui dona.

> Quant la femme fu aparceu
> De la grace et de la vertu
> Que à lui envéïe fu,
> "Des merci! j'o la véu."[55]

In the usual versions of "Sir Hugh" a boy kicks a ball into a lady's garden. The lady entices him in (with the sexual symbol of an apple, sometimes also with a cherry or fig), kills him, and throws the body into a well. His mother finds the body, which miraculously speaks to her. The relation of this ballad story to "Young Hunting" should be as obvious as that of the latter to fairy lover ballads. There is probably more than one tension explaining the "stuffing" of the legend of the 1255 affair into a fairy lover ballad. The well was fact. The mother's search for the body and the miraculous speaking corpse seem to have come from the singing boy legend. The supernatural denunciation has joined little Sir Hugh with Lord Hencry, the Wexford girl, Rosanna, Pretty Polly, and countless other "murdered sweethearts" whose memory exists in an otherworldly tension.

NOTES

[1]Albert B. Lord, *The Singer of Tales* (Cambridge, Mass.: Harvard University Press, 1960), p. 97.

[2]Examples include: Francis James Child, *The English and Scottish Popular Ballads* (Boston and New York: Houghton, Mifflin and Co., 1882-98), nos. 17, 252, 263; G. Malcom Laws, Jr., *American Balladry from British Broadsides* (Philadelphia: American Folklore Society, 1957), nos. M 12, N 28, N 29, N 30, N 31, N 32, N 33, N 34, N 35, N 36, N 37, N 38, N 39, N 40, N 41, N 42, N 43; Laws, *Native American Balladry*, rev. ed. (Philadelphia: American Folklore Society, 1964), nos. dB 39, H 28, H 29; Helen Creighton, *Maritime Folk Songs* (Toronto: Ryerson Press, 1962), pp. 160-61; Gavin Greig, *Folk-Song of the North-East* (1914; rpt. Hatboro, Pa.: Folklore Associates, 1963), nos. 23, 55, 81, 112, 153; Sam Henry, "Songs of the People," *Northern Constitution* (Coleraine, 1923-29), nos. 8, 78, 205, 529, 563, 570, 737, 795, 812; Edith Fowke, *Traditional Singers and Songs from Ontario* (Hatboro, Pa.: Folklore Associates, 1962), pp. 116-17; Robin Morton ed., *Come Day, Go Day, God Send Sunday* (London: Routledge and Kegan Paul, 1973), p. 7; John Ord, *Bothy Songs and Ballads* (1930: rpt. Edinburgh: J. Donald, 1974), p. 77; Kenneth Peacock, *Songs of the Newfoundland Outports*, 3 vols. (Ottawa: National Museums, 1965), 2: 530-31.

[3]Mircea Eliade, in *Myth, Rites, Symbols: A Mircea Eliade Reader*, 2 vols., eds. Wendell C. Beane and W. G. Doty (New York: Harper and Row, 1976), 1: 178-79. The period of sojourn in the "underground chamber" (initiatory death) varies among and apparently within cultures.

[4]David Buchan, *The Ballad and the Folk* (London and Boston: Routledge and Kegan Paul, 1972), pp. 127-31.

[5]Examples include: Child 105, 106, 293; Laws nos. N 6, N 7, N 10, N 11, N 14, N 15, N 16; Henry, "Songs of the People," nos. 203, 556, 584, 797; Colm O Lochlainn, *More Irish Street Ballads* (Dublin: Three Candles, 1965), pp. 176-77; Peacock, *Newfoundland Outports* vol. 1, p. 190. There are many ballads related to this pattern. Laws N 12 is a truncated form in that the girl resists the

captain (who wishes "he" was a woman) and never finds her love. The girl in Laws N 3 discovers her lover is dead. In many ballads the disguised girl accompanies her lover (e.g., Laws N 1, N 2, N 5, N 8, N 17, and in some variants of O 33). The male lover may reject the girl's offer to accompany him (Laws K 14, N 9), or she may simply sail in disguise for adventure (Laws N 4, N 13). Dianne Dugaw has completed a study of Anglo-American "female warrior" ballads which deal with these problems: "The Female Warrior Heroine in Anglo-American Popular Balladry" (Ph.D. dissertation, University of California, Los Angeles, 1982).

[6]Anne B. Cohen, *Poor Pearl, Poor Girl!* (Austin: American Folklore Society, 1973), p. 103. This study is extremely important in demonstrating the effect of traditional patterning on both ballads and journalistic reports of events.

[7]*Roxburghe Ballads*, ed. Charles Hindley (London: Reeves and Turner, 1873–74), vol. 8, pp. 143-44, 173-74.

[8]Irish Folklore Collections, University College, Dublin, *MSS na Scol.* no. 967, pp. 121-25 (Cavan, ca. 1938).

[9]I am not considering or citing ballads lacking *Denunciation*, as I am not arguing that the element is obligatory in murdered-sweetheart ballads. I do cite broadside texts not reported from traditional performers. The manifestation of traditional patterns in popular literature is significant, as demonstrated by Cohen, *Poor Pearl*.

[10]*The Pepys Ballads*, ed. Hyder Edward Rollins (Cambridge, Mass.: Harvard University Press, 1931), vol. 7, pp. 132-35.

[11]A full study of the ballads dealing with the Randolph Co., Va. murder of Naomi Wise remains to be made. It seems likely that the ghost was introduced in *later* versions of F 4 on the basis of local traditions and/or pamphlets on the events, the latter of which likely formed the basis for Carson Robison's "Naomi Wise" (F 31).

[12]Broadside, Trinity College, Dublin, 66.u.165; National Library of Ireland, Song Books (Limerick).

[13]"Sorrowful Lamentation of Stephen Sulivan," NLI. This 1819 murder was the basis for Gerald Griffin's *The Collegians* (Dublin, 1829 *et seq.*) and Dion Boucicault's *Colleen Bawn* (1860).

[14]IFC, *MSS na Scol,* no. 600, pp. 20a, 29 (Clare, 1937).

[15]TCD, 21.bb.52, p. 411.

[16]Broadside, "The Lamentation of Patrick Daly," TCD, 21.bb.51, p. 214.

[17]Broadside, "Murder of Mary Benfield," TCD, 66.u.165.

[18]Broadside, NLI.

[19]In some variants the ghost of the "Wexford Girl" seems to be manifesting itself in the murderer's dream: e.g., "And all that night the Wexford girl/Came trembling 'round his head" (Peacock, *Newfoundland Outports*, vol. 2, pp. 635, 637).

[20]Peter Buchan, *Gleanings of Scotch, English and Irish Scarce Old Ballads* (Peterhead: P. Buchan, 1825), pp. 46-51; William Christie, *Traditional Ballad Airs*, 2 vols. (Edinburgh: Edmonston and Douglas, 1876-81), 2: 78-79; Worthington Chauncey Ford, *Broadsides, Ballads, etc. Printed in Massachusetts, 1639–1800* (Boston: Massachusetts Historical Society, 1922), nos. 3255, 3325; Harvard University Library, 62.5; 100 (ii) .75; 102.56; 102.57; MS Book of Abba Adaline Ellsworth, West Bennington, Vt., 25241.60*; *Roxburghe Ballads*, vol. 8: pp. 68, 175-76.

[21]*Journal of the English Folk Dance and Song Society*, 6 (1951), 91.

[22]Mary O. Eddy, *Ballads and Songs from Ohio* (1939; rpt. Hatboro, Pa.: Folklore Associates, 1964), p. 235.

[23]"The Berkshire Tragedy of the Wittam Miller," *Roxburghe Ballads*, vol. 8, pp. 629-30.

[24]Peacock, *Newfoundland Outports*, vol. 2, p. 608.

[25]"The Millman and Turpin Song," *Northeast Folklore*, 5 (1963): 42-44; Louise Manny and James Reginald Wilson, *Songs of Miramichi* (Fredericton, New Brunswick: Brunswick Press, 1970), pp. 195-96.

[26]Broadside, NLI.

[27]"Lamentation for Miss Walker," broadside, NLI; Frank Kidson Folio Collection of Broadsides (Mitchell Library, Glasgow), no. 4, p. 18.

[28]"The Fork Hill Murder," broadsides, NLI; TCD, Gall.R.15.35; Royal Irish Academy, Dublin, 66.H.17.

[29]IFC, Donagh MacDonagh Collection, p. 89.

[30]IFC, *MSS na Scol*, no. 224, pp. 166, 260 (Leitrim).

[31]IFC, *MSS na Scol*, nos. 987, pp. 64-65 (Cavan, 1939); 1098, pp. 203-4 (Donegal, ca. 1938). The ballad is attributed to Francis (Francy the Fiddler) Kelly, blind itinerant musician, who died ca. 1928.

[32]Frank Kidson Folio Collection of Broadsides, no. 1, p. 79. For traditional versions see *Cecil Sharp's Collection of English Folk Songs*, ed. Maud Karpeles (London: Oxford University Press, 1974), pp. 308-9, 726 (there is also an unpublished tune and half stanza of text in the Sharp MSS., no. 4811).

[33]Donald McCormick, *The Red Barn Mystery* (South Brunswick, N.J.: A.S. Barnes, 1967). An examination of the sermons, journalistic reports, pamphlets, melodramas, etc. dealing with Maria Marten would undoubtedly reveal the same type of patterning discussed by Cohen, *Poor Pearl*.

[34]McCormick, *The Red Barn Mystery*, pp. 132-37.

[35]Ibid., p. 183.

[36]Clara Reeve, *The Old English Baron: A Gothic Story*, ed. James Trainer (London and New York: Oxford University Press, 1967), passim.

[37]McCormick, *The Red Barn Mystery*, pp. 183-87.

[38]Phillips Barry, "Fair Florella," *American Speech*, 3 (1928), 441-47.

[39]Laws, *Native American Balladry*, pp.61-62.

[40]Barry, "Fair Florella," ibid.

[41]Louise Pound, *American Ballads and Songs* (New York, Chicago, Boston: C. Scribner's Sons, 1922), p. 101; H.M. Belden, *Ballads and Songs Collected by the Missouri Folklore Society* (1940; rpt. Columbia, Mo.: University of Missouri Press, 1955), p. 326; etc.

[42]*The Frank C. Brown Collection of North Carolina Folklore*, vol. 2, *Folk Songs from North Carolina*, eds. Henry M. Belden and Arthur Palmer Hudson (Durham, N.C.: Duke University Press, 1952), p. 579; etc.

[43]Bruce A. Rosenberg, *The Folksongs of Virginia: A Checklist of the WPA Holdings, Alderman Library, University of Virginia* (Charlottesville, Va.: University Press of Virginia, 1969), no. 690 V (copy in my possession); etc.

[44]Ibid., 690 T and BB (copies in my possession); etc.

[45]Geneva Anderson, "A Collection of Ballads and Songs from East Tennessee" (M.A. Thesis, University of North Carolina, 1932), p. 35; *Brown Collection*, vol. 2, p. 386; Cohen, *Poor Pearl*, p. 57; John Harrington Cox, *Folk-Songs of the South* (1925; rpt. Hatboro, Pa.: Folklore Associates, 1963), p. 199; Rosenberg, *Folksongs of Virginia*, no.690 P, S, X (copies in my possession); etc.

[46]Cox, *Folk-Songs of the South*, p. 290.

[47]Tristram Potter Coffin, *The British Traditional Ballad in North America*, rev. ed. with a Supplement by Roger deV. Renwick (Austin and London: University of Texas Press, 1977); Holger Olof Nygard, *The Ballad of Heer Halewijn* (Folklore Fellows Communications 65, no. 169; Helsinki: Academia Scientiarum Fennica, 1958; Knoxville: University of Tennessee Press, 1958), pp. 284-86; Bertrand Harris Bronson, *The Traditional Tunes of the Child Ballads*, vol. 2 (Princeton, N.J.: Princeton University Press, 1962), p. 60.

[48]Iivar Kemppinen, *The Ballad of Lady Isabel and the False Knight* (Helsinki: n.p., 1954), p. 174.

[49]Svend Grundtvig et al., *Danmarks Gamle Folkeviser*, 13 vols. (Copenhagen: Universitets-Jubilæets Danske Samfund, 1853-1965; reissued 1966-67).

[50]See D. K. Wilgus, "A Type-Index of Anglo-American Traditional Narrative Songs," *Journal of the Folklore Institute*, 8 (1970), 169-73.

[51]"Song of a Lost Hunter," Frank Profitt, Folk Legacy FSA-1 (12" LP; recorded 1962).

[52]Gavin I. Langmuir, "The Knight's Tale of Young Hugh of Lincoln," *Speculum*, 47 (1972), 459-60.

[53]Ibid., 460.

[54]Francisque Michel, *Hughes de Lincoln* (Paris: Silvestre; London: Pickering, 1834), p. 1.

[55]Ibid., pp. 10-11.

Index of Names